Gender, Identity and the Culture of Organizations

Gender, Identity and the Culture of Organizations offers insights into the ways in which organizations operate as spaces in which minds are gendered and men and women constructed. This edited collection brings together four powerful themes that have developed within the field of organizational analysis over the past two decades: organizational culture; the gendering of organizations; postmodernism and organizational analysis; and critical approaches to management. It contains essays written by distinguished writers from a range of countries, including the UK, USA, Canada, Denmark, Sweden, Finland, and The Netherlands, and explores innovative methods for the critical theorizing of organizational cultures.

In particular, this book reflects the growing interest in the organizational identity formation and its implications for individuals and organizational outcomes in terms of gender.

In addition to its theoretical contributions, this volume aims at introducing research designs, methods and methodologies by which the complex interrelationships between gender, identity and the culture of organizations can be explored.

Iiris Aaltio is Professor of Management and Organization at the Department of Management, Lappeenranta University of Technology, Finland.

Albert J. Mills is Professor of Management at the Frank H. Sobey Faculty of Commerce, Saint Mary's University, Halifax, Canada.

Management, Organizations and Society
Edited by Professor Barbara Czarniawska, *Göteborg University, Sweden* and Professor Martha Feldman, *University of Michigan, USA*

'Management, Organizations and Society' presents innovative work grounded in new realities, addressing issues crucial to an understanding of the contemporary world. This is the world of organized societies, where boundaries between formal and informal, public and private, local and global organizations have been displaced or have vanished, along with other nineteenth-century dichotomies and oppositions. Management, apart from becoming a specialized profession for a growing number of people, is an everyday activity for most members of modern societies.

Similarly, at the level of enquiry, culture and technology, and literature and economics, can no longer be conceived as isolated intellectual fields; conventional canons and established mainstreams are contested. 'Management, Organizations and Society' will address these contemporary dynamics of transformation in a manner that transcends disciplinary boundaries, with work which will appeal to researchers, students and practitioners alike.

Contrasting Involvements: A Study of Management Accounting Practices in Britain and Germany
Thomas Ahrens

Turning Words, Spinning Worlds: Chapters in Organizational Ethnography
Michael Rosen

Breaking Through the Grass Ceiling: Women, Power and Leadership in Agricultural Organizations
Margaret Alston

The Poetic Logic of Administration: Styles and Changes of Style in the Art of Organizing
Kaj Sköldberg

Casting the Other: The Production and Maintenance of Inequalities in Work Organizations
Edited by Barbara Czarniawska and Heather Höpfl

Gender, Identity and the Culture of Organizations
Edited by Iiris Aaltio and Albert J. Mills

Gender, Identity and the Culture of Organizations

**Edited by Iiris Aaltio
and Albert J. Mills**

London and New York

For my sons Jaakko and Heikki, who give me so much presence
Iiris Aaltio

For Jeannie Helms Mills who gives my identity some meaning
Albert J. Mills

First published 2002 by Routledge
11 New Fetter Lane, London EC4P 4EE

Simultaneously published in the USA and Canada
by Routledge
29 West 35th Street, New York, NY 10001

Routledge is an imprint of the Taylor & Francis Group

© 2002 Editorial matter and selection, Iiris Aaltio and Albert J. Mills;
individual chapters the contributors

Typeset in 10/12pt Times by Wearset Ltd, Boldon, Tyne & Wear
Printed and bound in Great Britain by The Cromwell Press, Trowbridge,
Wiltshire

British Library Cataloguing in Publication Data
A catalogue record for this book is available from the British Library

Library of Congress Cataloging in Publication Data
A catalog record for this book has been requested

ISBN 0-415-27000-6 (hbk)
ISBN 0-415-27001-4 (pbk)

Contents

Illustrations

Plates

Figures

Tables

Contributors

Iiris Aaltio is Professor of Management at the Lappeenranta University of Technology, Finland. Her research interests focus on how organizational life becomes organized by ideals, archetypes and stereotypes that stem from the corporate culture as well as from broader institutional contexts. Her background is in business administration and organization psychology. She concluded her thesis on cultural change in Helsinki School of Economics and Business Administration using longitudinal data from an industrial enterprise, and later continued by studying it from a gender perspective. She is an author of two books (in Finnish), several book chapters, and her work has been published in *Organizational Change Management, Journal of Management Inquiry, Finnish Administrative Studies, Human Relations*, and *Scandinavian Journal of Management Studies*.

Mats Alvesson is a professor at the Department of Business Administration at Lund University, Sweden. He is interested in critical theory, organizational culture and symbolism, gender and the philosophy of science. Empirical work has mainly been conducted in professional service and knowledge-intensive companies. He is a co-editor of the journal *Organization*. Recent books include *Making Sense of Management: a Critical Introduction*, with Hugh Willmott (London, Sage, 1996), *Management of Knowledge-Intensive Companies* (Berlin and New York, de Gruyter, 1995), *Reflexive Methodology*, with Kaj Sköldberg (London, Sage, 2000), and *Understanding Organizational Culture* (London, Sage, 2002).

Yvonne Benschop is Associate Professor of Gender and Culture at the Nijmegen Business School, University of Nijmegen, The Netherlands. Fascination for the persistent gender division of labour underlies her research that focuses on the manifestations and meanings of gender in organizations. Her publications in English include articles in *Organization Studies, The International Journal of Human Resource Management and Gender, Work and Organization*. Current research projects explore the influences of diversity on organizational practices and representations of gender in corporate culture. She is also engaged in a project to integrate gender in the Human Resource Management of the Ministry of the Flemish Community in Belgium.

Yvonne Due Billing is associate Professor of Sociology at the Department of Sociology at the University of Copenhagen in Denmark. She has published on gender and organizations in various journals and her books on the subject include *Gender, Managers and Organizations*, with Mats Alvesson (Berlin, de Gruyter, 1994); and *Understanding Gender and Organizations*, again with Alvesson (London, Sage, 1997).

Pat Bradshaw is Associate Professor of Organizational Behaviour at York University in Toronto. Her research interests focus on organizational power and politics and how these impact on the possibilities for radical social change. In pursuing these questions she has done research on non-profit governance, women on boards, deep structures of power and dynamics of resistance in organizational settings. Pat has approached these research topics from a variety of qualitative approaches, including interviews, case studies and post-modern-feminist deconstruction, as well as from more quantitative methods.

Attila Bruni is a Ph.D. student at the Faculty of Sociology of the University of Trento, Italy. He is part of the Research Unit on Cognition and Organizational Learning and has just finished a research project at the Venice International University on Communities of Practice as systems of distributed knowledge. On gender and enterpreneurship he has published a recent book (*Gender and Entrepreneurship: An Ethnographic Approach*, Stanford University Press, California 2002) Co-authored with Silvia Gheradi and Barbara Poggio.

Erica Gabrielle Foldy is a Post Doctoral Fellow in Business Administration at Harvard Business School, a Researcher at the Center for Gender in Organizations at the Simmons Graduate School of Management, and an Assistant Professor at the Wagner School of Public Service at New York University. Her work has been published in the *Journal of Applied Behavioral Science and the Handbook of Action Research*, among other outlets. Her dissertation research explored how organizations influence their employees' race, gender and class identities. Her current research investigates whether and how broad principles of organizational learning can be applied to learning from social identity differences such as gender and race. Her general research interests include identities in organizations, action learning and reflective practice, the interaction of individual, organizational and social change, and non-profit organizations.

Silvia Gherardi is Full Professor of Sociology of Organization at the Faculty of Sociology of the University of Trento, Italy, where she co-ordinates the Research Unit on Cognition and Organizational Learning. Areas of interest include the exploration of different 'soft' aspects of knowing in organizations, with a peculiar emphasis for cognitive, emotional, symbolic and linguistic aspects of organizational process. Her last book is devoted to the theme of gender and organizational cultures (*Gender, Symbolism and Organizational Cultures*, Sage, 1995).

Jeff Hearn is Professorial Research Fellow, Department of Applied Social Science, University of Manchester, and Guest Professor and Academy Fellow at the Swedish School of Economics and Business Administration, Helsinki, Finland. His authored, co-authored and co-edited books include

The Gender of Oppression (Brighton, Wheatsheaf, 1987), *The Sexuality of Organization* (London, Sage, 1989), *Taking Child Abuse Seriously* and *Men, Masculinities and Social Theory* (both London, Unwin Hyman/Routledge, 1990), *Men in the Public Eye* (London, Routledge, 1992), *'Sex' at 'Work'* (Brighton, Harvester Wheatsheaf/Prentice-Hall, 1995), *Violence and Gender Relations* (London, Sage, 1996), *Men as Managers, Managers as Men* (London, Sage, 1996), *Men, Gender Divisions and Welfare* (London, Routledge, 1998), *The Violences of Men* (London, Sage, 1998), *Children, Child Abuse and Child Protection* (Chichester, John Wiley, 1999), *Consuming Cultures* and *Transforming Politics* (both London, Macmillan, 1999) and *Hard Work in the Academy* (Helsinki UP, 1999). His most recent book is *Gender, Sexuality and Violence in Organizations*, with Wendy Parkin (London, Sage, 2001). He is currently researching men, gender relations and transnational organizing, organizations and management.

Saija Katila is a Ph.D. (Econ.) and a researcher for the Academy of Finland. She is based in the Department of Management and Organization at the Helsinki School of Economics and Business Administration, Finland. Her personal experiences in the academic world inspired her to attempt to study and change the gendered practices of her own department, in collaboration with her colleague Susan Meriläinen. Their joint paper on this endeavour 'A Serious Researcher or Just Another Nice Girl? Doing Gender in a Male-Dominated Scientific Community', was published in *Gender, Work and Organization* (1999). Katila was a co-editor, along with Kovalainen, Meriläinen and Tienari, of the special issue 'Gender, Organization and Society' of *The Finnish Journal of Business Economics* (3/2000), and since the beginning of 2001 has acted as one of the associate editors for the journal *Gender, Work and Organization*. Her recent work has concerned the survival strategies of farm-business families in Finland. The study highlighted the local moral order (i.e. the norms and values which support and limit the actions of different family members) and the role of emotions in stabilizing it.

Hanne E. Meihuizen received a doctorandus degree from Erasmus University Rotterdam in 1989 and a Ph.D. from Texas A&M University in 1994, both in economics. She spent six years as an assistant professor of Finance and Investments at the Nijmegen Business School, University of Nijmegen, doing research on HRM, financial labour participation and gender studies. She is currently a fellow at the OSA Institute of Labour Studies in Tilburg, The Netherlands, where she is mainly concerned with labour market research in the health care and welfare sectors.

Susan Meriläinen is a research fellow in the Department of Management and Organization at the Helsinki School of Economics and Business Administration, Finland. She, together with Saija Katila, is currently engaged in a research project that concerns gendered academic practices. Their journal article on gendering of professional identities in academia was recently published in *Gender, Work and Organization*. Her research and writing has focused on gender and organization, especially on gendered social and discursive practices, gendering of professional identities and manifestations of equality and difference discourses in women managers' work histories. She has also researched environmental management practices from an ecofeminist point of view. She is a co-editor of a special issue 'Gender, Organization and Society' of *The Finnish Journal of Business Economics* (3/2000).

Albert J. Mills is Professor of Management at Saint Mary's University in Nova Scotia, Canada. His research activities centre on the impact of organizational realities upon people – focusing on organizational change and human liberation. This concern was formulated on the shop floor of British industry and through involvement in the movements for social change that characterized the 1960s. Leaving school at fifteen, Mills's early images of organization – images of frustration, sexually segregated work, power disparities, and conflict – were experienced through a series of unskilled jobs and given broader meaning through campaigns for peace, women's liberation, environmental survival and social change. His co-authored/co-edited books include *Organizational Rules* (Milton Keynes, Oxford University Press, 1991), *Gendering Organizational Analysis* (Newbury Park, Sage, 1992), *Reading Organization Theory* (Toronto, Garamond [1995] 1998), and *Managing the Organizational Melting Pot* (Thousand Oaks, Sage, 1997).

Anshuman Prasad received a Ph.D. from the University of Massachusetts at Amherst and teaches strategic management and organizational analysis at the School of Business, University of New Haven, Connecticut, USA. His research is primarily concerned with understanding organizational processes from a critical, symbolic, and non-instrumental perspective. Within this broad framework, his publications and conference presentations have dealt with such themes as strategic action in the global petroleum sector, postcolonialism, organizational ideology, workplace resistance and empowerment, management of technological change, critical pedagogy, and epistemological issues in management research. His work has appeared in such scholarly outlets as *Organization Science, Human Relations, Research in the Sociology of Organizations, Studies in Cultures, Organizations and Societies, Journal of Management Education,* and *Journal of Management Inquiry.* He is a co-editor of *Managing the Organizational Melting Pot: Dilemmas of Workplace Diversity* (Thousand Oaks, Sage Publications, 1997). Before joining academe, he was an executive in the State Bank of India for nine years.

Pushkala Prasad is the Zankel Chair Professor of Management and Liberal Studies at Skidmore College. She received a Ph.D. in management in 1992 from the University of Massachusetts at Amherst and has taught at Clarkson University in Potsdam, New York, the University of Calgary and Lund University in Sweden. Professor Prasad's research interests are somewhat eclectic and cover such areas as technological change, workplace resistance, multiculturalism and post-positivist methodologies. She has published widely on these topics in leading journals such as the *Academy of Management Journal, Human Relations,* the *Journal of Management Studies, Organization Science* and *MIS Quarterly.* She has also co-edited a book, *Managing the Organizational Melting Pot* (Thousand Oaks, Sage, 1997) and is currently writing a book on the different qualitative research traditions. More recently, she has been looking at deviant and socially controversial industries such as the tobacco, gun, armament and fur industries. Her current research project, entitled 'Narratives of Legitimacy in the Killing Industries', was given a grant of close to a quarter of a million dollars by the Bank of Sweden's Tercentenary Foundation. Pushkala Prasad has also received the 'Ascendant Scholar' Award from the Western Academy of Management, was named the Outstanding Researcher of the Year at the University of Calgary and is listed in *Who's Who in the Management Sciences*. She has been married for over seventeen years to Anshuman Prasad, who is also her partner in most of her scholarly adventures.

David Wicks gained his Ph.D. from York University and is Associate Professor of Management and Chairperson of the Department of Management in the Frank H. Sobey Faculty of Commerce at Saint Mary's University in Halifax, Nova Scotia. He teaches courses in management principles, strategic management, organizational behaviour and research methods. David's research interests are in compliance and resistance with institutional expectations and their effects on organizational stability/change and the formation/replication of gendered institutional practices and organizational cultures. His most recent study is a qualitative examination of how processes of institutionalization contributed to the explosion at Westray Mines in 1992. He has written several journal articles, serves as a referee for the Social Sciences and Humanities Research Council of Canada's grant programmes, and speaks regularly at the Academy of Management, European and Group Organization Studies and Administrative Sciences Association of Canada conferences.

Acknowledgements

The authors and publishers would like to thank the following for granting permission to reproduce material in this work: Philips, for the right to reproduce images from their 1996 financial report. Nestlé Ltd, for the right to reproduce images from their 1996 and 1999 financial reports. Scottish & Newcastle plc, for the right to reproduce images from their 1996/97 annual report. Fortis Corporate Communications for the right to reproduce images from their 1996 financial and social reports.

Every effort has been made to contact copyright holders for their permission to reprint material in this book. The publishers would be grateful to hear from any copyright holder who is not here acknowledged and will undertake to rectify any errors or omissions in future editions of this book.

The development of a book is the outcome of many people beyond those indicated on the front cover. We would like to take this opportunity to thank those who played a role in bringing this particular book to publication: Gerard Greenway of Harwood Press for his early commitment to the book, Barbara Czarniawska and Martha Feldman for their support and feedback on the initial proposal, Catriona King and Gavin Cullen of Routledge for their careful shepherding through the various processes, Gina Grandy and Dov Bercovici for insightful reviewing; and the folks at Wearset – Sarah Coulson and Alan Fidler – for making us all look good.

Part I

Introduction

1 Organizational culture and gendered identities in context

Iiris Aaltio and Albert J. Mills

There is no escape – the term FEMINIST is written across our foreheads – probably for the rest of our academic careers. We must admit, though, that we did something to deserve it.

(Katila and Meriläinen, Chapter 10, this volume)

Introduction

This edited collection brings together four powerful themes that have developed within the field of organizational analysis over the last two decades: organizational culture, the gendering of organizations, postmodernism and organizational analysis, and critical approaches to management. We view these themes as intertwined in research on the essence of organizational life with its multiple manifestations. In particular the book reflects the growing interest in the impact of organizational identity formation and its implications for 'individuals' and 'organisational' outcomes in terms of gender. These themes are integrated through a focus on new and varied research designs, methods and methodologies by which the complex interrelationships between gender, identity and the cultures of organizations are submitted to our understanding and can be explored. This book edition with its variety of methodological and conceptual approaches aims:

1 to promote diverse theoretically based, empirical explorations on crossing issues between gender and organizational culture,
2 to apply that understanding in the context of organizations and management, and
3 to support critical reflections within organizational research in terms of equality between women and men at the workplace.

Organizational culture

The cultural approach to organizations became popular in the 1980s. As remarked by Stablein and Nord (1985: 22), 'probably never before in organizational studies has an innovative area been given such attention so rapidly'. Reasons for the emergence of organizational culture studies are manifold. As suggested, there was a need to seek for new methods to study organizations and to find 'subjective' concepts to replace the old 'objective' concepts in order to understand organizational essence (Alvesson and Berg, 1988: 22–25). Culture became a theoretical tool to cross over the traditional micro- and macro-level organizational analysis (Morey and Luthans, 1985: 227–228). In general, internationalization gave impulses to study cultural aspects of business communication (Morgan, 1986). By now we can see the many branches stemming from the cultural perspective, its several theoretical and methodological contexts, and any idea of its simplicity, trend-like appearance or hegemony over other concepts, meets with a difficulty when facing this diversity. Among the approaches, the notion of organizations as 'mini-cultures' was raised by organizational educators and practitioners seeking more comprehensive ways of understanding organizational behaviour and management. This debate encouraged research that explored the complex factors influencing behaviour within organizations. The relationships between non-rational factors and multiple-level organizational outcomes were explored especially, and the focus was on the symbolism of organizational life in general. The first approaches of organizational culture emphasized its invisibility, whereas nowadays multiple methodologies and methods of analysis and interpretations are accepted. Exploring organizational cultures and their gendered nature means making them visible.

Culture debate as a heuristic for studying organizations is clearly acknowledged, but the impact of culture on gender and identity is largely ignored. By the late 1980s the culture debate subsided in the face of new theories of change (like re-engineering), on the one hand, and the growing popularity of postmodernist critique, on the other. However, there is evidence that the topic of organizational culture is finding renewed interest among scholars, as witnessed in the recently published *Handbook on Organizational Culture and Climate* (Ashkanasy *et al.*, 2000).

This edited collection sets out to contribute to the revised interest in organizational culture as a heuristic for understanding the relationship between organizational arrangements and outcomes, in particular the way that combinations of symbolic, non-rational factors contribute to our understanding of 'women' and 'men'.

Gender and organizational analysis

Sex is a biological classification of humans into women and men, whereas gender is a cultured knowledge that differentiates them. To understand what gender means is to understand its cultural dimensions. Thus, feminine and masculine genders consist of the values and ideals that originate from culture. The gender classification of men and women, male and female, as a biological or cultural definition is far from easy to handle in research and everyday life. Since the early 1970s a growing body of work has developed a focus on the gendering of organizations and its impact on individual and organizational outcomes. Why this growing interest in gender studies in management research today? There are several reasons for this. Besides the nowadays more explicitly expressed demand in Western societies for equality between the sexes, there is also a need for gender studies that connect the changing conditions for contemporary organizations. Gender is evidently an important aspect to take into account in business commu-

nication (see, for example, Hofstede (1980)). Applying ideas of gender for alternative ways to organizational change has also become a useful area of research.
'Gender at work' is the problematic issue in numerous accounts, among which the
relationship between organizational culture and the social construction of gendered identities is of special interest. Sadly, despite the development of extensive
scholarship on gender and organizations, the mainstream accounts, including the
organizational culture debate, continue to ignore the relationship between organizational arrangements and gender. The new *Handbook on Organizational Culture
and Climate* (Ashkanasy *et al.*, 2000), for example, includes only one chapter that
deals with gender. In addition, even when institutional contexts are accepted as
having a great impact on gender in organizational realities, the channels by which
they delve into the everyday life of people are still largely ignored. Multiple kinds
of interpretations are needed. In contrast, this edited collection brings together a
number of researchers noted for their work in exploring the relationship between
gender, institutional realities and the cultures of organizations.

Postmodernism

Natural bodies, voices and texts become questioned in postmodernism. Postmodernist thought has strongly influenced the debate on gender, identity and
the culture of organizations by highlighting the relationship between 'subjectivity' and 'discursive organizational practices', while, at the same time, questioning the viability of 'gender' and 'culture' as categories of understanding. In some
cases this has led to 'strategic' uses of postmodernist analysis in the production
of feminist accounts of gendering and organizational practices. In yet other
cases this has generated post-feminist angst and even the rejection of 'gender' as
a category of analysis. In all events, this has enriched the debate and sharpened
the interest in identity and organizational analysis (Hassard, 1999). Men and
women in organizations can be seen not only as carriers of bodies and voices,
but also of femininity and masculinity, which are both organizational and institutional categories. Texts produced in organizational contexts are related to
many questions of gender, not only as innocent and factual products by nature.
The symbolism of organizational realities is seen in postmodernists' understandings of organizations. While the early ideas of postmodernism emphasized the
death of the subject in discourse, concern is nowadays given to the complex
ways in which women and men seek to exert control over their lives (Elliott,
1999). As today's organizations are almost like global, anonymous cities, individuals in their identity formation processes come up against organizational
frames, and unavoidably meet gender aspects at the same time. They build their
individual identities based on gender, and at the same time organizational identities become built. This edited collection reflects the growing interest in identity
construction and the problematic of organizational discourse.

Critical approaches to management

Within the debate on gender and organizations, there is a feminist divide
between mainstream 'women in management' accounts and critical management theories. The former approach focuses on 'improvements' in the status of

women within existing organizational arrangements, accepting the notion of 'women' and 'men' as fixed, essential categories. In general, they emphasize equality and inequality issues in management, and focus on the means to achieve equality. The latter approach takes the problematic of social construction as its starting point, and seeks to identify the relationships between the social construction of organizational arrangements and the 'organizational construction of gender', seeing both men and women as important categories in the analysis. The approach also brings together an understanding of the multiple-level social, organizational and institutional factors beyond the issues of inequality and organizational culture. The wider environment of this approach can be located in the dilemmas of overall workplace diversity and its management (Prasad, Mills, Elmes and Prasad, 1997). Gender aspects are part of this diversity, and meet and cross the other diversity aspects in the melting pots of organizations. This edited collection contributes to a critical approach to management by raising questions about the impact of organizational arrangements on people and their sense of gendered self, exploring the relationship between the cultures of organizations as 'mini-societies' and as institutional constructs, and the construction of gendered selves or subjectivities. 'Showcases' (Prasad and Mills, 1997: 3–27) about how to critically explore gender in this organizational social construction, and how to promote equality issues in the process, are also presented throughout the book.

The structure of the book

The book is divided into three sections: the first is the Introduction (Chapter 1); the second, 'Theorizing Organizational Culture and Gendered Identities', is composed of Chapters 2–6; and the third, 'Methods: Beyond Explorations', is covered by Chapters 7–11. In the first section we introduce the book and its overall themes and discuss some of the issues raised.

Theorizing gender and organizational culture

The second section brings together five different approaches to the theorization of organizational culture and gender. It begins with the work of Attila Bruni and Silvia Gherardi (Chapter 2) who take a 'symbolic approach'. Here gender is viewed as 'the most powerful symbol of differences, culturally enacted and "positioned" through material and semiotic practices. Gender is something we "do" and something we think.' From this perspective organizational culture stands as 'a signification domain' within which gender is created as a discursive effect. Through a focus on organizational culture is revealed 'the boundaries in which identity and gender are allowed, as well as the permeability and the meaning of these boundaries'.

Within this chapter gender is disconnected from the realm of the biological (except where, implicitly, biology itself can be seen as a form of signification). Individuals are not so much absent from but blurred within the text, replaced by subject positions (i.e. 'a conceptual repertoire and a location for persons within the structure of rights pertaining to those who use the repertoire'). Here we are not so much concerned with what happens to women or men so much as the 'en-gendering' of persons. Through the concept of 'dual presence' – whereby persons experience conflicting aspects of en-gendering – Bruni and Gherardi suggest that organizational cultures provide boundaries across and within which conflicting experiences of en-gendering may occur. This viewpoint serves not only as 'a strategy for dismantling the taken-for-granted of any cultural representation of gender' but as an insight into the very real possibility of change.

Chapter 3, by Jeff Hearn, draws on pro-feminist, subtext and deconstructive approaches to problematize the notion of gender, identity and organizational culture. For Hearn the notion of organizational culture serves as a problematic construct for addressing gendered practices. Its potential for making gender more or less apparent lies in conceptualizing it as text and subtext. Yet it is limited as a heuristic by its rootedness in 'gendered differentiations' where organizational culture has been encoded as 'feminine' and 'female'. In particular a focus on organizational culture is particularly problematic for Hearn's concern with exposing maleness and masculinity in the processes of discrimination at work, arguing that it is far from clear what 'the implications of the feminine/female encoding of culture [are] for the analysis of men's gendered power'. Hearn concludes that 'notions of organizational culture may be deconstructed and recognized as a (misleading) shorthand for multiple, overlapping, paradoxical and contradictory processes of gendered othernesses, both women and men'.

In a similar vein to the previous chapter, Hearn moves us away from the notion of individual agency towards a social constructionist view of gendered categories (men/women; masculine/feminine). But the chapter moves us away from gender *per se* to a focus on 'men' and 'masculinity' and how these concepts have hitherto not been problematized within studies of discrimination at work. In so doing, the concept of 'man' has a more ontologically real feel to it than Bruni and Gherardi's en-gendered subject positions. In his treatment of organizational culture Hearn appears to press the notion of signification further than Bruni and Gherardi in contending that it helps to signify and thus marginalize 'femininity'.

In Chapter 4 Anshuman and Pushkala Prasad use a postcolonial 'theoretical lens' forged to an institutional approach to understand the contemporary dynamics of difference and identity in organizational cultural milieux. Here the concern is not simply with the social construction of womanhood within and by organizational settings but also the intersection of gender with 'race, ethnicity, religion, national origin, etc.' in the constitution of a spectrum of 'other' identity categories. To achieve this, the Prasads explore the impact of 'neo-colonial and neo-imperial discourses of otherness' on the cultures of organizations, viewed as 'identity spaces' and as sites for the transmission of and adjustments to globalization.

This approach focuses less on organizational cultures as 'local' sites but on the meta-discourses that influence institutional processes in the construction of cultural formations in organizational arrangements. In so doing the chapter raises issues about the viability of a study of gender divorced from the other 'major axes of difference' (e.g. race, class, ethnicity, sexuality, and religion), and a concept of organizational culture that is divorced from 'geopolitical realities and global hegemonies that mediate the formation of identity spaces in organizational and institutional locations'. To that end, the chapter differs from the previous chapters in attempting to *decontextualize* subjectivity from purely localized influences.

Mats Alvesson and Yvonne Due Billing return us, in Chapter 5, to an organizational-level analysis in which the cultures of organizations serve as sites for the social construction of gender. In this perspective a crucial distinction is made between masculinity/femininity and male/female, with the first pair viewed as 'more abstract and detached from biological sex' and the second pair seen as 'closer to what men and women actually do'. This, at one and the same time, sets up gender as an organizing process rather than a fixed system, while retaining some oblique notion of the biological. As with Hearn, Alvesson and Due Billing draw attention to the underlying gendered assumptions of the term 'organizational or corporate culture', but see the associations as problematic but potentially more enabling of feminist debate. For them the notion of organizational culture 'send[s] signals about the importance of feelings, communities, social relations and teams, which are more in accord with femininity'.

In Chapter 6 Erica Foldy brings to the fore the problematic relationship between organizational culture and gendered identities through an exploration of the impact of diversity management on identities. Using a Foucauldian lens, Foldy's interest in the relationship between power and identity is illustrated through analysis of the impact of diversity management programmes on identities. Here, more than in any of the previous chapters, we are focused on individual agency and the problem of multiple identities. In this framework, the gendered self is one of several identities that are contested within the context of work organizations and 'their less visible and more embedded aspects, such values and underlying assumptions, which constitute their cultures'. Foldy's analysis of diversity programmes helps to illustrate how, in recent years, the cultures of organizations – referencing the work of Schein (1985) – have become a 'central arena' for contests over identity, with diversity programmes having 'their most immediate impact on observable manifestations of the culture, including representation of different demographic groups and organizational policies'. In contrast to Hearn's rejection of 'identity politics', Foldy contends that a focus on 'the politics of identity' reveals the problematic nature of attempting to divorce or isolate gender from other aspects of identity (e.g. race, ethnicity, sexual orientation, etc.). In some ways this accords with the approach of the Prasads, but differs by focusing on the organizational-level of analysis and localized outcomes.

Ways of studying the gendering of organizational culture

The third section of the book presents the work of several researchers who have grappled with various methods for making sense of gender through an organizational culture lens. Although more centrally concerned with methods these chapters can also be seen as continuing the theoretical debate on gender and organizational culture.

In Chapter 7 Albert J. Mills deals with the issue of historiography and the study of organizational culture over time. More than in any of the preceding discussions, this chapter embraces the organizational culture lens as a heuristic for addressing discriminatory practices. In this perspective organizational culture is used as a tool for conceptualizing the configuration of rules (e.g. expectations, constraints, methods of control) that impact on the experiences of people at work. Similarly, gender is viewed as a fluid set of rules with different meanings and outcomes within different configurations: this has something in common with Alvesson and Due Billing's notion of gender (Chapter 5). Arguing for the study of organizational cultures over time, the chapter draws on Jenkins's postmodernist reading of 'history' to explore some of the key problems involved in developing an historical account of discrimination and organizational change.

In contrast to Mills's longitudinal approach and Alvesson and Due Billing's rejection of 'body counting' research, David Wicks and Pat Bradshaw (Chapter 8) provide detailed analysis of the usefulness and limitations of value survey instruments in the study of contemporary aspects of gendered organizational cultures. Through the development and application of a values survey in a cross-section of Canadian work organizations, Wicks and Bradshaw explore 'the systematic effects of culture', contending that 'self-reported values are reflections of the deeper structures of basic assumptions underlying cultural artefacts and observable behaviour'. Here Wicks and Bradshaw address the concerns of Alvesson and Due Billing by arguing that their focus is not on *representation* of biologically rooted differences but rather on 'the presence of differing social norms relating to women and men and the possibility of uncovering *patterns of perception* within a seemingly heterogeneous sample' [our emphasis]. The study, thus, was designed to reveal 'the pervasiveness of particular values and the ways in which they are differentially held in women and men'.

Wicks and Bradshaw view gender as locations within a system of relationships that are a 'set of social constructions that create ideas about appropriate roles for women and men'. This focus of gender as relational shadows elements of Hearn's approach in which the biological is not discounted but is rather overlaid by processes of social construction. It also shadows the work of Foldy, both in referencing gender as embodying a set of power relationships and in its conceptualization of men and women as individual agents within organizational cultures. Also like Foldy, they draw on Schein's (1991, 1985) notion of organizational culture to reveal not only its value for understanding gendered realities but also in exposing the neglect of gender within mainstream studies.

In Chapter 9 Yvonne Benschop and Hanne Meihuizen explore the use of content analysis in the examination of representations of gender in texts, figures and photos in corporate financial and social annual reports. In a similar way to Wicks and Bradshaw, this chapter draws attention to the value of quantitative methods for studying 'differences in opportunities for men and women within . . . organizations'. While Meihuizen and Benschop differ from Bruni and Gherardi in their referencing of embodied persons they argue that their approach 'connects to the symbolic approach to gender', viewing 'the cultural representations of gender in annual reports [as producing] meanings that relate to a symbolic gender in organizations'. Similarly, they share a symbolist view of organizational culture, viewing such things as annual reports as 'cultural products of organizations . . . [that] contribute to the construction of the organizations' values, norms and beliefs both at a symbolical and at a practical level'.

Chapter 10 deals with the issue of 'self in research'. Long discounted in objectivist mainstream approaches to the study of organizations (Kirby and McKenna, 1989; Stanley and Wise, 1983), Katila and Meriläinen argue that 'placing self in the centre of research ... can be a meaningful and fruitful research strategy' for uncovering the gendered practices of organizational life. This framework challenges methodologies based on the 'disembodied knower', whereby 'good' research is seen as rational and independent, distanced from the research object. For Katila and Meriläinen the self, as a culturally devised/symbolically positioned phenomenon, cannot easily be divorced from the study of culture and identity. Drawing on Foucauldian and symbolist lens (see, respectively, Foldy, Chapter 6 and Bruni and Gherardi, Chapter 2), it is argued that gender is culturally enacted and 'positioned' through discursive practices. Organizational culture is viewed as a moral order 'where rituals, confirmations of respect and contempt and displays of proper character and moral commentary are permitted only to those who are members of these communities'.

In Chapter 11 Iiris Aaltio deals with the issue of 'the interview'. Through a focus on the relationship between self and the social construction of 'the interview', this final chapter bridges the focus on method (as a way of collecting 'data') with that of issues of the self in enquiry discussed by Katila and Meriläinen. Here 'beside a method, an interview is a socially constructed, localized interactional process'. While Aaltio is concerned with 'local, contextually situated stories' her work resonates with that of the Prasads in contending that identities are 'rooted in global and local organizational contexts'. The chapter also resonates with the work of Foldy and of Katila and Meriläinen in bringing individual agency to the fore. Aaltio is interested in the interplay between individual identity, gender, and the cultures of organizations. In this framework, 'men and women in organizations' are seen as having multiple identities, among which gender is an 'integral component'. Gender is viewed as socially constructed notions of difference that impact how one 'thinks and understands the nature of one's self'. But the diverse, localized character of organizational cultures – defined as underlying values and basic assumptions (see also the chapters by Foldy, and Wicks and Bradshaw), ensures that 'gender identity is a complex, dynamic and multifaceted social phenomenon'. Through analysis of 'the interview' Aaltio brings to the fore the interrelationship between self, method and organization culture, these being seen as intertwined, not clearly separate or separable issues. 'Gender and organizational culture are knit together' in a framework (and dynamic) that form a 'gendered cultural context' in which people are interviewed and both interviewer and interviewee construct gendered notions of self.

Opening the space

> It is within a particular discourse that a subject (the position of a subject) is constructed as a compound of knowledge and power into a more or less coercive structure which ties it to an en-gendered identity.
>
> (Bruni and Gherardi, Chapter 2: 25)

An important starting point of this edited collection is that the organizational culture debate has opened up an important theoretical space for exploration of gender within organizational analysis. In many ways, the space has remained unfurnished and neglected, but it is a fixer-upper and there are already a number of squatters. The problem is that until recently the property has been condemned and is still in danger of being torn down, but is a worthwhile structure for the exploration and exposure of gender at work.

As a theoretical space organizational analysis developed through the establishment of a number of concrete structures. The edifices were built from hard, objectivist materials that were impervious to issues of subjectivity (Burrell and Morgan, 1979). By the late 1970s many of the buildings operated as condominiums, offering a partial view of the organizational landscape. Some apartments, for example, allowed an exploration of structure, others motivation, and yet others strategy. Most of the occupants were men but no one really noticed; it was certainly not an issue (Collinson and Hearn, 1994). Few seemed interested in the other people in the building.

For the most part feminist theorists seemed happy to stay away from this overly rationalized structure, feeling more at home in other communities with pathways through areas of emotionality and gendered selves. But there were some feminists in the building, checking out the opportunity structures and the tenancy agreements (see, for example, Kanter, 1977).

In the 1980s new developers moved in with holistic approaches to interior design. Gone was the condominium approach with its focus on partial analysis. In came the new culture approach with its focus on the interrelationships between the structures of the buildings and the building process itself. Many of the objectivist materials continued to structure the buildings, but new porous materials introduced were more open to the subjectivist elements (see Alvesson and Due Billing, Chapter 5). This new (organizational culture) approach proved extremely popular and led to a proliferation of buildings and building types. Planning permission for the new approach helped legitimize study of the subjectivist and symbolic elements or organizations, encouraging socially constructed edifices to arise alongside the more concrete buildings.

In the midst of this building boom, spaces were opened for exploration of the relationship between self and the structuring of organizational realities. The spaces offered a legitimate place within the mainstream of organizational analysis for exploration and exposure of the discriminatory nature of organization (Aaltio-Marjosola and Mills, 2000). The problem is that, despite the fact that a number of squatters moved in (e.g. Aaltio-Marjosola, 1991, 1994; Gherardi, 1995; Mills, 1988; Morgan, 1988; Smircich, 1985), the spaces were often neglected (Hearn and Parkin, 1983) and for a time fell into disrepair in the wake of new concerns with 'quality' (i.e. Total Quality Management) and the tearing down of old structures to make way for re-engineered buildings. That the organizational culture framework retains some resilience within organizational analysis can be seen in responses to recent rebuilding efforts (cf. Ashkanasy *et al.*, 2000). That resilience has been greater among feminist organizational theorists (Aaltio-Marjosola and Lehtinen, 1998; Aaltio-Marjosola and Sevøn, 1997; Alvesson and Due Billing, 1997; Helms Mills and Mills, 2000; Korvajarvi, 1998; Maddock, 1999; Marshall, 1992; Wilson, 1997, 2000) who are less susceptible to the fads and fashions of organizational theory (Abrahamson, 1996; Kieser, 1997). To be clear, while we argue that the organizational culture debate opened theoretical space for feminist research, we do not mean to suggest that it was directly, or even indirectly, sympathetic to feminism nor that it was the only or main avenue for developing feminist research. Clearly much of feminist organizational analysis has drawn on broader feminist scholarship outside of management research, but the organizational culture debate did at least two things:

i   it provided a perspective and a range of conceptual tools that were useful to feminist research, and, in so doing,
ii   it served to provide a framework of 'plausibility' for that research.

Nonetheless, as a theoretical frame, organizational culture does not 'as such' lead towards gendered understanding of organizations. Cultural studies that do not recognize the gendered nuances of organizational realities can create blindness of gender issues as well as any other approach. While the organizational culture debate moved attention away from the rational to the emotional elements of the organization, from fixed to the social construction of individuality, from macro to micro aspects of organizing, it continued to ignore gender.

Beyond metaphor: organizational culture as a heuristic for studying gender in organizations

> The study of cultural meanings, and of how different forms of masculinity dominate in companies, technologies, sciences, politics, organization, management, etc., provides the major alternative to gender-as-a-variable/body-counting research.
>
> (Alvesson and Due Billing, Chapter 5: 77)

We contend that the lens of organizational culture provides a useful way of studying gender at work. Simply put, gender is a cultural phenomenon whereby culturally specific patterns of behaviour come to be associated with the biological differences between 'males' and 'females' (Oakley, 1972). Organizations are important sets of social arrangements that dominate the cultural landscape of industrial society (Denhardt, 1981), and thus important cultural sites in the construction of gendered identities (Burrell, 1992). Studies of gender and such things as organizational symbolism (Acker, 1992), communication (Borisoff and Merrill, 1985), structure (Savage and Witz, 1992), dress (Rafaeli et al., 1997), and discourse (Ferguson, 1984) have been invaluable in exposing the cultural processes whereby gendered identities and discriminatory practices are constructed. An organizational culture framework builds on these different elements to provide a holistic account of the interrelationships between different elements of organizational reality and gendering. Certainly this approach mirrors legislative change in some jurisdictions, including Canada and the US, where anti-discrimination laws have moved the focus from individual actions to 'system-wide' practices (see Helms Mills and Mills, 2000).

   Certainly this approach is not without its problems. We are in danger of authorizing one approach to the exclusion of others (Jacques, 1996), engaging in culture war games (Martin and Frost, 1996), and disempowering others through engagement in the creation of a powerful discourse (Calás and Smircich, 1996). And that is only what our friends would say! For the sake of friendship as well as scholarship, let us deal with those potential critiques.

Authorizing

It is not always easy to understand symbolic representations, nor to define the way in which they structure social experience. The difficulty stems from the nature itself of the symbol itself, which is so much the *significans* as to be indeterminate and constantly defer its *significandum*, and which requires an indirect language, one which establishes relations and conserves transformative power.

(Bruni and Gherardi, Chapter 2: 22)

[A focus] on identity and organizational culture should not be taken to suggest ... any favour with narrowly defined identity politics or culturalist explanations ... [T]endencies towards essentialism in the theorizing of both identity and culture should be strongly guarded against.

(Hearn, Chapter 3: 39)

To be clear, we are excited about the possibilities of an organizational culture framework for addressing the processes of gender discrimination at work. That enthusiasm has led us to numerous explorations of the cultural roots of organizational inequities and, to be sure, we certainly prefer this approach to what Alvesson and Due Billing (Chapter 5) call body-counting. By 'selling' the idea to others – particularly in a book of this nature – we are constructing a story, which authorizes the 'good' method of organizational culture analysis and downplays other 'lessor' approaches. We have already done this by cues which suggest that the 'bad' mainstream has shut out subjectivist accounts and ignored gender. We have introduced demons in the form of body-counters and we will go on to 'reveal' the value of the organizational culture approach through introduction of the other chapters in the book. Sadly, we also position ourselves as something of experts in the field (see our contributors' pages and citations). Yet we do want to encourage further research in this field. We do see it as an important way to address discrimination at work. Thus, our only redress is, like the warning on the cigarette packet, to advise that you may be in danger from authorizing if you read further. If it will help, you may want to deconstruct us as purveyors of unhealthy habits. But please read on ...

War games

Symbolists differ from many culture researchers in that they emphasize the aesthetic, ethical and emotional dimensions of human life, rather than simply examine its cognitive and axiological dimensions.

(Bruni and Gherardi, Chapter 2: 22)

The notion of culture as an 'island' of given norms and values that is separate from the rest of the world, whether it is a societal culture, an organizational culture, or a local sub-culture, is extremely problematic. While the concept of culture continues to be of ever-increasing interest in organizational, managerial and academic discourses ... it remains contested.

(Hearn, Chapter 3: 40)

The concept of organizational culture arises from viewing organizations less as machines, and more as social entities, possessing socialization processes, social norms and structures. Organizational culture, therefore, can be viewed as a set of widely shared attitudes, values and assumptions that give rise to specific behaviours and physical manifestations which become entrenched in the minds and practices of organizational participants.

(Wicks and Bradshaw, Chapter 8: 137)

Our contribution to the culture war games is limited somewhat by an avoidance of (a) an overarching definition of organizational culture, (b) any explicit attempt to favour one perspective over another, and (c) a revisiting of the central debates and definitional wars within the area. In the last regard we would direct those of you interested in the nature and extent of the debate to re/visit any or all of the following – Allaire and Firsirotu (1984), Ashkanasy *et al.* (2000), Brown (1998), Martin (1992), Martin and Frost (1996), Ott (1989) and Smircich (1983). A useful summary of the development of feminist accounts of the organizational culture debate can be found in Wilson (2000) – see also Fiona Wilson's (1995) discussion of culture and socialization. We have also worked to ensure a diversity of critical approaches towards the framing of an organizational culture perspective.

As editors we – Iiris and Albert – share an interest in the relationship between 'cultural artefacts' (e.g. symbols, language, values, beliefs, rules, ways of doing things, etc.) and gendered practices, but we differ on our exact definition of organizational culture. Iiris holds to a more symbolist approach and Albert to a rules approach [see Aaltio-Marjosola, 1994 and Chapter 11 of this collection; Mills, 1988 and Chapter 7 this collection]. It will be clear from a reading of the other chapters that most of the other contributors share a similar interest in organizational culture but hold varying institutional, materialist, symbolist, postmodernist, feminist, and postcolonialist perspectives. Jeff Hearn (Chapter 3) goes so far as to warn us that his discussion of identity and organizational culture should not be confused as a commitment to 'narrowly defined identity politics or culturalist explanations'. In the process we are reminded of the limits of the approach. Anshuman and Pushkala Prasad (Chapter 4) prefer a different *level* of analysis, locating the organizational culture focus within a wider context of the construction of otherness through post/colonial relationships. This helps to frame the limitations of the organizational culture heuristic within broader socio-political concerns. And Erica Foldy (Chapter 6) draws political distinctions between the current interest in 'diversity management' and the problematic of an organizational culture focus, reminding us of the dangers of ignoring the potential abuses of the concept of organizational culture. Further, we wish to underline that the researcher's reflective subjectivity in the study of gender and organizational culture is of importance: there is no escape from the methodological issues that our learning capacity and our own experiences as females and males are of importance in any research processes where gender is an issue. We do not need to face gender empowerment ourselves to be able to understand gender inequality issues, but we need intelligence to describe and essentialize cultural processes that outline gendered organizational reality. Cultural sensitivity towards gender issues in needed.

The privileging of an organizational discourse perspective

A subject position is what is created in and through conversations as speakers and hearers construct themselves as persons: it creates a location in which social relations and actions are mediated by symbolic forms and modes of being.

(Bruni and Gherardi, Chapter 2: 25)

As with all perspectives, a focus on the relationship between organizational culture and gendered identities has the effect of silencing other ways of seeing. It may, for example, deflect attention from structural arrangements (Kanter, 1977), the role of the state (Grant and Tancred-Sheriff, 1992), or 'a wide variety of social forces, gender notably among them' which inform the historical development of organizational arrangements (Witz and Savage, 1992: 57). Further, where we raise discussion to the level of discourse – encouraging others to join with us in a set of ideas and practices that reinforce a particular view of reality – we contribute to the creation of subject positions, in which some may be disempowered as 'lay readers' and others empowered through their location as 'experts'. That this is 'true' of all academic approaches should not blind us to the responsibility to draw attention to the process that we are engaged in. We do contend that an organizational culture focus provides a useful, albeit problematic, framework for uncovering patterns or configurations of discriminatory practices. Nonetheless, it is, in the end, a heuristic not a truth. Through this collection we hope that you will be able to gain insights into the use of the organizational culture lens in research. The problematic and contested nature of gender, gendered identity, and organizational culture is laid bare but in a way, we hope, that will encourage further research and debate into the multifarious ways that discriminatory practices become embedded in the meanings and understandings of organizational realities.

References

Aaltio-Marjosola, I. (1991). *Cultural Change in a Business Enterprise: Studying a Major Organizational Change and its Impact on Culture.* Helsinki School of Economics and Business Administration.

Aaltio-Marjosola, I. (1994). Gender stereotypes as cultural products of the organization. *Scandanavian Journal of Management*, 10(2): 147–162.

Aaltio-Marjosola, I. and Lehtinen, J. (1998). Male managers as fathers? Contrasting management, fatherhood and masculinity. *Human Relations*, 51(2): 121–136.

Aaltio-Marjosola, I. and Mills, A.J. (2000). The Organizational Culture Debate and the Gendered Understanding of Organizational Realities. Paper presented at the Women in Management Division of the ASAC/IFSAM conference, Montreal, July.

Aaltio-Marjosola, I. and Sevøn, G. (1997). Gendering organization topics. *Hallinnon Tutkimus (Finish Journal of Administrative Studies)*, 4: 269–71.

Abrahamson, E. (1996). Management fashion. *Academy of Management Review*, 21(1): 254–285.

Acker, J. (1992). Gendering organizational theory. In A.J. Mills and P. Tancred (eds), *Gendering Organizational Analysis* (pp. 248–260). Newbury Park, CA: Sage.

Allaire, Y. and Firsirotu, M. (1984). Theories of organizational culture. *Organization Studies*, 5: 193–226.

Alvesson, M. and Berg, P.O. (1988) *Företagskultur och organisationssymbolism. Unveckling, teoretiska perspektiv och aktuell debatt*. Lund: Studentlitteratur.

Alvesson, M. and Due Billing, Y. (1997). *Understanding Gender and Organizations*. London: Sage.

Ashkanasy, N., Wilderom, C. and Peterson, M. (eds) (2000). *Handbook of Organizational Culture and Climate*. Thousand Oaks, CA: Sage.

Borisoff, D. and Merrill, L. (1985). *The Power to Communicate: Gender Differences as Barriers*. Prospect Heights, Ill.: Waveland Press, Inc.

Brown, A. (1998). *Organizational Culture*. London: Financial Times/Pitman Publishing.

Burrell, G. (1992). Sex and organizational analysis. In A.J. Mills and P. Tancred (eds), *Gendering Organizational Analysis* (pp. 71–92). Newbury Park, CA: Sage.

Burrell, G. and Morgan, G. (1979). *Sociological Paradigms and Organizational Analysis*. London: Heinemann.

Calás, M.B. and Smircich, L. (1996). From 'the woman's' point of view: feminist approaches to organization studies. In S.R. Clegg, C. Hardy and W.R. Nord (eds), *Handbook of Organization Studies* (pp. 218–257). London: Sage.

Collinson, D. and Hearn, J. (1994). Naming men as men: implications for work, organization and management. *Gender, Work and Organization*, 1(1): 2–22.

Denhardt, R. (1981). *In the Shadow of Organization*. Lawrence, Kans.: Regents Press of Kansas.

Elliott, A. (1999) *Social Theory and Psychoanalysis in Transition*. (pp. 1–11). London: Free Association Books.

Ferguson, K.E. (1984). *The Feminist Case against Bureaucracy*. Philadelphia, PA: Temple University Press.

Gherardi, S. (1995). *Gender, Symbolism, and Organizational Culture*. London: Sage.

Grant, J. and Tancred-Sheriff, P. (1992). A feminist perspective on state bureaucracy. In A.J. Mills and P. Tancred-Sheriff (eds), *Gendering Organizational Analysis*. Newbury Park, CA: Sage.

Hassard, J. (1999) Postmodernism and organizational analysis: an overview. In J. Hassard and M. Parker (eds), *Postmodernism and Organizations* (pp. 1–25). London: Sage.

Hearn, J. and Parkin, P.W. (1983). Gender and organizations: a selective review and a critique of a neglected area. *Organization Studies*, 4(3): 219–242.

Helms Mills, J.C. and Mills, A.J. (2000). Rules, sensemaking, formative contexts and discourse in the gendering of organizational culture. In N. Ashkanasy, C. Wilderom and M. Peterson (eds), *Handbook of Organizational Culture and Climate* (pp. 55–70). Thousand Oaks, CA: Sage.

Hofstede, G. (1980) *Culture's Consequences. International Differences in Work-Related Values*. London: Sage.

Jacques, R. (1996). *Manufacturing the Employee: Management Knowledge from the 19th to 21st Centuries*. London: Sage.

Kanter, R.M. (1977). *Men and Women of the Corporation*. New York: Basic Books.

Kieser, A. (1997). Rhetoric and myth in management fashion. *Organization*, 4(1): 49–74.

Kirby, S. and McKenna, K. (1989). *Experience, Research, Social Change. Methods from the Margins*. Toronto: Garamond.

Korvajarvi, P. (1998). *Gendering Dynamics in White-Collar Work Organizations*. Tampere, Finland: University of Tampere.

Maddock, S. (1999). *Challenging Women. Gender, Culture, and Organization*. London: Sage.

Marshall, J. (1992). Organizational cultures: attempting change often means more of the same. *Women in Organization and Management* 3: 4–7.

Martin, J. (1992). *Cultures in Organizations: Three Perspectives*. Oxford: Oxford University Press.

Martin, J. and Frost, P. (1996). The organizational culture war games: a struggle for intellectual dominance. In S.R. Clegg, C. Hardy and W.R. Nord (eds), *Handbook of Organization Studies* (pp. 599–621). London: Sage.

Mills, A.J. (1988). Organization, gender and culture. *Organization Studies*, 9(3): 351–369.

Morey, N. and Luthans, F. (1985) Refining the displacement of culture and the use of scenes and themes in organizational studies. *Academy of Management Review* 10 (2): 219–229.

Morgan, G. (1986) *Images of Organization*. USA: Sage.

Morgan, N. (1988). *The Equality Game: Women in the Federal Public Service (1908–1987)*. Ottawa: Canadian Advisory Council on the Status of Women.

Oakley, A. (1972). *Sex, Gender and Society*. London: Temple Smith.

Ott, S.J. (1989). *The Organizational Culture Perspective*. Pacific Groves, CA: Brooks/Cole Publishing Co.

Prasad, P. and Mills, A. (1997) From showcase to shadow: understanding the dilemmas of managing workplace diversity. In P. Prasad, A. Mills, M. Elmes and A. Prasad (eds),: *Managing the Organizational Melting Pot. Dilemmas of Workplace Diversity*. (pp. 3–27). USA: Sage.

Prasad, P., Mills, A., Elmes, M. and Prasad, A. (1997) *Managing the Organizational Melting Pot. Dilemmas of Workplace Diversity*. USA: Sage.

Rafaeli, A., Dutton, J., Harquail, C.V. and Mackie-Lewis, S. (1997). Navigating by attire: the use of dress by female administrative employees. *The Academy of Management Journal*, 40(1): 9–45.

Savage, M. and Witz, A. (eds) (1992). *Gender and Bureaucracy*. Oxford: Blackwell.

Schein, E. (1991). What is culture? In P.J. Frost, L.F. Moore, M.R. Louis, C.C. Lundberg and J. Martin (eds), *Reframing Organizational Culture* (pp. 243–253). Newbury Park, CA: Sage.

Schein, E.H. (1985). *Organizational Culture and Leadership*. San Francisco, CA: Jossey-Bass.

Smircich, L. (1983). Concepts of culture and organizational analysis. *Administrative Science Quarterly*, 28: 339–358.

Smircich, L. (1985). Is the concept of culture a paradigm for understanding organizations and ourselves? In P.J. Frost, L.F. Moore, M.R. Louis, C.C. Lundberg and J. Martin (eds), *Organizational Culture* (pp. 55–72). Beverley Hills, CA: Sage.

Stablein, R. and Nord, W. (1985) Practical and emancipatory interests if organizational symbolism: a review and evaluation. *Journal of Management*: 11(2): 13–28.

Stanley, L. and Wise, S. (1983). *Breaking Out: Feminist Consciousness and Feminist Research*. London: Routledge & Kegan Paul.

Wilson, E.M. (1997). Exploring gendered cultures. *Hallinon Tutkimus*, 4: 289–303.

Wilson, E.M. (2000). Organizational culture. In E.M. Wilson (ed.), *Organizational Behaviour Reassessed* (pp. 168–187). London: Sage.

Wilson, F.M. (1995). *Organizational Behaviour and Gender*. London: McGraw-Hill.

Witz, A. and Savage, M. (1992). The gender of organizations. In M. Savage and A. Witz (eds), *Gender and Bureaucracy* (pp. 3–62). Oxford: Blackwell.

Part II

Theorizing organizational culture and gendered identities

2 En-gendering differences, transgressing the boundaries, coping with the dual presence

Attila Bruni and Silvia Gherardi[1]

Introduction

Gender is a linguistic artefact, a theoretical concept, a feminist invention, a quasi-object shaped in order to deal with bodies, sexualities, the desire, power, and the politics of knowledge. All these are elements which, in the material existence of everyday life, are closely bound up with each other and resist separation. The 'embracing' of the previous elements in the concept of gender is produced by social practices of knowledge representation, and social practices are so adept at engendering differently gendered subjectivities that their cultural construction becomes invisible, and the final assemblage appears entirely 'natural'. Therefore de-naturalizing the social and socializing the natural may be a good strategy for dismantling the taken-for-granted of any cultural representation of gender.

Playing with words, Teresa De Lauretis inserts a hyphen in the verb 'to engender', thus producing an ironic neologism: to en-gender. While 'to engender' signifies to produce but has no gender connotation, 'to en-gender' denotes the process of gender attribution, and self-attribution, as the effect of technologies of gender (De Lauretis, 1987) and more broadly as the effect of the technology of the self (Foucault, 1984).

En-gendering is a neologism which follows (and allows) the same logic as similar concepts – like racializing or sexualization – which point to the production of subjectivities as a socio-political process, and communicate the idea that race, sexuality, gender are not natural properties of the body but Western cultural representations. Insofar as sex, sexuality, race or gender are cultural artefacts enacted in and through social practices of signification which result in effects of reality, it is socially important for a political subject to understand how knowledge production works since it can be done differently.

By thinking, being and doing in particular ways, human agents create 'truths' about the world, and the objects and people within it; but Foucault (1984) argues that there are other, possibly limitless, ways of being, thinking and doing which are no more or less 'true' than those which we currently practise.

In this chapter we intend to focus on social processes of en-gendering subjectivities in organizational dynamics, our purpose being to argue that we currently practise both the signification and re-signification of gender, thereby contributing to the deferral of the meaning of gender, to its dissemination, and to the change or maintenance of gender relations. We shall use a symbolic approach to gender relations in order to analyse how professional subjectivities are produced and reproduced as the heterogeneous engineering of persons, objects, technologies, texts in everyday organizational life (Bruni and Gherardi, 2001). En-gendering subjectivities will be described as the active self-formation of gendered subjects in interactive process which takes place on symbolic terrain at the boundaries of the great divides – like female/male and homosexual/ heterosexual – where similarity and difference are in the process of differentiation, where the one and the other split, and where what was united becomes separate. At the same time, en-gendering subjectivities will be framed as the effect of the constant 'labour of division' (Cooper, 1989; Hetherington and Munro, 1997) inspired by an organizational culture. That is, one of the affordances provided by an organizational culture is to show the boundaries in which identity and gender are allowed, as well as the permeability and the meaning of these boundaries.

In the sections that follow, after presenting the theoretical framework for our analysis, we shall explore two territories of signification and re-signification, the first relating to the experience of being a woman in a male-dominated organizational culture and the second to the experience of being a male heterosexual doing research in a homosexual community. In accordance with a feminist methodological principle for critical knowledge production we choose to start from our own experience in order to expose the collusive process – and the resistance to it as well – that takes place when handling the ambiguity of crosswise gender presence.

A symbolic approach to gender

It is not always easy to understand symbolic representations, nor to define the way in which they structure social experience. The difficulty stems from the nature of the symbol itself, which is so much the *significans* as to be indeterminate and constantly defer its *significandum*, and which requires an indirect language, one which establishes relations and conserves transformative power. The invention of a symbol is a creative act which rests upon the ability to see a thing as what it is not (Castoriadis, 1987: 137). Symbolic understanding is therefore generated on the borders of ambiguity, where being and non-being merge, where the indeterminate is about to transform itself into the determinate, and where possibilities are emergent.

Symbolists differ from many culture researchers in that they emphasize the aesthetic, ethical and emotional dimensions of human life, rather than simply examining its cognitive and axiological dimensions (Alvesson and Berg, 1992: 118–126). Symbolists dissolve the difference between the subjective and the objective; they link symbols, images, metaphors, etc. together: 'the mythic mode of symbolling' (Witkin and Berg 1984). Therefore the symbol of difference resides within a symbolic approach to gender; it subsumes a dyadic code which entails constant relation and tension; it symbolizes what is separate and inseparable.

In organization studies a symbolic approach to gender may be traced back to organizational symbolism and cultural studies of organizing processes (Gherardi, 1995). Nevertheless it has more ancient roots in a conception of gender as a discursive effect created within a signification domain.

In fact, French and Italian feminism view the body as the symbolic rather than physical origin of the subject 'woman' (Irigaray, 1974; Cavarero, 1990; Muraro, 1991). This subject is unable to 'auto-signify herself' because Western philosophical thought has imposed itself as male thought, devising a universal and neutral subject which defines and represents the world in its own terms. As a consequence, women have been denied access to the symbolic. This is the position aptly expressed by Kristeva (1981) in the title of her article 'Women can never be defined'. As to a definition of the subject Woman, during a first phase of feminist theorizing, women were signified as 'the Other' (de Beauvoir, 1949; Irigaray, 1974) in the same way as Frantz Fanon (1961) represented blacks as 'the Other' to Western culture. In so doing, feminist thought produced the cultural effect of de-legitimizing the unity and stability of the Cartesian subject.

A second phase in the genealogy of the concept of gender was the shift, in the 1980s, from the concept of difference (in the singular and mainly as Female/Male difference) to differences among women and men and in the inter-sections of gender, race, class and other situated differences. The subject Woman now splits in a multiplicity of subjectivities. The radical difference of the subject Woman has come to symbolize an ontological paradox, a paradox inscribed in language and in dichotomous thought. Deconstructionism is there-fore a feminist practice which encourages women to demonstrate that the prac-tices which define them are a fiction and that they are historically situated in power relations. Feminism takes a critical stance towards the postmodern debate on contemporary subjectivity by emphasizing that the crisis of subject-ivity mainly affects the Western male, while 'other' subjectivities are now moving to centre stage. The concept of difference now evokes Derrida's word game as he plays with difference and *différance*. And the third phase is labelled the post-woman period (Braidotti and Cavarero, 1993) or in Teresa De Lau-retis's (1999) terms the rise of eccentric subjects. We may say that the move from women studies to gender studies has been accomplished when the subject becomes a grammatical need (Braidotti and Cavarero, 1993), or when the subject is conceived as existing only as a citation effect (Butler, 1990), or when the body is only a symptom and the passage from sex to gender is mediated, translated, enacted (De Lauretis, 1999).

A symbolic approach to gender may be historically situated within the third phase of the feminist debate, when gender is taken to be the most powerful symbol of differences, culturally enacted and 'positioned' through material and semiotic practices. Gender is something we 'do' and something we think (Gher-ardi, 1994). The social construction of gender and its en-gendering in situated subjectivities is the effect of discursive practices and cultural representations (in films, literature, arts) rooted in power relations and social institutions like the family, language, scientific disciplines, the welfare system.

In order to illustrate the passage from the theoretical definition of gender as a symbol of differences to a symbolic methodology for analysing gender rela-tions in organizing, more careful exploration is required of the concepts of dif-ference in the deconstructive tradition, of positioning as the collaborative process of taking a discursive subject position, and of dual presence as the process of transgressing the boundaries of oppositional categories.

Several currents of thought are involved in the project to deconstruct the self and to create a relational self (Sampson, 1989). Alongside feminism, social constructionism has contributed analysis of the individual as a social and historical construction; systems theory has given ontological primacy to relations rather than to individual entities; critical theory – the Frankfurt School – has unmasked the ideology of advanced capitalism; and deconstructionism has developed as a perspective internal to post-structuralism. Although these approaches belong to very different disciplinary traditions, they converge on a conception of subjectivity in which

> the subjects are constituted in and through a symbolic system that fixes the subject in place while remaining beyond the subject's full mastery. In other words, persons are not at the centre [. . .] but have been decentred by these relations to the symbolic order.
>
> (Sampson, 1989: 14)

The symbolic order of gender that separates the symbolic universes of the female and the male sanctions a difference whereby what is affirmed by the One is denied by the Other. The One and the Other draw meaning from this binary opposition, which forms a contrast created *ad hoc* which maintains a hierarchical interdependence (Derrida, 1967, 1971). The interdependence-based symbolic order is a relational order which rests upon difference and the impossibility of its definition. Male and female are undecidable, their meaning is indeterminate and constantly deferred.

The origins of the widely used concept of 'difference' (Derrida, 1971) warrant examination. By 'difference' is meant a form of self-reference 'in which terms contain their own opposites and thus refuse any singular grasp of their meanings' (Cooper and Burrell, 1988: 101). In order to stress the processual nature of difference, Derrida invented the term *différance*, which in French is pronounced the same as *différence* and incorporates the two meanings of the verb *différer*: defer in time, and differ in space. Male and female are not only different from each other (static difference) but they constantly defer each other (processual difference), in the sense that the latter, the momentarily deferred term, is waiting to return because, at a profound level, it is united with the former. The difference separates, but it also unites because it represents the unity of the process of division. Because of their multi-individual dimension and supra-individual duration, male and female as symbolic systems possess a static aspect which creates a social perception of immutability, of social structure and institution. But male and female is also a social relation dynamic whereby meaning is processually enucleated within society and individual and collective phenomena. The symbolic order of gender is static difference and processual difference. Put better, it is the product of their interdependence: the impossibility of fixing meaning once and for all sanctions the transitoriness of every interpretation and exposes the political nature of every discourse on gender. The crucial theoretical issue is whether a male epistemology can/must be replaced by a female one, or whether the concept itself of epistemology must/can be replaced by an explanation of the discourse processes by which human beings acquire understanding of their common world. Within the latter, the subject position (Foucault, 1984) becomes a 'positioning' enacted and performed within an institutionalized use of language and of other similar sign systems.

It is within a particular discourse that a subject (the position of a subject) is constructed as a compound of knowledge and power into a more or less coercive structure which ties it to an en-gendered identity. A subject position incorporates both a conceptual repertoire and a location for persons within the structure of the rights pertaining to those who use the repertoire (Davies and Harré, 1990).

A subject position is what is created in and through conversations as speakers and hearers construct themselves as persons: it creates a location in which social relations and actions are mediated by symbolic forms and modes of being. Performing gender relations entails both reproducing the impression of a static symbolic order in which gender difference arises from an oppositional categorial system (the logic of either/or differentiation) and the dynamic symbolic order in which the meaning of gender relation is deferred, situated in interactions, institutionalized in historical systems of thought. Therefore, the performativity of gender relations may be seen at the border between mutually exclusive categories: in the slash that divides and unites the opposite symbolic universes of female/male, private/public, nature/culture, science/technology. It is in the ambiguity of the slash that the symbolic approach gains heuristic power.

Ambiguity and duality are the distinctive features of every symbol, since the symbolic function resides simultaneously in the force of coagulation (i.e. in the synthesis, by images and correspondences among symbols, of a multiplicity of meanings into one) and in the force of dissolution (i.e. in a return to chaos, to the mixing of meanings, to dissolution). Crossing the boundaries between the symbolic universes of female/male, and acting in this symbolic liminal territory for the deferral of the meaning of gender, may be expressed and synthesized in the concept of 'dual presence'.

Dual presence in liminal territories

The 'dual presence' (Balbo, 1979; Zanuso, 1987) is a category invented by Italian feminists in the 1970s to indicate cross-gender experiences and the simultaneous presence (in the imaginary, consciousness and experience of women) of public and private, of home and work, of the personal and the political. The expression 'dual presence' denotes a frame of mind which, midway through the 1970s, came to typify a growing number of adult women who thought of themselves in a 'crosswise' manner with respect to different worlds – material and symbolic – conceived as different and in opposition to each other and, not coincidentally, pertaining to one or the other of the symbolic universes of gender: public/private, the family/the labour market, the personal/the political, the places of production/the places of reproduction (Zanuso, 1987: 43). In social practices, more and more women found themselves operating in a plurality of arenas; they broke with traditional role models, and they created a space which was practical and mental, structural and projectual, adaptive to given constraints and productive of new personal and social arrangements. In short, the dual presence may be seen as the symbolic presence in a liminal territory of signification and re-signification where the boundaries between the symbolic universes of male and female became fluid, negotiable, intersect and merge.

The positioning of gender as a social practice which en-genders specific individuals is a 'liminary' activity, (van Gennep, 1909; Turner, 1969). That is, it is an activity which relates to the metaphor of the 'threshold' (*limen* in Latin): the invisible line (the slash) that separates and unites the inner and the outer, a symbol of transition and transcendence. The state or condition of liminarity enables communication between the structure – the institutional organization of positions and/or actors – and what Victor Turner (1969) calls 'antistructure'; that is, the social dynamic unit. The structure differentiates individuals, it renders them unequal within relatively rigid social positions. The antistructure is *communitas*, contact with the totality, an arena in which the individual or the group redefines the universal function of the structure in contact with age-old symbols.

In other words, one may talk of persistence and change, of structure and process, of institution and movement: all these are dualities which enable communication between static difference and processual difference. Just as the threshold between waking and sleeping represents what no longer is and what is not yet, so liminarity is the state of difference, of the 'original unifying unity of what tends apart' (Heidegger, 1969: 75). The dialectical tension between structure and antistructure is the dynamic between the totality in the individual and the individual in the totality; it is structural ambivalence. The structuring of the symbolic world of gender differences is expressed in institutions, processes and dynamics which erect a symbolic order of gender based on static difference, but at the same time the collective and global meaning of gender differences is historicized into radically different symbolic and social structures, where the threshold between male and female is crossed innumerable times. Female experiences in the male symbolic universe or heterosexual experiences in homosexual symbolic domains – as we shall see in the next sections – give dynamic redefinition to the concrete meaning of en-gendering subjectivities. Handling the dual presence entails competence in transgressing the boundaries and shaping the boundaries of the liminal territory where the symbolic order of gender is redefined through the suspension of pre-existing gender significations, and it re-emerges with its contents changed to redefine successive meanings. But en-gendering subjectivities is not only the effect of discursive practices, as some post-structuralist and deconstructive scholars assume, or as the so-called 'transgender' approach argues. The materiality of en-gendering the individual is inscribed in the technologies of gender and in the institution of compulsory heterosexuality which sustains the gender ideology.

The concept itself of subject is grounded in ambiguity and in that ambiguity the eccentric subject – as Teresa De Lauretis (1999) points out – may represent a knowing position as the subject who is affected by gender, who is inside gender determinations, but at the same time is critical, ironic, eccentric to the ideology of gender. The concept of subject in fact activates two meanings: one is 'being subject to' (i.e. subjection to social constraints); the second is tied to the grammatical sense of 'being the one who acts' (i.e. self-determination). The eccentric subject is the one whose subjectivity takes shape in the translation process from being subject to becoming the one who signifies self-determination within a network of socio-material relations. In recent years, numerous figures of discourse similar to the eccentric subject have appeared as cultural representations of postmodernity: the ironist (Rorty, 1989), the nomadic (Braidotti, 1994), the cyborg (Haraway, 1991), the mestiza (Anzaldùa, 1987), the hybrid (Bhabba, 1994). All these subjectivities have a common element: they are simultaneously inside and outside, at the borders of cultures, and committed to practices of re-signification. In our terminology, they inhabit liminal territories and are committed to practices of handling the dual presence; in other terms they delimit 'transitionary spaces' (Holvino, 1996) where hybridization may occur. The distinctive feature of the practice of the dual presence (and hybridization as well) is that change and resistance are intertwined: contradictions, oppositions, paradoxes, tensions are not resolved but re-signified in discursively, socially and materially new forms. The proliferation of metaphors for translation (from one language into another, from one place to another, from global to local, from a natural world to an artefactual one) testifies to how knowledge and ideas travel, and in travelling are transformed and engender different realities.

A note on method

In order to illustrate the practical working of the dual presence we have chosen the liminarity between female/male and between homosexual/heterosexual in the experience of a female scholar entering a male-dominated organizational culture, and in the experience of a male heterosexual doing research in a gay and lesbian magazine managed by homosexual men. The two sections illustrating the heterogeneous engineering of our gendered subjectivities may be considered two episodes of self-ethnography, or two exercises in reflexive methodology in which the knowing subject and the known object are subjected to the same objectifying gaze (see also Chapter 10 by Katila and Meriläinen for an extensive discussion of the methodological and ethical implications of conceptualizing self both as subject and object of research).

In fact, the symbolist scholar has the following distinctive features (Turner, 1992):

- S/he is a qualitative researcher who prefers to see things through the eyes of the subject. S/he is interested in meanings, in the process of their attribution, in how they are sustained, in the way that some meanings prevail while others disappear.
- S/he is a participative researcher, who knows that s/he is part of the production of meaning and of the narration of stories, as both the narrating and the narrated subject.
- S/he is the product of contextual understanding of actions and symbols, not only because they are inseparable but because all symbols are value-laden and meaningful only in terms of their relationship to other symbols.
- S/he is a wanderer among the realms of knowledge seeking to reconstruct the links among the various levels of reality created by a symbol through individual symbolic production, the collective unconscious and artistic production: the immanent with the transcendent, the mental with the physical, with action, with transformation.

The meaning of our methodological choice is also political: it represents a form of resistance to one of the founding values of the professional community to which we belong. Academia, in fact, may be considered an organization devoted to knowledge production and to celebration of the superiority of objective knowledge. The epistemological position of objective knowing produces objectified objects and subjects, since it separates the subject of knowledge by distancing it from its object, denies any emotional bond between the two, and represents the obsession of controlling through distancing and objectifying. The knowledge thus produced in and through academia pretends to be objective, dispassionate, universal and neutral. We shall illustrate the process by which 'gender neutrality' is achieved: the erasure of the body, sexuality, and desire. But the erased terms tend to reappear in disguised forms.

A female newcomer enters a male-dominated community

I shall begin my ethnographic journey through Italian academic culture by recounting how I became a competent member of the community of practice of organizational scholars, starting from a poster which hangs on the wall of my office (see Plate 2.1).

I bought the poster at a Magritte exhibition in Rome where I went with a male colleague to celebrate my awarding of tenure. On showing him the picture, I asked him if he would like it in the office which we shared. He commented, 'It suits you!' At the time I ignored his remark, suspecting some sexual innuendo, but since then – and almost twenty years have passed – whenever I look at Magritte's image, I find new meanings and realize how I use that poster to symbolize my acceptance of the profession's 'rules of the game'. But at the same time, the symbol is the ostensible sign of my resistance to a culture which claims to be gender-neutral and requires me to silence my difference.

A nightgown is hanging in Magritte's wardrobe but it still retains the form of a body and of provocative breasts. In achieving tenure I put my nightdress in the wardrobe – leaving the door open – and from studying the female labour market I moved to organizational decision-making. From sociology of work I moved to sociology of organization. In my choice of research topic and disciplinary field, the move was towards centrality, leaving behind so-called 'women issues' and a declining discipline. In Magritte's poster I see the symbol of what I left behind when I assumed a professional identity and community membership in a male-dominated environment. I was obeying three silent orders issued by my community: leave the body, leave a female body, respect a principle of order.

Leave the body: the nightdress has no head. The head does not belong to the wardrobe, but to the outside world. And the head symbolizes the upper functions: cognition, wisdom, intelligence, rationality. In order to gain initiation to knowledge, the body should be put aside: knowledge is abstract, mental, universal, disinterested and disembodied. Knowledge has no body and no gender: it is neutral and pure.

Leave a female body: the nightdress has breasts and desire belongs to the night, the dark, the wardrobe. When entering the professional community, desire should be set aside: better not be attractive, nor be attracted. Knowledge is separation; the act of knowing is the act of introducing distance and distinction between the knowing subject and the known object. In the Cartesian

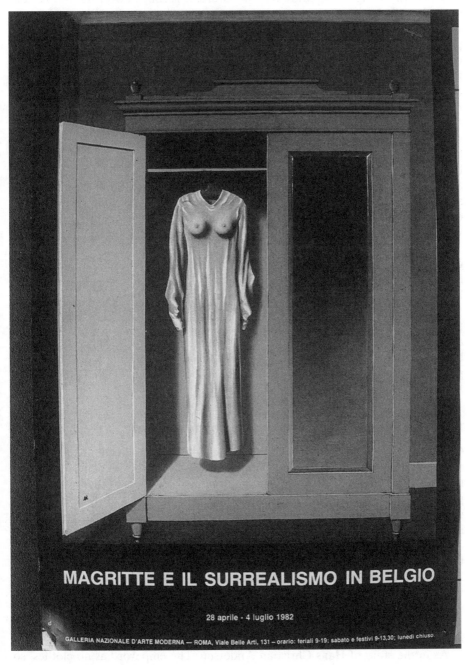

Plate 2.1 'Magritte e il surrealismo in Belgio'.

Source: Copyright permission granted by the Galleria Nazionale di Arte Moderna-Rome (I)

tradition knowledge is separation from nature, it is control over nature. A nurturing knowledge is an oxymoron.

Respect a principle of order: the nightdress belongs to the wardrobe like a piece of cheese belongs to the fridge. In our Western civilized culture, we usually keep the two items separate, even if we can do so in different ways. Putting the nightdress in the wardrobe and the cheese in the fridge is an act of classification; it is obedience to a principle of order whose logic we understand, respect and take for granted. In becoming affiliated to a scientific discipline, we should also agree to be disciplined in the body and in the mind. Knowing and mastering a discipline means understanding its system of classification and the logic behind it, on the implicit assumption that there is a single logic. A discipline is not ordered like the Chinese encyclopaedia cited by Borges, where animals are classified as: (a) belonging to the emperor, embalmed; tamed; sucking-pigs; sirens; fantastical; stray dogs; included in the present classification; on heat; several; designed with a brush made of camel hair, and so on; animals which have just broken the water jug; those which have long looked like flies.[2]

But the classifications we use to keep our wardrobe in order (where the socks go and where the pants), which we take for granted and whose logic we assume is self-evident, break down and become difficult to explain as soon as we start living with somebody else and share a wardrobe with our beloved.

The logic which keeps a discipline (and its followers) in order is called 'objective' and 'scientific', but it could also be called 'grounded in power/knowledge dynamics' or simply 'no different from housekeeping'. The three definitions bring with them different resources of legitimization. Entering a community of practice means participating in a reputational social system which fights for classifications, legitimacy and symbolic resources.

Leaving Magritte, leaving the body, reapproaching gender

Gender and reputation are indeed in the same drawer, and becoming an organizational scholar entails becoming competent at mastering a gendered practice, not only according to one's own gender but also to maleness as the invisible and prime standard. Like in the *Epistemology of the Closet* by Eve Kosofski Sedgwick (1990), the closet focuses metaphorically on the relations between the known and the unknown, on the 'subjective practice in which the oppositions of private/public, inside/outside, subject/object are established, and the sanctity of their first term kept inviolate' (Miller, 1988: 207, quoted in Sedgwick, 1990: 67). As a woman professional I have learnt how to hide and how to be forgiven for my femaleness: a competence rule in academia is that gender, body and sexuality must not intrude into the profession if reputation is at stake. And more reputation can be gained by colluding to save the invisible masculinity – the gender honour – of a discipline claiming to be gender-neutral.

As in the story of Hans Christian Andersen 'The emperor has no clothes' so in organization studies 'the discipline has no gender' (nor race, Nkomo, 1992), and its neutrality is the artful cultural product of a community of scholars, many of whom – even when they study gender – equate gender with 'women' and women issues and in so doing contribute to render masculinity invisible.

But a thought system based on dichotomous categories is always a poor system. On the one hand, it is unavoidable because it is inscribed in the language; on the other it leads to oppositional thought and perpetuates the hierarchical order of one term over the other (the second term becomes second-sexed). If gender studies in the organizational field follow the line of reasoning of either/or (either male or female, either men or women), they will end up by 'adding the female', adding the women in organization studies, or by being enrolled in the mainstream in an ancillary role.

It is more challenging to reason in terms of both/and, because this breaks with a linear, consequential order, giving rise to resistance, subversion, transgression, perversion, playfulness, creativity. Accommodating both/and in our thought and life is to face up to our feelings of unease, of ambivalence, of feeling upset at the onset of disorder.

We cannot escape the gender trap, but we can bring resistance and subversion in reading and reproducing organizational literature and academic culture. To do so, we need an oppositional gaze.

The term 'oppositional gaze' comes from bell hooks (1994) and film theory. It refers to the possible positioning of the black spectator – woman – in American film production. The black woman has two alternatives. Either she identifies with the white character and enjoys the film, denying her race identity and being disappointed once back to reality, or she suffers from the beginning at her exclusion from the film's imagery and she does not enjoy the film. The oppositional gaze deconstructs the fabric of a cultural text in order to understand how racializing is achieved and to resist it. An oppositional gaze in organization studies would be the one used by those scholars – women and men – who do not feel at ease in reproducing texts of invisible masculinity.

A heterosexual man doing research in a homosexual community

The episode about to be narrated occurred during ethnographic fieldwork conducted as part of a research study on gender and entrepreneurship (Bruni, *et al.*, 2000). Five business initiatives were examined and 'read' in terms of their gender aspects: the entrepreneurs were both male and female, but they were all heterosexuals, except from the one that I am about to describe.

The episode happened during a period (one week) spent in the Milan editorial offices of the only gay and lesbian magazine currently published in Italy, a setting peopled entirely by (male) homosexuals. The person 'shadowed' was the only male entrepreneur in the sample belonging to a homosexual organizational culture, and it was decided to include him because the issue of homosexual identity is a particularly delicate aspect of the discourse on the formation of the Male/Female position (Weed and Schor, 1997). Sexual orientation, in fact, involves the bodily practices of people, and thus focuses attention on how one can talk about gender identity (as a category which transcends merely genetic sexual membership) while also involving people's bodies.

The surprises of ethnographic research

One day the person I was 'shadowing' said to me: 'Have you got a boyfriend or are you single?' Seeing that I'm a male I realized that he thought I was homosexual. As it happened I had no partner at the time, and so I simply answered that I was 'single'. The conversation stopped there for the time being. I knew that he thought I was gay, but I couldn't understand why. I found this odd but not particularly embarrassing. Yet it seems strange that I should be able to 'confuse' a homosexual. In a sense it was a problem of culture, and here a brief aside on my 'image' is required. I have long hair (tied back), a goatee, and ear-rings (three), I wear cardigans and slacks, and I am what is usually called 'soft-spoken'. It was not the first time that someone has thought I was gay, but it has usually been heterosexuals who do so. This is because (I presume) my 'image' corresponds to the stereotype that Western heterosexual culture has produced of homosexuals. And this is why a homosexual who knows his 'culture' (and who does not have long hair, ear-rings or a goatee, and is decidedly more 'in-your-face' than I am) often takes me the wrong way. Moreover, I have homosexual friends, both gay and lesbian, and none of them has ever mistaken my heterosexuality – which I therefore presume is reasonably obvious.

In the days that followed, because I was in close contact with the person for entire workdays, I found myself discussing just about everything with him – politics, films, travel, hobbies, and so on. We obviously did not think in the same way, but there emerged a world which both of us to some extent shared, at least at the level of key words.

On my last day, during the final interview, we began to talk about the situation of the gay community in Italy and how nice it would be if things were otherwise. I wanted him to tell me something about the relations between male, female and homosexuality. If there is a (symbolic) construction of male and female, I was interested in whether and how homosexuality is likewise constructed. I realized that this meant asking a declaredly homosexual person about prejudices against homosexuals, and I also realized that this was not a particularly 'polite' thing to do. In fact I did not know how to ask him. But I then remembered that he thought I was homosexual as well, and at a certain point asked: 'But, for example, the other day why did you ask me so confidently if I had a boyfriend?'

'Why?'

'Well, I'm usually asked if I have a girlfriend . . .'

'Yes, but you can see!'

'You can see what?'

'That you're homosexual!'

'And how can you see?'

'Well, a straight would have settled the gender question simply by doing research on women. And then a straight would never have been interested in the homosexuality issue in particular . . . and he would never have managed to get so far into the editorial offices as you have done . . .'

And so on, but with the oddity that the more the conversation continued, the more his remarks about heterosexuals became insults. I listened, merely smiling and nodding from time to time.

'But you're gay, aren't you?' This was the final phrase in his explanation of why he thought I was gay. As a question it left no room for evasion; the answer could only be yes or no. I was seriously embarrassed, more than anything else because saying 'yes' would have been an outright lie, while saying 'no' would reveal that I had been dishonest with him.

'No'

'Ah, how strange, I could have sworn ...'

'Yes, I know ... yet ... no, I'm not homosexual.'

'So ... have you got a girlfriend?'

'No, I really am single.'

It is not a pleasant sensation to face someone to whom you have just admitted that although you have not been lying, neither have you been telling the truth. Of course, I could have explained the value of being considered an 'insider' for my participant observation. But this did not seem a good excuse from a human point of view. Indeed, it seemed shabby. The problem is that when he had asked me (three days previously) about my sentimental situation, and I had decided 'not to tell a lie' (but not in the sense that I told the truth), I never imagined that I would again find myself in a similar situation. I did not know what was going to happen some days later, nor did I know whether I would be able to handle the interviews without committing 'heterosexual' gaffes. But I think I managed it.

The role of the researcher: what does being 'single' mean?

As I have tried to illustrate with the episode recounted, calling oneself 'single' in a setting where the presumption of heterosexuality is inoperative may be 'ambiguous'. Consider again the process that led to the subject's conviction that I was homosexual:

1 *'Yes, but you can see! ... That you're homosexual!'* My outward appearance, although physically in keeping with the male gender (I sport a beard), is also contaminated by features that might be related to the female (I wear ear-rings and have long hair). My outward appearance, in association with my role as a researcher, is therefore somewhat ambiguous. The occupational community to which I belong is founded on abstract and universal knowledge. The organizational culture which springs from that knowledge is prescriptive in nature, and the space granted for dissent and assertion (even only aesthetic) by individuals is rather limited. Moreover, compliance with the social practices of the community is even more forcefully required of newcomers ('young researchers' like myself) who are not yet an integral part of the community and must display their acquiescence by assuming the dominant gender identity (even if only aesthetically). In the same way, the symbolic realm of masculinity asserts the culture of heterosexuality as a practice common to and shared by all 'men'. It thus constructs a hetero-normative knowledge which rejects 'ambiguous' and 'contaminated' identities like, for example, gayness (Connell, 1995). My interlocutor took it for granted that I knew this, and in some way this awareness was common to both of us.

2 *'Well, a straight would have settled the gender question simply by doing research on women.'* Here, a 'straight' is somebody who takes for granted that, when talking about gender, one talks about the female (worse, about 'women') with the male (i.e. 'men') being treated as obvious or normal, exploiting the advantages of a culture which a priori assumes the masculine as a given element. The equations gender = sex and sex = women are not only misunderstandings

due to inexperience or to a linguistic operation which attenuates the social embarrassment caused by the word 'sex', replacing it with a more 'polite' one, they are an ideological operation which allows gender studies to continue without calling the gender relation – that is, the relation between the male and female – into question. In this manner, maleness is made invisible, removed from critical reflection and continues to be the prime term, the one in relation to which the other is defined by default. My interviewee reminded me that numerous studies share this basic assumption, and that the organizational culture of the academic community is not only hetero-normative but identifies 'women' as the residual category.

3   *'And then a straight would never have been interested in the homosexuality issue in particular.'* The dominant model of sexual desire, what Connell calls 'cathexis' (1995), is one of the most covert assumptions of masculinity, justified as it is by being 'biologically normal'. It seemed strange to the person interviewed not only that a 'straight' could interrogate masculinity but also, and especially, that he would be interested in sexual (we would say bodily) practices in organizations. In other words, if he found it difficult to understand that a 'straight' could be interested in the gender processes underlying organizations and the market, he found it even more incomprehensible that a 'straight' would want to investigate one of the most covert aspects of individuals in organizing: sexual orientation.

4   *'and he would never have managed to get so far into the editorial offices as you have done ...'* Bodily practices are not necessarily 'sexual' practices. They belong to the broader category of 'relational' practices that sustain them. His discourse evinces that this relation is very close, so much so that those who do not engage in these practices are not accepted by their organizational community.

Thus, the implicit elements on which his discourse grounded were:

- respecting aesthetic (and external) categories of Male/Female;
- assuming the coincidence (or otherwise) of gender identity with biological identity;
- taking for granted the model of socially shared bodily practices;
- the relational dimension, proving membership (or otherwise) of a community.

These are probably the same criteria that the interviewee saw applied to himself when he was no longer recognized as a member of the male community. But he was also implicitly revealing to me the shared gender assumptions of the organizational culture to which I belong, showing that my non-compliance with them automatically places me in other communities. Calling myself 'single' caused such confusion in my interlocutor that he committed the error of interpreting my non-recognition of any gender rules as signalling adherence to 'other' sexual practices. He probably thought it normal that somebody interested in homosexuality, and knowledgeable on gay issues, should also be a member of the homosexual community, taking it for granted that sexual orientation in organizing was not under discussion. Just as I committed the opposite error of interpreting our membership of 'peripheral' categories of masculinity as proof of one (and only one) difference: it was obvious to me that my heterosexuality required no justification, or clarification, and that it could never be the subject of confusion or deception, taking for granted that 'research' has nothing to do with sexual practices.

Thus both of us were trying to cancel our difference, falling into the 'gender trap' of the mutual exclusiveness of different gender identities, In seeking to distinguish ourselves from the gender order of our respective organizational cultures, we were both reaffirming one of its cardinal principles: the cancellation of difference and the assumption that what is 'diverse' must be internally homogeneous.

Conclusions

Gender attribution and self-attribution are precarious achievements, learnt and enacted on appropriate occasions in situated social and organizational practices. The codes of coherence between sex, sexuality, desire and appropriate gender performances are inscribed in cultural norms and values which operate at a discursive and material level. 'En-gendering subjectivities' has been described as a process of active self-formation which transforms individuals into subjects who secure their meaning and reality through identifying with a particular sense of their own gender and sexuality. At the same time, 'en-gendering subjectivities' is a process strongly rooted in (and linked with) the organizational culture assumption regarding gender and identity.

En-gendering a professional subjectivity is an interactive process of collective signification and re-signification which takes place in symbolic territories at the borders of ambiguity, where being and non-being merge. Through the personal experiences of crosswise presence – as an academic woman in a male-dominated environment and as a heterosexual man doing research in an homosexual community – we have illustrated the artful cultural practice of handling our dual presence as competent members of those communities.

The aim of the chapter has been, in fact, to argue that the symbolic order inscribed in language which separates dyadic and hierarchical categories and oppositional belongings – either female or male; either homosexual or heterosexual – is constantly deferred, subverted, translated, hybridized by the permeability of boundaries. Liminary is the state and the activity of signifying differences; it symbolizes the original unifying unity of what tends apart and the possibility of disrupting dichotomic categories and their subversive re-signification, proliferation and dissemination beyond the binary frame.

The category of 'dual presence' allows us to focus on the slash between categories of thought and on the activities involved in the deferral of meanings. In situated encounters, the skilful handling of the dual presence goes unnoticed because it is part of our taken-for-granted world and our tacit competence in moving through it.

When we focus on dual presence as a social process we are able to see how meanings are generated as both a discursive practice and a material one. Heterogeneous engineering (Law, 1994) is the image for the alignment of material and non-material elements into a coherent – but unstable – whole. In citing the example of the academic woman we have highlighted how the neutrality of academia and of academic knowledge is a process of symbolic representation based on the disembodiment of the person (which represents knowledge as mental), on the suppression of the female body (which represents 'Man' as an universal knowing subject), and on the production of disembodied texts (which hide the authorization of the knowledge production behind the invisible authority of scientific writing). The gender-neutrality of disciplines is the social outcome of a process of disciplining the minds and the bodies of those who belong to knowledge production organizations, and it is also enacted through their active involvement and resistance to it. The material artefact, the image of the female body in the closet, introduces irony and subversion, and it symbolizes belonging and non-belonging. Moreover, it highlights metaphorically the organizational practices in which gender and identity are established and where organizational culture roots its oppositions of Private vs. Public, Inside vs. Outside, Subject vs. Object.

In the second experience, at the borders of sexuality and desire attribution, the engineering of a gendered subjectivity is achieved through the mobilization of discursive and relational practices based on a 'reading' of cultural codes of what is taken for granted in two organizational communities. The clash between implicit assumptions about homosexual/heterosexual categorical systems reveals the pervasiveness of the institution of compulsory heterosexuality and its framing of the situation in which gender attribution is mobilized through linguistic artefacts. But this time the clash also symbolizes a shifting and a failing in the alignment of organizational culture, identity and gender, thus highlighting the precarious nature of every process of ordering.

It is therefore evident that en-gendering subjectivities is an artful social process of ordering bodies, sexualities, desires, symbols of belonging and exclusion, discourses, artefacts and texts into a coherent arrangement. Some of these arrangements hold longer than others, but all of them are historical products and fragile social enactments, partially under our control some of the time. The dissemination of the meaning of 'gender relation' is such a case.

A symbolic approach to gender, and a methodology to analyse the skilful engineering of heterogeneous elements into a social practice, yields deeper understanding of the following points:

- how the decentring of the 'self' as the privileged site of thinking and knowing, of identity and gender, may be pursued further on stressing the material and the discursive construction of the subject position within situated practices of subjectivization and objectification;
- how highly negotiated the belonging to an organizational culture is and how belonging is inscribed in ritualized semiotic and material practices;
- how gender and identity are staged through the workings of power and how a subject position is constituted by power relations;
- how the achievement of belonging is a construction that conceals its genesis and obscures the collective agreement which sustains a situated professional identity.

Therefore, an en-gendered subjectivity is the outcome of a process of negotiation, of acculturation, of acceptance/refusal of gender codes, of assertiveness/erasure of the identity of the 'Other'. Gender is learnt and enacted as a situated practice, and the codes of an organizational gendered subjectivity are passed on to new participants as an integrative part of an organizational culture.

The concept of dual presence enables us to deconstruct essential gender identities and to recognize the contingency and ambiguity of every identity and the political conflicts associated with the permeability of boundaries between female and male symbolic universes, between heterosexuality and homosexuality. Therefore, how to handle the dual presence is a matter of the micro-politics of everyday life for both women and men who do not wish to reproduce invisible masculinity.

Notes

1 The present paper is a totally collaborative effort by the two authors whose names appear in alphabetical order. If, however, for academic reasons individual responsibility has to be assigned, Attila Bruni wrote pp. 31–5 and the conclusions; Silvia Gherardi wrote the introduction, and pp. 22–31.
2 Foucault (1973), in *The Order of Things* (p. xv) quotes this passage from Borges and concludes that: 'in the wonderment of this taxonomy, the thing we apprehend in one great leap, the thing that, by means of a fable, is demonstrated as the exotic charm of another system of thought, is the limitation of our own'.

References

Alvesson, M. and Berg, P.O. (1992). *Corporate Culture and Organizational Symbolism*. Berlin: de Gruyter.
Anzaldùa, G. (1987). *Borderlands: The New Mestiza = La Frontera*. San Francisco, CA: Aunt Lute Books.
Balbo, L. (1979). La doppia presenza. *Inchiesta*, 32: 3–6.
Beauvoir, S. de (1949). *Le deuxieme sexe*. Paris: Gallimard.
Bhabba, H. (1994). *The Location of Culture*. London: Routledge.
Braidotti, R. (1994). *Nomadic Subjects: Embodiment and Sexual Difference in Contemporary Feminist Theory*. New York, NY: Columbia University Press.
Braidotti, R. and Cavarero, A. (1993). Il tramonto del soggetto e l'Alba della soggettività femminile. *Donna, Women, Femme*, 4: 69–90.
Bruni, A. and Gherardi, S. (2001). Omega's story: the heterogeneous engineering of a gendered professional self. In M. Dent and S. Whitehead (eds), *Knowledge, Identity and the New Professional*. London: Routledge.
Bruni, A., Gherardi, S. and Poggio, B. (2000). *All'ombra della maschilità. Storie di imprese e di genere*. Milano: Guerini e Associati.
Butler, J. (1990). *Gender Trouble: Feminism and the Subversion of Identity*. London: Routledge.
Castoriadis, C. (1987). *The Imaginary Institution of Society*. Oxford. Polity Press.
Cavarero, A. (1990). *Nonostante Platone*. Roma: Editori Riuniti.
Connell, R.W. (1995). *Masculinities*. London: University of California Press.
Cooper, R. (1988). The visibility of social system. In N.C. Jackson, T. Keys and S.A. Cropper (eds), *Operational Research and the Social Sciences*. New York, NY: Plenum Press.
Cooper, R. (1989). Modernism, postmodernism and organizational analysis 3: the contribution of Jacques Derrida. *Organization Studies*, 10(4): 479–502.
Cooper, R. and Burrell, G. (1988). Modernism, postmodernism and organizational analysis: an introduction. *Organization Studies*, 9(1): 91–112.

Davies, B. and Harré, R. (1990). Positioning: the discoursive production of selves. *Journal of the Theory of Social Behaviour*, 1: 43–63.

De Lauretis, T. (1987). *Technologies of Gender. Essays in Theory, Film and Fiction*. Bloomington: Indiana University Press.

De Lauretis, T. (1999). *Soggetti Eccentrici*. Milano: Feltrinelli.

Derrida, J. (1967). *De la grammatologie*. Paris: Les Editions de Minuit.

Derrida, J. (1971). *L'écriture et la difference*. Paris: de Seuil.

Fanon, F. (1961). *Les damnés de la terre*. Paris: Francois Maspéro éditeur/La Dècouverte & Syros.

Foucault, M. (1973). *The Order of Things*. NY: Vintage.

Foucault, M. (1984). *L'usage des plaisirs*. Paris: Gallimard.

Gennep, A. van (1909). *Les rites de passage*. Paris: Nourry.

Gherardi, S. (1994). The gender we think, the gender we do in everyday organizational life. *Human Relations*, 47(6): 591–609.

Gherardi, S. (1995). *Gender, Symbolism and Organizational Culture*. London: Sage.

Haraway, D. (1991). *A Manifest for Cyborg*. New York, NY: Routledge.

Heidegger, M. (1969). *Zur Sache des Denkens*. Tübingen: Niemeyer.

Hetherington, K. and Munro, R. (eds) (1997). *Ideas of Difference*. Oxford: Blackwell.

Holvino, E. (1996). Reading organization development from the margins: outsiders within. *Organization*, 3(4): 520–534.

Hooks, B. (1994). *Teaching to Transgress: Education as the Practice of Freedom*. New York, NY: Routledge.

Irigaray, L. (1974). *Speculum. De l'autre femme*. Paris: Les Editions de Minuit.

Kristeva, J. (1981). Women can never be defined. In E. Harks (ed.), *New French Feminism*. New York: Schocken.

Law, J. (1994). *Organizing Modernity*. Oxford: Blackwell.

Muraro, L. (1991). *L'ordine simbolico della madre*. Roma: Editori Riuniti.

Nkomo, S. (1992). The emperor has no clothes: rewriting 'Race in Organizations'. *Academy of Management Review*, 17(3): 487–513.

Rorty, R. (1989). *Contingency, Irony and Solidarity*. Cambridge: Cambridge University Press.

Sampson, E. (1989). The deconstruction of the self. In J. Shotter and K. Gergen (eds), *Texts of Identity*. London: Sage.

Sedgwick, E.K. (1990), *Epistemology of the Closet*. London: Penguin.

Turner, B.A. (1992). The symbolic understanding of organizations. In M. Reed and M. Hughes (eds), *Rethinking Organization*. London: Sage.

Turner, V. (1969). *The Ritual Process. Structure and Anti-Structure*. Chicago: Aldine.

Weed, E. and Schor, N. (eds) (1997). *Feminism Meets Queer Theory*. Bloomington and Indianapolis: Indiana University Press.

Witkin, R. and Berg, P.O. (1984). Organization Symbolling: Towards a Theory of Action. Paper presented at SCOS Conference in Lund.

Zanuso, L. (1987). Gli studi sulla doppia presenza: dal conflitto alla norma. In M.C. Marcuzzo and A.R. Doria (eds), *La ricerca delle donne. Studi femministi in Italia*. Torino: Rosemberg e Sellier.

3 Alternative conceptualizations and theoretical perspectives on identities and organizational cultures

A personal review of research on men in organizations[1]

Jeff Hearn

Introduction

In recent years there have been extensive debates on both the social position of men, and the theoretical and practical significance of identity and organizational culture. To connect 'men', 'identity' and 'organizational culture' is both a very obvious thing to do and yet still rather unfamiliar. Its obviousness comes from the myriad ways that men and thus their associated identities often dominate and are formed by organizations and organizational cultures; its unfamiliarity comes from the fact that this connection is rarely made, and may indeed actively be avoided. In this chapter I review some of my recent research on gender, sexuality and organizations in terms of possible connections that can be recognized between men, identity and organizational culture. Significantly, much of this work has been collaborative with other researchers. Before addressing alternative conceptualizations and theoretical perspectives on these issues, some introductory remarks are necessary to set the scene.

First, I have chosen to use the topic of 'men' rather than 'masculinity' as my main theme. This is primarily because the term 'masculinity' has become used in so many different and variable ways – as behaviour, expectations, identity, psychodynamics, and so on (Hearn, 1996b). My own preference is to see 'masculinity' as ideology, as the set of signs that someone is a man. This question is not, however, the main focus of this chapter. In contrast, 'men' is a much clearer and less ambiguous social category – people defined as such that are assumed to exist in relation to males and maleness (Hearn, 1994c). The general task is to name men as men (Hanmer, 1990; Collinson and Hearn, 1994), to deconstruct the dominant (Hearn, 1996a) within a clearly critical perspective (Hearn, 1998b).

Second, focusing on identity and organizational culture should not be taken to suggest that I hold any favour with narrowly defined identity politics or culturalist explanations. Similarly, I consider that tendencies towards essentialism in the theorizing of both identity and culture should be strongly guarded against. Culture is one of the most complex concepts in the English language (Williams, 1976), and it is thus advisable to remember that 'culture' is 'not a "thing" but a political process of contestation over the power to define concepts, including that of culture itself' (Wright, 1998: 12). The notion of culture as an 'island' of given norms and values that is separate from the rest of the world, whether it is a societal culture, an organizational culture, or a local sub-culture, is extremely problematic. While the concept of culture continues appears to be of ever-increasing interest in organizational, managerial and academic discourses (see Harlow and Hearn, 1995), it remains contested.[2]

The concept of identity is more closely connected to the self and the individual; it stands at the intersection of self-perception and the perception of others; it is also subject to many different interpretations and approaches, and is becoming increasingly disputed. Identity can be understood as relatively fixed sense of self, as a form of subjectivity, as multilayered and multiple, as the object of identity-work and self-monitoring, as the object of material and discursive regulation. Like culture, the notion of identity as a fixed and isolated island, in this case of the self, is misguided. While the concept has a long history of use in psychoanalytic studies, social psychology and symbolic interactionist, social action and kindred sociologies, it has in recent years been taken up much more widely in other sociological traditions, in cultural studies and in social theory. Sasha Roseneil and Julie Seymour (1999: 2–5), in a review of recent developments in the theorizing of identity in sociology, have drawn attention to two main strands: what they call a social theory strand,[3] and a post-structuralist cultural theory strand.[4] The former builds partly on earlier symbolic interactionist work in casting 'the problem of identity' largely in terms of the changing form of identity, agency and the self within modernity and late modernity. The latter strand derives its inspiration from post-structuralism and deconstructionism, and accordingly has emphasized 'the instability, fluidity, fragmentary and processual character of identities'. It has also had a much greater engagement with feminism, postcolonialism and queer theory, than has been the case within much of the more modernist first strand. Much discussion has centred on the growing multiplicity, fragmentation, fracturing and threatening of (what can indeed be contradictory or potentially contradictory) identities (for example, Weeks, 1990: 88; Bradley, 1996); on the understanding of identity as in a process of 'becoming' as well as 'being' (Hall, 1990); and on the shift from personal identity to social identity, related to social realities and social divisions (Bradley, 1996). These kinds of debates have impacted to a considerable extent upon organization studies in recent years (for example, Kondo, 1990; Collinson, 1992; Hatch and Schultz, 2000).

Third, it is necessary to locate this chapter within the context of feminist, pro-feminist and other critical scholarship on men, masculinities, organizations and management This includes in particular that by Cynthia Cockburn (1983, 1985, 1990, 1991, 1994), Michael Roper (1991, 1994, 1996), David Collinson (1992), and Deborah Kerfoot and David Knights (1993, 1996), as well as the contributions to the collection, *Men as Managers, Managers as Men* (Collinson and Hearn, 1996b). Such studies have examined, amongst other things, men's power on the shop floor, in management, and in relation to technology. In focusing on men in organizations, my assumption is that the public world of organizations can be best understood in the context of the foundation of unpaid, domestic, 'non-organizational' labour outside organizations (Hearn, 1983, 1987; Hearn and Parkin, 1986–7, 1988), and in the context of patriarchy and specifically public patriarchies (Hearn, 1987, 1992b; Hearn and Parkin, 1995).

Fourth, my focus throughout will be on gender, sexuality and power. Despite the growth of research on sexuality in and around organizations, sexuality remains relatively neglected within organizational analysis, especially so in mainstream research. It does not, however, involve any competition between the concepts of gender and sexuality. While in a variety of work, particularly in collaboration with Wendy Parkin, I have been at pains to show the underdevelopment of work on sexuality and organizations, I have also been insistent in analysing gendered power relations.[5] In this, the very construction of the concepts of 'gender' and 'sexuality' is important. Shifts in their definition and use are indicative of shifts in power relations that are themselves gendered and 'sexualed'.[6] The following analysis has to be considered in the context of these ongoing debates on the very relation of gender, sexuality and organizations.

In the remainder of this chapter, I present four main conceptual and theoretical ways of linking the actions, activities and discourses of 'men' to 'identity' and 'organizational culture'. These approaches are not mutually exclusive; rather they are ways of building up a more complex understanding of that relationship. Each of these four main ways of linking 'men', 'identity' and 'organizational culture' is a commentary on both particular types of organizational cultures and particular analyses of organizational culture. These four approaches are now described in brief.

First, there is the persistent taken-for-grantedness of identities and organizational cultures being men's identities and men's cultures. This is so much so that it is not usually even talked of. This applies in both academic analysis and organizational processes. The apparent or presumed degendering of organizational cultures and identities remains a powerful form of men's power.

Second, there is the increasing recognition of the explicit domination by men of particular organizational cultures and identities. This is becoming an important part of current debates in organizational studies, women's studies and critical studies on men. Examples of relevant cultures and identities include careerist, entrepreneurial, informalistic and paternalistic forms, which persist through gender and sexual domination of various kinds of men and men's actions.

Third, there is the significance of 'men' in the construction of less obvious subtexts of identities and organizational cultures. Here we are concerned with interpretations of identities and organizational cultures that are not only about directly observable behaviour (for example, physical sexual harassment) but also about less obvious meanings that are less directly observable and may occur over time. A prime example of such interpretative processes is the sexual subtext of organizational cultures and identities, including the 'male (hetero)sexual narrative' and the 'homosexual' subtext of organizations.

Fourth, there is a more general question of the deconstruction of the connections between men and the very ideas of 'identity' and 'organizational culture'. This is the least developed of the four approaches. It refers to the ways in which 'gender' is made more apparent or less apparent through the use of the concepts of identity and organizational culture. While identity and organizational culture have often been used, both by analysts and managers, as a repository for that which is not structure, including the 'feminine', what this means for men is far from clear. This could be a way of opening up an exploration of the complexities of men's relations to organizations.

Taken-for-granted (men's) identities and (men's) organizational cultures

Organizational cultures are routinely taken for granted as men's cultures, and as routine locales of men's identities. This assumption pervades both particular organizations (with their organizational cultures) and particular (academic) organizational analyses. Indeed, the majority of debates on identities in organizations and organizational cultures – that is, the patterns of behaviour, beliefs, symbols and identity reproduced by organizational participants – have taken their ungenderedness as given. Identity and organizational culture are themselves presented here as relatively non-problematic concepts. They may be presented in either everyday perceptions or academic analyses as non-problematic 'wholes'. In terms of debates on organizational culture, there are clear links with Martin's (1992) integration perspective, that is itself easily compatible with a centred, relatively unproblematic notion of the self or 'whole identity'.

In order to interrogate these gendered questions, let us begin by taking a fairly typical example of the extensive literature on organizational culture, Mats Alvesson and Per Olof Berg's (1992) book *Corporate Culture and Organizational Symbolism*. They distinguish national culture, regional and industrial culture, department culture and worker culture. They also identify the following cultural elements within corporate culture: physical and visual artefacts, collective mental frameworks and manifestations (sagas, epochs, legends, myths, stories) and collective action patterns (rites, rituals, ceremonies, celebrations). Yet throughout all this they hardly mention gender, even though all of these are clearly gendered.[7] An interesting example in the field of identity studies might be the classic text, *The Organization Man* (Whyte, 1956), which despite its title does not problematize the notion of identity that lurks behind men's corporate 'belongingness'.

Examples of comparable taken-for-grantedness within particular observed organizations can be drawn from research on men's violence to known women.[8] This has involved interviewing men about their violence to known women. A separate but linked project has interviewed women's experience of violence from known men. Both projects have also investigated organizational reponses to the violence concerned – both organizational policy responses and more informal responses of organizational staff. What this research from these two projects has shown is the distinctiveness of women's organizations (for example, women's aid, women's refuges, black women's organizations) and what might be called 'men's organizations' (for example, the criminal justice system, men's programmes that are designed to work against men's violence). These organizations are not only managed and staffed differently by women and men, but they also define violence and relate to violence very differently. These men's organizations are taken for granted as men's cultures and as locales of men's identities. In such organizations, violence may be brought into the routine processes of the organization and used in men's conversation in ways that are taken for granted as non-problematic (Hearn, 1994b). Men's identities and men's cultures can be said to be formed, or to appear to be formed, accordingly.

There are several ways in which this taken-for-grantedness works. Organizational cultures and identities may be taken for granted just as 'cultures' and 'identities', rather than by being recognized as peopled or dominated by men. This involves not naming men as men. Men are present as an absence (see Hearn, 1998b). These absences obscure, through degendering, the political process of contestation of identities and culture. This can persist both in particular organizations and in particular organizational analyses, through simple lack of consciousness of these issues or through keeping them off the agendas in more proactive ways.

Bringing these taken-for-granted men's organizational cultures and identities to the fore illustrates the need to develop macro/societal conceptualizations that locate organizations, cultures and identities in the context of patriarchy and patriarchal social relations (Hearn, 1992b; Hearn and Parkin, 2001). Considering men's cultures and identities in this way necessitates the analysis of the societal location of different organizations within patriarchy, public patriarchy and patriarchies.[9] This refers to the relative position of different organizations within public patriarchies – for example, within or outside the state. It also refers to the very formation of organizations, particularly their dominant form, and is located within patriarchal structures, including the patriarchal separation of the public and private domains.

This and many other studies highlight the obvious – that many, perhaps most, organizations are predominantly men's organizations; and that most organizational cultures are predominantly men's organizational cultures. Mainstream organizations provide the homes for the 'real' 'men's groups' (Hearn, 2000). Furthermore, where organizations are women's organizations, very different concerns are usually dominant to those of men's organizations. I do not say this in terms of essentialism, but rather in recognition of the different social locations and social experiences of women and men. This is clear when women organize consciously as women. These differences are especially clear between women's organizations and men's organizations that are organized in relation to the problem of men's violence. Differences exist in organizational structure, ideology, process, as well as specifically in the definition, understanding and response to violence.[10]

Men's domination of particular identities and particular organizational cultures

This leads us on to a second form of connection between 'men', 'identity' and 'organizational cultures'; namely, the particular ways in which men's organizational cultures and identities operate and men's domination thereof. Thus here we are not so much concerned with the taken-for-grantedness of men's organizational cultures and identities but with the forms that they may take in particular organizations. Indeed, contrary to the 'wisdom' (or lack of wisdom) of much malestream (O'Brien, 1981) organization theory, that has been persistently ungendered, we are now move on to an acceptance of the all too obvious fact that organizational cultures are profoundly affected by and constructed through gender and gender relations. This involves naming men as men (Hanmer, 1990; Collinson and Hearn, 1994), in both everyday organizational life and academic analyses thereof. It is not only a question of making this gendering explicit as asking in what ways that gendering works, with what forms of gendered agency, selves and personal projects. There is in effect a need to progress beyond the simple recognition that cultures are gendered to the investigation of the specifics of how men dominate particular organizational cultures in particular ways, behaviours, practices and indeed identities. Thus this perspective connects with the more modernist strand of theorizing identified by Roseneil and Seymour (1999).

There are many particular aspects and elements of organizational culture, identities, process and dynamics that have been persistently described and analysed in gender-neutral terms, within both practical and theoretical discourses. These include management, hierarchy, control, labour process. Instead there is a strong need to develop gendered concepts of management, hierarchy, control, labour process, and so on. This has been attempted by Kathy Ferguson (1985) in *The Feminist Case Against Bureaucracy*, in which the very notion of bureaucracy is subjected to critique as carrying patriarchal ideology into social form (Sheppard, 1989; Bologh, 1990; Morgan, 1996; cf. Due Billing, 1994).

This line of enquiry has been developed in more particular ways in both historical and contemporary works. For example, in *Men in the Public Eye* (Hearn, 1992b), I consider the history of the British Civil Service and Post Office. The important point is that this history can be re-read as a history of men controlling both each other and women in distinct vertical and horizontal organizational locations. While it would be wrong to see bureaucracy as essentially male, the connections between bureaucracies and men are socially and historically intense. A question that remains is whether current non-gendered concepts like bureaucracy can be salvaged by 'adding on' gendering; or whether there is a need to build in gender into the concepts themselves, or with notions of femocracy or mascocracy (Hearn, 1998d).

In work with a more contemporary focus, David Collinson and I (Collinson and Hearn, 1994) have outlined a variety of different discourses of men and masculinities that may characterize particular organizational and managerial cultures (also see Parkin and Maddock, 1993, 1995).[11] These include:

- *Authoritarianism*, in which aggressive and violent behaviour by men is maintained and reinforced.
- *Paternalism*, in which moral bases of co-operation are emphasized. This may involve younger men separating themselves from women and identifying with older men. It may also involve strong relations between younger and older men and attempts by men to place women, especially younger women, in conventional female locations.
- *Entrepreneuralism*, in which men operate relatively independently and competitively, whilst identifying with similar other men. This may be particularly helpful to younger men (for example, men engaged in saleswork), where being over 45 may sometimes be constructed as past the ideal. It may also exclude women.
- *Informalism*, in which men maintain contact with other men through infor-

mal contacts and the use of men's currency of conversation (for example, cars, drink, sport). This can be important in academic organizations, as pointed out by David Morgan (1981) and in a different way by Caroline Ramazanoglu (1987).

- *Careerism*, in which concern with impressive management and elevation of self are paramount. Competition for career progress mutually reinforces dominant forms of being men. This is likely to involve increasingly unrealistic demands on self and home life.

These can be understood as examples of (men's) dominant forms of discourses of multiple masculinities, identities and organizational cultures. This link with or emphasis on multiplicity opens up the possibility of exploring 'multiple masculinities', in which other social divisions, such as class, ethnicity or age, are invoked (Collinson and Hearn, 1994; Hearn and Collinson, 1994). Discourses of 'authoritarian masculinity' bring together gender and force, 'careerist masculinity' gender and work, 'paternalist masculinity' gender and family.

This approach is also a way of analysing and understanding how men's material discursive practices simultaneously reproduce management and masculinities (Collinson and Hearn, 1996b). As such, it is part of the more general growth of interest in studies that address the power of men as managers. The various ways in which men dominate particular organizational cultures can be understood in terms of the interrelations of unities and differences between men; that is, what brings men together as a gender class and what differentiates men (Hearn and Collinson, 1994, 1997), and the dominant forms of identities of men that are so formed, within the context of multiple workplaces (Collinson and Hearn, 1996b).

This perspective also has major policy and practical implications for changing men in organizations and managers, leaders, workers and colleagues – for example, in the development of equal opportunities policies, which adequately address men's power and oppression in organizations (Hearn, 1989, 1992a, 1994a, 2000). This involves attention to the proscription of specific behaviours by men in organizations, as elsewhere (Moyer and Tuttle, 1983) – for example, 'hogging the show', talking in capital letters, interrupting and not listening, always trying to be the problem-solver. Meanwhile alternative non-oppressive behaviours may be promoted.

Men's domination of subtexts of identities and organizational cultures

So far, I have considered some of the explicit ways in which men relate to and dominate organizational cultures and identities. In addition, there are many other less obvious and more implicit ways in which that connection can be made. In particular, it may be helpful to conceptualize organizational cultures and identities as texts (Linstead and Grafton-Small, 1992), which therefore may also have subtexts. The idea of subtext comes from cultural studies, and textual analyses that postulate the text as having a less obvious, but structurally determining, meaning. The notion of subtext may also draw on psychoanalytic metaphors in the interpretation of meaning (Wood, 1987). While psychoanalytic traditions have been very influential within organizational analysis, most obviously in the work of the Tavistock Institute, these have usually ignored gendered power relations.

Alternatively, the notion of subtext may be useful in conceptualizing the less obvious and more implicit aspects of gender relations (Smith, 1987, 1989, 1990), and thus gendered organizational cultures and identities. This may include attention to those aspects of culture subject to social silencing (Harlow *et al.*, 1995; Collinson and Hearn, 1996a; Benschop and Doorewaard, 1998; Hearn and Parkin, 2001). An example of this is the way in which organizational cultures may be understood in terms of sexual subtexts. This is an approach which is developed in collaborative work with Wendy Parkin (for example, Hearn and Parkin, 1987, 1995). This focus on sexuality in organizations is part of our work on gendered power relations in organization(s) within patriarchy. As such, a focus on sexuality in organization's is, in our view, part of the development of more accurate conceptualization of patriarchy and public patriarchy. This includes men in organizations operating within what might be thought of as mini-patriarchies.

In considering the sexual subtexts of organizational cultures and identities it is first necessary to recognize them as arenas of sexuality, which are accordingly dominated by men's sexualities. As before, this involves naming men as men. Thus, for example, in this view, sexual harassment in organizations needs to be understood in relation to men's sexualities, not as some individually held possession but as a socially structured power relation (Collinson and Collinson, 1989). Analysing sexual harassment involves naming men as men (Collinson and Collinson, 1996). The sexual subtext of many particular organizational cultures is hierarchic (Hearn, 1987); there heterosexuality and hierarchy are mutually reinforcing in management, control and communication; that pattern of domination is typically men's domination of women.

Furthermore, the process of the heterosexual subtexts of organizational cultures and identities takes place over time and often with a certain direction of development – what Richard Dyer (1985) has called 'the male sexual narrative'. This refers to the construction of narratives in accordance with dominant models of men's sexuality, including objectification, targeting (fixation), pursuit and conquest (see Betzold, 1977; Coveney *et al.*, 1984; Buchbinder, 1987).

There is, however, at least one major complication to this picture of men's domination of the sexual subtexts of organizational cultures. It is that many heterosexual-dominated organizational cultures are also characterized by men's preference for men, men's company and men's spaces. This may be understood in terms of a variety of ways, for example, men's homosociality (Lipman-Blumen, 1976; Morgan, 1981), men's use of women as currency between men (Cockburn, 1983; Game, 1989), homosexuality between men (Seidenberg, 1970; Irigaray, 1985), circuits and pyramids of desire between men (Hearn, 1992b; Roper, 1996). The contradiction of men's heterosexual and men's homosociability/homosexuality is perhaps clearest in such practices as horseplay. These may be performed by and between heterosexually identified men in the form of (parodies of) homosexuality (Hearn, 1985).

Similarly, we may also conceptualize men's identities in terms of the presence of subtext. Indeed much of the inspiration for the analysis of subtexts in socio-political situations can be traced to the application of psychoanalytic thinking from the individual to the textual, the social and the political. Many men's identities and organizational cultures are characterized by a combination of heterosexual, even heterosexist/homophobic, and homosocial/homosexual subtexts. Such sexual subtexts are a further arena of men's domination of organizations. They also point to the complex ways in which unities and differences between men may interrelate. To put this in a slighly different way, there are complex interplays between homosexual reproduction, stressing the unities of men, and men's difference from women, and homosocial reproduction, stressing the differences among men (Kanter, 1977, 1993).[12] While unities among men may carry a homosexual subtext, differences among men may carry a heterosexual subtext.[13] Subtexts of identity and subtexts of organizational culture may reciprocally reproduce each other.

The deconstruction of 'men, identity and organizational culture'

In recent years the 'cultural turn' has led to a prioritizing of deconstruction. For my purposes, such deconstruction of unities and simple dichotomies applies not just to the making of organizational 'men' but also to the making of identities and organizational cultures. This is not just a move from unified organizational cultures (for example, Deal and Kennedy, 1988; Peters and Waterman, 1982) to dominant and dominated or counter-cultures (Martin and Siehl, 1983), but on to fragmented organizational cultures and the fragmentation of identities and organizational cultures. It is the movement from differentiation to fragmentation (Martin 1992), and thence the possible movement to de-differentiation. Above all, there can no longer be no fixed, a priori set of relations between men, identity and organizational culture.

Thus far, I have considered a variety of ways in which men dominate organizational cultures and identities; however, in doing so, it is still possible for the concepts of identity and organizational culture to be used as if they were ungendered. There thus remains what is, in some ways, a more fundamental question around the connection between men and the very ideas of identity and organizational culture. 'Gender' may be made more apparent or less apparent through the use of the concepts of identity and organizational culture. In particular it is necessary to ask in what ways are gender and gendered power relations made more apparent by the use of the concepts of identity and organizational culture, and in what ways are they obscured, made less apparent.

In simple terms, the very notions of culture and identity, and thus organizational culture and organizational identity, rest on gendered differentiations. Both identity and organizational culture have often been used by analysts and managers as a repository category for that which is not structure, including the 'feminine'. Most obviously, this is the case when 'culture' is used to summarize that which is marginal, other, and of which one is not a part. Culture acts in contrast to the one/centre of the dominant/structure. Accordingly, culture can be used to refer to that which is other, either elsewhere from or within a given situation. This has been particularly important in modernist uses of culture (Harlow and Hearn, 1995). Organizational culture has thus often been encoded as 'feminine' and 'female'.

Thus the concept of culture can easily obscure gender, and so also obscure the naming of men as men (by reducing men's apparentness in organizations). The indexical use of 'culture' can obscure 'men' and indeed men's cultures (Hearn, 1998a). To put this another way, we may ask what are the implications of the feminine/female encoding of culture for the analysis of men's gendered power. This is particularly so when the use of culture is set within a modernist framework that reproduces dichotomous thinking about organizations, paralleling dichotomous thinking about gender (Hearn, 1996a).

This apparent impasse can be interrogated more closely through the lens of postmodernism,[14] and associated deconstructive approaches (for example, Martin, 1990; Calás and Smircich, 1991). For example, Stephen Linstead and Robert Grafton-Small (1992) have approached organizational culture as text, paradox, otherness, seduction, discourse. A weakness of their work, and of much similar work, is the neglect of gender and other oppressions (Hearn and Parkin, 1993). The strength of their work is that it provides a way into a critique of unified, dichotomous and overly simply gendered views of culture (Harlow and Hearn, 1995). Postmodern approaches to culture and organizational culture are of interest in critiquing false unities, dichotomies and simplicities. Instead, notions of organizational culture may be deconstructed and recognized as a (misleading) shorthand for multiple, overlapping, paradoxical and contradictory processes of gendered othernesses, of both women and men.

Somewhat similarly, Mary Jo Hatch and Majken Schultz (2000) have recently presented a synthesizing and programmatic review of the relation of identity, image and culture in organizations. In analysing identity through relational differences, they catalogue the shifts towards both external and internal positioning, the intersections of self and other, multiplicity rather than singularity, contextualization of texts, the intermingling of tacit and explicit meanings, and the instrumental use of emergent cultural symbols. Though their analysis here is non-gendered, it opens up possibilities for examining the provisonal nature of gendered identities and gendered organizational cultures, and their intersections.

While identity and organizational culture have been used as a gendered repository for that which is not structure, what this means for analysing men is far from clear. This could open up an exploration of the ambiguities and complexities of men's relations to organizations. For example, the categories of men and particular groups of men in organizations can also be understood in terms of otherness – both in particular organizations and in a more general societal sense. While the other has mainly been employed as a concept for making sense of the construction of subordinated groups, categories and classes, the possibility of remaking those that are dominant as other has been little developed. Sometimes there are avenues for approaching this conundrum of dominance through the association of two or more social categories of identity, of which one or more are each subordinated and superordinate. For example, 'black gay men' may be seen as other by virtue of their 'blackness' and 'gayness', and the links between those aspects and being a man (Mercer and Julien, 1988). Deconstructing the dominance of men, as, for example, with the category 'white, heterosexual, able-bodied men', from within may appear more difficult. It involves subjecting that which is taken for granted as dominant to ambiguous distancing and critique (Hearn, 1996a).

Men simultaneously form identities and cultures, and are formed as identities and as subjects in organizational cultures. Men are simultaneously static and continuously reproduced in power, and continually provisional, absent, lacking, fragmented and fractured. This does not refer to any sense of men's individuation but rather to the provisional nature of men's existence in structures. The idea of the individual, the individual man, is constructed in their way as a unifying subject gloss on these fracturings and other paradoxes. Thus, this is a way of connecting men and organizational culture that is significant in the production of the supposedly unified identity subject of individual men in the first place (Hearn 1992b: ch. 9). It addresses attention to the processes whereby the emotional hooking of men to organizations is translated to become the construction of the 'rational' actor, manager or analyst. The concept of organizational culture both obscures that process and opens up a space for reviewing this 'second nature', cathexis, formation of male subjects, restimulation and reproduction of everyday organizational desire, whether between men and women, between men, or between men and 'bits' of the organization, such as the technology or the fascination of the work task. Such a perspective fits closely with the rich debate in cultural studies, and especially with film theory on masculine, more or less conscious identification processes with texts and parts of texts (Nixon, 1997).

Concluding remarks

I would like to conclude this tour with two brief points: one theoretical, the other empirical and practical. First, there is a general theoretical question of the epistemological and methodological implications of these debates. One of my own major concerns in recent years has been the development of understandings of social phenomena, including identity and organizational culture, that are simultaneously materialist and discursive.[15] By outlining some major ways in which men, identity and organizational culture may be interrogated and connected, I hope that the simultaneously material and discursive nature of organizations has been highlighted.

Second, and finally, I would simply say: beware men's monoidentities and monocultures. These various dominations and yet fragmentations outlined here often find expression in men's continuing attempts to assert monocultures in organizations and elsewhere: 'the dominant presumption of a single culture of cause, system or experience, either within an organization or brought about by an organization upon the outside world' (Hearn, 1992b: 199). Such reproductions and productions of false universals are a particularly dangerous aspect of the connections between men, identity and organizational cultures. Where it is confidently asserted there is only one way of this or that identity or only one way of doing, developing, analysing, even changing this or that particular organizational culture, the attempted reproduction of men's organizational power is rarely far away. Whatever the persistence of men's collective power, within and outside organizations, multiplicity and fragmentation of identities and organizational cultures still seem to speak to this particular historical age. At the same time, domination, including men's domination, seems increasingly to be a matter without a 'centre that holds' (Bauman, 1995; Hearn, 1997). Such cultural matters still need structural analysis.

Notes

1 I am grateful to David Collinson and Iiris Aaltio for comments on an earlier draft of this chapter.
2 Debates on organizational culture have been notorious in their neglect of gendered power relations. Exceptions to this include Mills (1988, 1989), Hollway (1991: ch. 8), Cockburn (1991), Alvesson and Due Billing (1992), Ramsay and Parker (1992), Gherardi (1994, 1995), Itzin and Newman (1995), Rantalaiho and Heiskanen (1997), Rutherford (1999), Wilson (2001). A very important analytical contribution to the study of organizational cultures has been made by Joanne Martin (1992) in her distinction between integration, differentiation and fragmentation conceptualizations of cultures in organizations, as well as her postmodernist/deconstructive critique of that framework. Though elements of Martin's framework might be detected in my approach, they are distinct and different frameworks, in particular in that Martin's fragmentation and postmodernist perspectives are both relevant to and overlap with both the subtext and deconstructive approaches outlined here.
3 Citing Giddens (1991), Beck (1992), Kellner (1992), Beck *et al.* (1994), Calhoun (1995), Bauman (1996).
4 Citing Weedon (1987), Butler (1990, 1992, 1993), Hall (1990, 1996), Scott (1992, 1993).
5 See, for example, Hearn and Parkin (1983, 1986–7, 1995, 2001), Burrell and Hearn (1989), Parkin and Hearn (1994).
6 By 'sexualed', I mean having meaning in relation in sexuality. This includes meaning in terms of power differences. Such 'sexualation' does not necessarily imply sexualization.
7 This is despite other work on gender and organizations by Alvesson and Due Billing (1992).
8 See Hanmer and Hearn (1993), Hanmer (1995), Hearn (1995, 1996c, 1998c, 2001), Hanmer *et al.* (1995).
9 Walby's (1986) six structures of patriarchy include that of 'culture', which presumably could include 'organizational culture' and identity formation. The other structures are capitalist work, the family, the state, violence, sexuality.
10 This is not to suggest any kind of argument of essentialist difference between women and men; rather that the different social conditions of women's and men's organizations, and women and men there, are likely to be different.
11 Parkin and Maddock describe the following 'male cultures': the gentlemen's club, the barrack yard, the locker room, the gender blind, paying lip-service and the feminist pretender, the smart macho.
12 For a sympathetic critique of Kanter's landmark study, see Collinson and Hearn (1995).
13 There is room here for further examination of the relevance of queer theory to organizational analysis or management studies; this is a connection that has been little explored thus far (cf. Gibson-Graham, 1999; Parker, 2001, 2002).
14 To avoid misunderstanding, this use of postmodernism should not read as any general subscription to postmodernism, and certainly not if this is taken to be antagonistic to materialism and the analysis of power and oppression (Hearn and Parkin, 1993). My interest in postmodernism comes from an attempt to amplify and extend an understanding of the complexities and subtleties of materialism and gender power relations, not to dilute them in any way.
15 See Hearn (1992b, 1993, 1998c); Hearn and Parkin (2001).

References

Alvesson, M. and Berg, P.O. (1992). *Corporate Culture and Organizational Symbolism.* Berlin: de Gruyter.
Alvesson, M. and Due Billing, D. (1992). Organizations and gender: towards a differentiated understanding. *Organization Studies*, 13: 75–105.

Bauman, Z. (1995). Searching for a centre that holds. In M. Featherstone, S. Lash and R. Robertson (eds), *Global Modernities*. London: Sage.

Bauman, Z. (1996). From pilgrim to tourist – or a short history of identity. In S. Hall and P. du Gay (eds), *Questions of Cultural Identity*. London: Sage.

Beck, U. (1992). *Risk Society: Towards a New Modernity*. London: Sage.

Beck, U., Giddens, A. and Lash, S. (1994). *Reflexive Modernization. Politics, Tradition and Aesthetics in the Modern Social Order*. Cambridge: Polity.

Benschop, Y. and Doorewaard, H. (1998). Six of one and half a dozen of the other: the gender subtext of Taylorism and team-based work. *Gender, Work and Organization*, 5(1): 5–18.

Betzold, M. (1977). The socialized penis. In J. Snodgrass (ed.), *A Book of Readings for Men Against Sexism*. Albion, CA: Times Change Press.

Bologh, R.W. (1990). *Love or Greatness? Max Weber and Masculine Thinking: A Feminist Inquiry*. London and Boston: Unwin Hyman.

Bradley, H. (1996). *Fractured Identities: Changing Patterns of Inequality*. Cambridge: Polity.

Buchbinder, H. (1987). The socialized penis revisited. In H. Buchbinder, V. Burstyn, D. Forbes and M. Steedman (eds), *Who's on Top? The Politics of Heterosexuality*. Toronto: Garamond.

Burrell, G. and Hearn, J. (1989). The sexuality of organization. In J. Hearn, D. Sheppard, P. Tancred-Sheriff and G. Burrell (eds), *The Sexuality of Organization*. London: Sage.

Butler, J. (1990). *Gender Trouble: Feminism and the Subversion of Identity*. New York, NY: Routledge.

Butler, J. (1992). Contingent foundations: feminism and the question of 'postmodernism'. In J. Butler and J.W. Scott (eds), *Feminists Theorize the Political*. New York, NY: Routledge.

Butler, J. (1993). *Bodies that Matter. On the Discursive Limits of Sex*. New York, NY: Routledge.

Calás, M.B. and Smirich, L. (1991). Voicing seduction to silence leadership. *Organization Studies*, 12(4): 567–602.

Calhoun, C. (1995). *Critical Social Theory*. Cambridge, MA: Blackwell.

Cockburn, C.K. (1983). *Brothers. Male Dominance and Technological Change*. London: Pluto.

Cockburn, C.K. (1985). *The Machinery of Dominance. Women, Men and Technical Know-how*. London: Pluto.

Cockburn, C.K. (1990). Men's power in organizations: 'equal opportunities' intervenes. In J. Hearn and D. Morgan (eds), *Men, Masculinities and Social Theory*. London and Boston: Unwin Hyman.

Cockburn, C.K. (1991). *In the Way of Women. Men's Resistance to Sex Equality in Organisations*. London: Macmillan.

Cockburn, C.K. (1994). Play of power: women, men, and equality initiatives in a trade union. In S. Wright (ed.), *Anthropology of Organizations*. London: Routledge.

Collinson, D.L. (1992). *Managing the Shopfloor. Subjectivity, Masculinity and Workplace Culture*. Berlin: Walter de Gruyter.

Collinson, D.L. and Collinson, M. (1989). Sexuality in the workplace: the domination of men's sexuality. In J. Hearn, D. Sheppard, P. Tancred-Sheriff and G. Burrell (eds), *The Sexuality of Organization*. London: Sage.

Collinson, D.L. and Hearn, J. (1994). Naming men as men: implications for work, organizations and management. *Gender, Work and Organization*, 1 (1): 2–22.

Collinson, D.L. and Hearn, J. (1995). Men managing leadership? Men and women of the corporation revisited. *International Review of Women and Leadership*, 1(2): 1–24.

Collinson, D.L. and Hearn, J. (1996a). Breaking the silence: on men, masculinities and managements. In D.L. Collinson and J. Hearn (eds), *Men as Managers, Managers as Men*. London: Sage.

Collinson, D.L. and Hearn, J. (eds) (1996b). *Men as Managers, Managers as Men*. London: Sage.

Collinson, M. and Collinson, D.L. (1996). 'It's only Dick': the sexual harassment of women managers in insurance sales. *Work, Employment and Society*, 10(1): 29–56.

Coveney, L., Jackson, M., Jeffreys, S., Kaye, S. and Mahoney, P. (1984). *The Sexuality Papers. Male Sexuality and the Social Control of Women*. London: Hutchinson.

Deal, T.E. and Kennedy, A.A. (1988). *Corporate Cultures*. Reading, MA: Addison-Wesley.

Due Billing, Y. (1994). Gender and bureaucracies: a critique of Ferguson's 'The Feminist Case Against Bureaucracy'. *Gender, Work and Organization*, 1(4): 179–193.

Dyer, R. (1985). Male sexuality in the media. In A. Metcalf and M. Humphries (eds), *The Sexuality of Men*. London: Pluto.

Ferguson, K.E. (1985). *The Feminist Case Against Bureaucracy*. Philadelphia, PA: Temple University Press.

Game, A. (1989). Research and writing: 'secretaries and bosses'. *Jounal of Pragmatics*, 13: 343–361.

Gherardi, S. (1994). The gender we think, the gender we do in our everyday lives. *Human Relations*, 47(6): 591–610.

Gherardi, S. (1995). *Gender, Symbolism and Organizational Cultures*. London: Sage.

Gibson-Graham, J.K. (1999). *The End of Capitalism (as we knew it)*. Cambridge, MA: Blackwell.

Giddens, A. (1991). *Modernity and Self-Identity. Self and Society in the Late Modern Age*. Cambridge: Polity.

Hall, S. (1990). Cultural identity and diaspora. In J. Rutherford (ed.), *Identity: Community, Culture, Difference*. London: Lawrence & Wishart.

Hall, S. (1996). Introduction. Who Needs 'Identity'? In S. Hall and P. du Gay (eds), *Questions of Cultural Identity*. London: Sage.

Hanmer, J. (1990). Men, power and the exploitation of women. In J. Hearn and D. Morgan (eds), *Men, Masculinities and Social Theory*. London and Boston: Unwin Hyman.

Hanmer, J. (1995). *Patterns of Agency Contacts with Women Who Have Experienced Violence from Known Men*. Bradford: Violence, Abuse and Gender Relations Research Unit, University of Bradford.

Hanmer, J. and Hearn, J. (1993). Gendered research and researching gender: women, men and violence. British Sociological Association Conference, Essex University.

Hanmer, J., Hearn, J., Dillon, C., Kayani, T. and Todd, P. (1995). *Violence to Women from Known Men. Policy Development, Interagency Approaches and Good Practice*. Bradford: Violence, Abuse and Gender Relations Research Unit, University of Bradford.

Harlow, E. and Hearn, J. (1995). Culture constructions: contrasting theories of organizational culture and gender construction. *Gender, Work and Organization*, 2(4): 180–191.

Harlow, E., Hearn, J. and Parkin, W. (1995). Gendered noise: organizations and the silence and din of domination. In C. Itzin and J. Newman (eds), *Gender, Culture and Organizational Change*. London: Routledge.

Hatch, M.J. and Schultz, M. (2000). Scaling the Tower of Babel: relational differences between identity, image and cultures in organizations. In M. Schultz, M.J. Hatch and M.H. Larsen (eds), *The Expressive Organization: Linking Identity, Reputation, and the Corporate Brand*. Oxford: Oxford University Press.

Hearn, J. (1983). *Birth and Afterbirth: A Materialist Account.* London: Achilles Heel.
Hearn, J. (1985). Men's sexuality at work. In A. Metcalf and M. Humphries (eds), *The Sexuality of Men.* London: Pluto.
Hearn, J. (1987). *The Gender of Oppression. Men, Masculinity and the Critique of Marxism.* Brighton: Wheatsheaf, and New York: St Martin's.
Hearn, J. (1989). Leading questions for men: men's leadership, feminist challenges and men's reponses. *Equal Opportunities International,* 8(1): 3–11.
Hearn, J. (1992a). Changing men and changing managements: a review of issues and actions. *Women in Management Review,* 7(1): 3–8.
Hearn, J. (1992b). *Men in the Public Eye: The Construction and Deconstruction of Public Men and Public Patriarchies.* London: Routledge.
Hearn, J. (1993). Emotive subjects: organizational men, organizational masculinities and the (de)construction of emotions. In S. Fineman (ed.), *Emotion in Organizations.* London: Sage.
Hearn, J. (1994a). Changing men and changing managements: social change, social research and social action. In M.J. Davidson and R. Burke (eds), *Women in Management. Current Research Issues.* London: Paul Chapman.
Hearn, J. (1994b). The organization(s) of violence: men, gender relations, organizations and violence. *Human Relations,* 47(6): 731–754.
Hearn, J. (1994c). Researching men and masculinities: some sociological issues and possibilities. *Australian and New Zealand Journal of Sociology,* 30(1): 40–60.
Hearn, J. (1995). *Patterns of Agency Contacts with Men Who Have Been Violent to Known Women.* Bradford: Violence, Abuse and Gender Relations Research Unit, University of Bradford.
Hearn, J. (1996a). Deconstructing the dominant: making the one(s) the other(s). *Organization,* 3(4): 611–626.
Hearn, J. (1996b). Is masculinity dead? A critique of the concept of masculinity/masculinities. In M. Mac an Ghaill (ed.), *Understanding Masculinities. Social Relations and Cultural Arenas.* Buckingham: Open University Press.
Hearn, J. (1996c). Men's violence to known women: men's accounts and men's policy development. In B. Fawcett, B. Featherstone, J. Hearn and C. Toft (eds), *Violence and Gender Relations. Theories and Interventions.* London: Sage.
Hearn, J. (1997). Searching for the centre of men and men's power?: historical, geographical and theoretical perspectives. International Colloquium on Masculinities, University of Natal, South Africa, July.
Hearn, J. (1998a). Context, culture and violence. In R. Kauranen, E. Oinas, S. Sundback and Ö. Wahlbeck (eds), *Sociologer om Sociologi och Metod: Festskrift till Kirsti Suolinna.* Åbo: Meddelanden Från Ekonomisk-Statsvetenkapliga Fakulteten vid Åbo Akademi, Sociologiska institutionen Ser.
Hearn, J. (1998b). Theorizing men and men's theorizing: men's discursive practices in theorizing men. *Theory and Society,* 27(6): 781–816.
Hearn, J. (1998c). *The Violences of Men: How Men Talk About and How Agencies Respond to Men's Violence to Women.* London: Sage.
Hearn, J. (1998d). The welfare of men? In J. Popay, J. Hearn and J. Edwards (eds), *Men, Gender Divisions and Welfare.* London: Routledge.
Hearn, J. (2000). Men, (pro-)feminism, organizing and organizations. *Finnish Journal of Business Economics,* 3: 350–372.
Hearn, J. (2001). Men, social work and men's violence to known women. In A.Christie (ed.), *Men and Social Work.* Houndmills: Macmillan.
Hearn, J. and Collinson, D.L. (1994). Theorizing unities and differences between men

and between masculinities. In H. Brod and M. Kaufman (eds), *Theorizing Masculinities*. Newbury Park, CA: Sage.

Hearn, J. and Collinson, D.L. (1997). *Men, Masculinities and Managements. Unities, Differences and their Interrelations*. Working Paper Series No. 17. Manchester: International Centre for Labour Studies, University of Manchester.

Hearn, J. and Parkin, W. (1983). Gender and organizations: a selective review and a critique of a neglected area. *Organization Studies*, 4(3): 219–242.

Hearn, J. and Parkin, W. (1986–7). Women, men and leadership: a critical review of assumptions, practices and change in the industrialized nations. *International Studies on Management and Organizations*, 16(3–4): 3–32.

Hearn, J. and Parkin, W. (1987). *'Sex' at 'Work'. The Power and Paradox of Organisation Sexuality*. Brighton: Wheatsheaf, and New York, NY: St Martin's.

Hearn, J. and Parkin, W. (1988). Women, men and leadership: a critical review of assumptions, practices and change in the industrialized nations. In N. Adler and D. Izraeli (eds), *Women in Management Worldwide*. New York, NY: M.E. Sharpe.

Hearn, J. and Parkin, W. (1993). Organizations, multiple oppression and postmodernism. In J. Hassard and M. Parker (eds), *Postmodernism and Organizations*. London: Sage.

Hearn, J. and Parkin, W. (1995). *'Sex' at 'Work'. The Power and Paradox of Organisation Sexuality*. Hemel Hempstead: Prentice-Hall/Harvester Wheatsheaf, and New York: St Martin's.

Hearn, J. and Parkin, W. (2001). *Gender, Sexuality and Violence in Organizations: The Unspoken Forces of Organization Violations*. London: Sage.

Hollway, W. (1991). *Work Psychology and Organizational Behaviour*. London: Sage.

Irigaray, L. (1985). *This Sex Which Is Not One*. New York, NY: Cornell University Press.

Itzin, C. and Newman, J. (eds) (1995). *Gender, Culture and Organizational Change*. London: Routledge.

Kanter, R.M. (1977). *Men and Women of the Corporation*. New York, NY: Basic Books.

Kanter, R.M. (1993). *Men and Women of the Corporation*. New York, NY: HarperCollins.

Kellner, D. (1992). Popular culture and the construction of postmodern identities. In S. Lash and J. Friedman (eds), *Modernity and Identity*. Oxford: Blackwell.

Kerfoot, D. and Knights, D. (1993). Management, masculinity and manipulation: from paternalism to corporate strategy in financial services in Britain. *Journal of Management Studies*, 30(4): 659–679.

Kerfoot, D. and Knights, D. (1996). 'The best is yet to come': the quest for embodiment in managerial work. In D.L. Collinson and J. Hearn (eds), *Men as Managers, Managers as Men*. London: Sage.

Kondo, D. (1990). *Crafting Selves: Power, Gender, and Discourses of Identity in a Japanese Workplace*. Chicago, IL: The University of Chicago Press.

Linstead, S. and Grafton-Small, R. (1992). On reading organizational culture. *Organization Studies*, 13(3): 331–356.

Lipman-Blumen, J. (1976). Towards a homosocial theory of sex roles: an explanation of the sex segregation of social institutions. In A. Blaxall and B. Reagan (eds), *Women and the Workplace*. Chicago, IL: University of Chicago Press.

Martin, J. (1990). Deconstructing organizational taboos: the suppression of gender conflict in organizations. *Organizational Science*, 1(4): 339–359.

Martin, J. (1992). *Cultures in Organizations*. New York, NY, Oxford University Press.

Martin, J. and Siehl, C. (1983). Organizational culture and counterculture: an uneasy symbiosis. *Organizational Dynamics*, 12: 52–64.

Mercer, K. and Julien, I. (1988). Race, sexual politics and black masculinity: a dossier. In R. Chapman and J. Rutherford (eds), *Male Order. Unwrapping Masculinity*. London: Lawrence & Wishart.

Mills, A.J. (1988). Organization, gender and culture. *Organization Studies*, 9(3): 351–369.

Mills, A.J. (1989). Gender, sexuality and organization theory. In J. Hearn, D. Sheppard, P. Tancred-Sheriff and G. Burrell (eds), *The Sexuality of Organization*. London: Sage.

Morgan, D. (1996). The gender of bureaucracy. In D.L. Collinson and J. Hearn (eds), *Men as Managers, Managers as Men*. London: Sage.

Morgan, D.H.J. (1981). Men, masculinity and the process of sociological enquiry. In H. Roberts (ed.), *Doing Feminist Research*. London: Routledge & Kegan Paul.

Moyer, B. and Tuttle, A. (1983). Overcoming masculine oppression in mixed groups. In *Off Their Backs ... and On Our Own Two Feet*. Philadelphia, PA: New Society Publishers.

Nixon, S. (1997). Exhibiting masculinity. In S. Hall (ed.), *Representation: Cultural Representations and Signifying Practices*. London: Sage.

O'Brien, M. (1981). *The Politics of Reproduction*. London: Routledge & Kegan Paul.

Parker, M. (2001). Fucking management: queer, theory and reflexivity. *Ephemera*, 1(1): 36–53 (www.ephemeraweb.org).

Parker, M. (2002). Queering management and organization. *Gender, Work and Organization*, 9(2): 146–166.

Parkin, D. and Maddock, S. (1993). Gender cultures. *Women in Management Review*, 8(2): 3–9.

Parkin, D. and Maddock, S. (1995). A gender typology of organizational culture. In C. Itzin and J. Newman (eds), *Gender, Culture and Organizational Change*. London: Routledge.

Parkin, W. and Hearn, J. (1994). Frauen, Männer und Führung. In A. Kieser, G. Reber and R. Wunderer (eds), *Handwörterbuch der Führung* (2nd. edn). Stuttgart: C.E. Poeschel.

Peters, T. and Waterman, R. (1982). *In Search of Excellence*. New York, NY: Harper & Row.

Ramazanoglu, C. (1987). Sex and violence in academic life or you can keep a good woman down. In J. Hanmer and M. Maynard (eds), *Women, Violence and Social Control*. London: Macmillan.

Ramsay, K. and Parker, M. (1992). Gender, bureaucracy and organisational culture. In M. Savage and A. Witz (eds), *Gender and Bureaucracy*. Oxford: Blackwell.

Rantalaiho, L. and Heiskanen, T. (eds) (1996). *Gendered Practices in Working Life*. Houndmills: Macmillan.

Roper, M. (1991). Yesterday's model: product fetishism and the British company man 1945–85. In M.R. Roper and J. Tosh (eds), *Manful Assertions. Masculinities in Britain since 1800*. London: Routledge.

Roper, M. (1994). *Masculinity and the British Organization Man Since 1945*. Oxford: Oxford University Press.

Roper, M. (1996). 'Seduction and succession': circuits of homosocial desire in management. In D.L. Collinson and J. Hearn (eds), *Men as Managers, Managers as Men*. London: Sage.

Roseneil, S. and Seymour, J. (1999). Practising identities: power and resistance. In S. Roseneil and J. Seymour (eds), *Practising Identities: Power and Resistance*. London: Macmillan.

Rutherford, S. (1999). Organisational Cultures, Patriarchal Closure and Women Managers. Doctoral thesis, Bristol, University of Bristol.

Scott, J.W. (1992) 'Experience'. In J. Butler and J.W. Scott (eds), *Feminists Theorize the Political*. New York, NY: Routledge.

Scott, J.W. (1993). Women's history. In L.S. Kauffman (ed.), *American Feminist Thought at Century's End*. Cambridge, MA: Blackwell.

Seidenberg, R. (1970). *Marriage in Life and Literature*. New York: Philosophical Library.

Sheppard, D. (1989). Organizations, power and sexuality: the image and self-image of women managers. In J. Hearn, D. Sheppard, P. Tancred-Sheriff and G. Burrell (eds), *The Sexuality of Organization*. London and Beverly Hills, CA: Sage.

Smith, D.E. (1987). *The Everyday World as Problematic. A Feminist Sociology*. Boston: Northeastern University Press.

Smith, D.E. (1989). Sociological theory: methods of writing patriarchy. In R.A. Wallace (ed.), *Feminism and Sociological Theory*. Newbury Park, CA: Sage.

Smith, D.E. (1990). *The Conceptual Practices of Power. A Feminist Sociology of Knowledge*. Boston, MA: Northeastern University Press.

Walby, S. (1986). *Patriarchy at Work*. Cambridge: Polity.

Weedon, C. (1987). *Feminist Practice and Poststructuralist Theory*. Oxford: Blackwell.

Weeks, J. (1990). The value of difference. In J. Rutherford (ed.), *Identity: Community, Culture, Difference*. London: Lawrence & Wishart.

Whyte, W.H. (1956). *The Organization Man*. New York, NY: Simon & Schuster.

Williams, R. (1976). *Keywords*. Glasgow: Fontana.

Wilson, E. (2001). Organizational culture. In E. Wilson (ed.), *Organizational Behaviour Reassessed: The Impact of Gender*. London: Sage.

Wood, R. (1987). Raging Bull: the homosexual subtext in film. In M. Kaufman (ed.), *Beyond Patriarchy: Essays by Men on Power, Pleasure and Change*. Toronto: Oxford University Press.

Wright, S. (1998). The Politicisation of 'Culture'. Presidential address 1997, Section H, British Association for the Advancement of Science. London. Royal Anthropological Institute. Available at: http.//lucy.ukc.ac.uk/rai/AnthToday/wright.htm

4 Otherness at large

Identity and difference in the new globalized organizational landscape

Anshuman Prasad and Pushkala Prasad

[W]hat is now before us nationally, and in the full imperial panorama, is the deep, profoundly perturbed and perturbing question of our relationship to others – other cultures, other states, other histories, other experiences, traditions, peoples and destinies.

Edward Said, *Representing the Colonized: Anthropology's Interlocuters*

Introduction

The spectre of 'otherness' has been haunting Western organizational landscapes for a long time. Relationships between dominant majority groups (typically Euro-American/Western men) and 'different' or 'other' social identity groups (e.g. women, African-Americans, gays, Latinos, etc.) have been recognized as central issues affecting the advancement, legitimacy and survival of organizations themselves. These questions of otherness have further intensified as national boundaries become more permeable and workplaces are swamped by the tides of diversity and cosmopolitanism. In sum, the currents of globalization have altered the contours of difference and otherness, simultaneously rendering them more immediate, more exciting and profoundly more problematic.

One thing is for sure – under conditions of postmodernity and globalization, otherness looms very much at large: an integral part of everyday organizational life, impossible to ignore and constantly holding the potential for conflict, creativity and disruption. Arguing that these new conditions require alternative conceptual frameworks, our chapter uses postcolonialism as a theoretical lens to understand the contemporary dynamics of difference and identity in organizational cultural milieus.

Woman as 'other' in organizations

Most serious discussions of 'otherness' in organizations have been conducted within different strands of feminist theory, explicitly seeking to understand how the 'other' is coded as female and constructed within the context of hierarchical and bureaucratic relations of patriarchy (Mills, 1988; Oseen, 1997). In essence, many feminists argue that core organizational principles (e.g. hierarchy, standardization, etc.) are constantly involved in constituting and reproducing woman as a distinct and subordinate 'other' with significant implications for male and female identities in diverse organizational spheres (Ferguson, 1984; Mills, 1988). The focus within this genre of feminism is more on 'the *inscription* of woman as other' in the language and discourse (Mascia-Lees, 1989) of organizations, workplaces and other areas of institutional life.

In analysing the discursive construction of woman as 'other', writers like Smith (1987) call for a close examination of the 'relationships of ruling' that make this possible. As Smith (1987: 19) points out, these discursive formations of woman 'have been either produced by men or controlled by them. In so far as women's work and experience have been entered into it, it has been on terms decided by men and because it has been approved by men.' In this process, biological characteristics, such as appearance and maternity (Martin, 1992), and so-called female or 'feminine' social traits, such as collaboration and nurturing skills, become systematic liabilities in the predominantly male world of institutional workplaces (Maier, 1997).

While focusing predominantly on woman as 'other', some organizational feminist writings remain fully aware of the intersections between womanhood and multiple categories of otherness, notably race, ethnicity and sexual preference. Mighty's (1997) exploration of the dynamics whereby race, foreignness and womanhood come together to produce a 'triple jeopardy' of identity in professional organizations is a case in point. Moreover, understanding woman as the 'other' in organizations offers many insights into the production of different forms of 'otherness' in institutional work domains. Increasingly, however, two material and intellectual currents convincingly argue for the need to reassess contemporary genres of Western feminism, and to examine questions of otherness from alternative theoretical positions. The first is what is popularly referred to as globalization, and the second is postcolonialism.

Globalization and otherness

With the advent of globalization, a range of identity questions have become exponentially complicated. To Hall *et al.* (1992: 299), globalization refers to 'those processes operating on a global scale which cut across national boundaries, integrating and connecting communities and organizations in new time–space combinations, making the world in reality and in experience more interconnected'. While different nations and cultures may well be brought into closer contact, globalization does not necessarily make these relationships any easier. What globalization does is to transmit difference everywhere while making it more problematic (Robertson, 1992).

Globalization's impact on questions of identity is immense. In the late twentieth century, questions about cultural identity have taken on a vibrant urgency. Questions such as 'who are we?', 'where do we really belong?', 'what do we mean by we?', etc. are repeatedly raised in diverse spheres such as national policy, media entertainment and organizational restructuring (Hall, 1996). Global systems and a growing global consciousness are held to be responsible for the demarcation of new *identity spaces* (Friedman, 1995) in which traditional identifications with nation, religion and ethnicity are sometimes called into question, and at other times substantially strengthened. What we are witnessing, according to Friedman (1995), is a paradox of *compression* – diminished phys-

ical distance among different cultures – and *implosion* – an increased consciousness of one's own cultural or national identity. Others, such as Larrain (1994),
observe that the more profound the tendencies of globalization, the more that
ethnic and other identity groups seek to reaffirm their differences.

Organizations of all kinds (i.e. corporations, non-profit ventures, NGOs and
national governments) are sites for the transmission of globalization and adjustments to it. In many ways, globalization increases the range of organizational
options, and permits individuals to identify themselves with multiple social and
cultural groupings. Increasingly, therefore, 'globalization is the framework for
the *amplification* and *diversification* of sources of the self' (Pieterse, 1995: 52). In
sum, globalization profoundly alters the nexus of identities available to the self,
and their enactment in organizational spheres.

While globalization often results in increased contact between different identity groups, it by no means diminishes the hierarchical distances between them.
Relationships between older identity formations (e.g. the First World and the
Third World) or between newer ones (e.g. software designers and maquilladora
workers) are invariably overshadowed by structures and discourses of domination, though these are frequently resisted in a number of different ways. At the
heart of globalization are a set of *centre–periphery relationships* that mediate the
repackaging of older categories of otherness, and the initiation of newer ones.
Understanding otherness in the new globalized landscape therefore involves
paying attention to (a) the nexus of shifting identities and alignments that are
brought together in the process of constituting the 'other', and (b) the current
geopolitical realities and global hegemonies that mediate the formation of identity spaces in organizational and institutional locations. Enloe's (1989) work
examining the constitution of female otherness within the institutional fields of
tourism, national defence and the United Fruit Company is an outstanding
exemplar using feminism within a context of global relations of power and dominance. Enloe's work deviates from the more customary attempts to understand
female otherness in organizations in its move from micro to macro relations
without a loss of female subjectivity.

The other speaks back

Challenges to Western feminism of both the more liberal and radical stripe have
been mounting in diverse intellectual fields such as women's studies, history,
anthropology and literature. These challenges have emerged from both within
the West itself – from African-American, Latina and Native American scholars
– and from outside it – mainly from scholars in Eastern Europe and the so-
called 'Third World'.

Local challenges to feminism charge it with primarily serving white middle-
class values and interests, and condemn it for its lack of commitment to understanding and acknowledging the diametrically different worlds inhabited by
Blacks, Latina, Native American and Aboriginal women even in Western societies (Carby, 1982; Irwin, 1991; Lugones and Spelman, 1990). A major concern
for these writers is what Bulbeck (1998: 5) calls 'the incessant refrain of rights
and freedoms' that dominates the discourse of Western feminism at the expense
of other questions of relevance to women on the margins. In following its own

trajectory, strands of Western feminism either ignore concerns of immediate relevance to certain women, or relegate them to the margins of the discourse wherein their otherness is further reproduced.

Black, Latina and Native American feminists also join with feminists from 'other' parts of the world in interrogating the discursive constitutions of Third World women as uniformly passive, irrational and subordinate subjects of male patriarchal exploitation (Davies, 1983; Mohanty, 1988) without an awareness of either (a) the multitude of complex identity positions occupied by women of the so-called Third World, or (b) the role played by Western discourses in representing both its own marginal groups and women from the Third World. In essence, these discussions seek to make Western feminism more conscious of its own cultural imperialism and eventually to rescue it from the pitfalls of Eurocentrism into which it often falls.

Like much of the globalization literature, these newer feminist writings also call for an acute awareness of the wider backdrop against which 'women' have been systematically constituted as other. This would definitely mean at least two things. First, is the necessity for more attention to differences within the constituted category of woman. As Moore (1994: 61) argues, 'all major axes of difference, race, class, ethnicity, sexuality and religion intersect with gender in ways which proffer a multiplicity of subject positions within any discourse'. Second, is the need for a recognition of the complex historical contexts against which these discourses are played out. This would imply an interweaving discussion of phenomena such as the history of colonialism, the economics of imperialism, the domination of English as a global language and the overwhelming institutional pressures to conform to Western cultural forms in many parts of the world (Bulbeck, 1998; Emberly, 1993). The emergence of these multiple urgent concerns strongly supports the use of postcolonialism as a theoretical lens for understanding and critiquing the practices whereby otherness is systematically constituted in and by organizations. Not surprisingly, perhaps, such questions have hardly been raised within organization and management studies, wherein discussions of otherness remain largely isolated from both the political tinges of globalization and the critiques of postcolonialism. Our chapter hopes to illustrate how postcolonialism can offer very different visions of identity questions in organizations.

A brief overview of postcolonialism

Postcolonialism has simultaneously emerged from and influenced a wide number of academic disciplines including literature, political science, anthropology, history and women's studies (Ashcroft *et al.*, 1995). It has strong affinities with certain strands of feminism and post-structuralism, and, like both these genres, is also concerned with the study and advocacy of marginalized others within historical and contemporary structures of domination (Gandhi, 1998). However, postcolonialism's starting point is (a) a recognition that colonialism is one of the most significant influences on the West's interpretation of people belonging to different races and ethnicities, and (b) a belief that past and continuing neo-colonial encounters hold important ramifications for gender, ethnic, national, religious and other identities in all walks of social life (Spurr, 1993).

Postcolonial theory is a valuable perspective for examining organizational identity issues because colonialism was one of the most profound and significant experiences that shaped the Western world's perception of peoples belonging to non-Western races and ethnicities (i.e. the West's *others*) (Said, 1979). Colonialism's legacy can be found in contemporary Western views of immigrants and people of colour, which are distinctly tinged with shades of imperialism (Hulme, 1985). Hence postcolonialism can serve as a useful device for probing the complicated dilemmas of race and ethnic identity that intersect with those of gender in contemporary Western organizations. In addition, the colonial encounter holds important implications for questions of sexual and gender identity in the West, as well as for experiences of social and cultural marginality (Nandy, 1983; Stoler, 1997). Postcolonial theory is therefore of obvious relevance for any examination of gender and cultural identities at the workplace, and for analysing the ways in which identities of otherness are produced out of dominant-group/marginal-group dynamics.

Few writers are as central to postcolonialism as Edward Said whose classic work, *Orientalism* (1979) established postcolonial theory as a prominent field of scholarly inquiry. Based on his landmark analysis of scholarship on the subject of the Middle East and Islam produced during the nineteenth and twentieth centuries in Britain, France and America – the so-called 'three great empires' (Said, 1979: 15) – Said sought to lay bare the inner workings of orientalism, which he characterized as both a specialized field of Western scholarship as well as a general tendency in Western (colonial) thought. *Orientalism* was followed by a flood of postcolonial research in a number of disciplines, including anthropology, cultural studies, history and literature. Lately, postcolonial theory has made an appearance even in management scholarship (e.g. Prasad, 1997a, Prasad, 1997b; Priyadarshini, 2000).

Given the magnitude of the overall postcolonial oeuvre, a comprehensive review of this literature's contributions is clearly beyond the scope of this chapter. At the risk of some simplification, however, we can state that postcolonial theory is based on the assertion that the project of Western colonization of the rest of the world was based upon the social and cultural construction of a fundamental *ontological* distinction between 'the West' and 'the non-West', with the latter occupying the position of the West's *other*, and serving as the focal point for distilling the *opposites* of all those moral, ethical and aesthetic attributes that gradually accreted to constitute the very core of the West's own self-image.

Given this, colonialism attempted simultaneously to produce and naturalize the subjectivities of both the colonizer and the colonized. As Said (1979: 1–2) observes, the West needed the non-West in order to 'define ... the West as ... [the non-West's] contrasting image, idea, personality, experience'. Or, as Achebe (1989: 3) explains, colonialism sought to constitute the West itself by setting up the non-West 'as a foil to Europe, as a place of negations ... in comparison with which Europe's own state of spiritual grace would be manifest'.

The construction of the West/non-West dichotomy was premised on the fiction of an elaborate system of hierarchical binary oppositions (e.g. active/passive, centre/periphery, civilized/savage, developed/underdeveloped, masculine/feminine, modern/archaic, scientific/superstitious, etc.). Table 4.1 provides a brief list of

Table 4.1 The hierarchical system of colonialist binaries

Constitutions of the West	Constitutions of the non-West
Active	Passive
Adult	Child
Centre	Periphery
Civilized	Savage/primitive
Completeness/fullness	Lacking/inadequate
Developed	Backward/undeveloped
Liberated	Exploited
Masculine	Feminine/effeminate
Modern	Archaic
Nation	Tribe
Occidental	Oriental
Scientific	Superstitious
Secular	Religious
Subject	Object
Superior	Inferior
Vanguard	Followers
White (European)	Coloured (non-European)

these binaries. These binaries were hierarchical in the sense that the first term in each of the foregoing examples was constituted as the *privileged* term, and was considered superior to, and more desirable than, the second term.

Essentially, colonialism linked the West (colonizer) with the superior pole of these binaries, and relegated the colonized (non-West) to the inferior pole. According to postcolonialism, such a conceptual manoeuvre was necessary for providing a moral justification for colonialism. Once the identity of the colonized had been thoroughly amplified with terms designating 'inferiority', colonialism could successfully claim to be a project intended to civilize, improve and even *help* those cultures that were 'lagging behind' in the march of history and civilization. Indeed, once this manoeuvre had been made, colonialism was virtually transformed into a moral obligation for the West.

Along with this, however, colonialism also evinced considerable ambivalence towards the non-West. For instance, even though colonialism sought clearly to identify the non-West as inferior and undesirable, the non-West was also regarded in the colonial discourse as a highly desirable and prized object of Western possession. Similarly, although colonialism sought to define the non-West as weak and effeminate, it simultaneously viewed the non-West as a grave threat capable of destroying the Western world. Further, while colonialism was spurred by the moral imperative to 'improve' the non-West in the West's own image, paradoxically colonialism also evinced an intense desire to preserve the 'authenticity' of the non-West, usually in terms of safeguarding some changeless essence of non-Western cultures.

In addition, although the discourse of colonialism claimed that its moral purpose was the civilization of the 'dark' and savage races, it simultaneously posited savagery as a fixed and immovable biological condition, incapable of being changed. Ambivalence can also be found in the colonial discourse of miscegenation (especially when it involved Westerners) that was typically presented as a nightmare to be avoided at all costs. At other times, it also recommended a policy of careful inbreeding between whites and non-whites in order to extinguish non-Western races altogether (Loomba, 1998: 173).

What the foregoing suggests is that the Western colonizer's approach towards the non-Western colonized was fraught with a sense of deep schizophrenia. Not surprisingly perhaps, the shadows of such colonialist schizophrenia continue to fall over contemporary Western organizations' engagements with other identities. Take the current interest in promoting workplace diversity and multiculturalism. While diversity is frequently promoted as desirable for organizations (Cox, 1993), many organizations continue to resist and oppose genuine diversity initiatives in both formal and informal ways (Martin, 1992; Prasad and Mills, 1997), and workplace diversity is often regarded as a source of 'confusion, disorder and hostility' (Thomas, 1994: 61).

The colonial experience also casts its shadows on other identity issues in organizations. For instance, the tendency in colonialist thought to see the white man as embodying the active principle (and the only subject in history) may find expression within contemporary organizational inclinations to regard immigrants and peoples of colour (and often even white women) as passive beings lacking in forcefulness, drive and initiative. Similarly, the colonial ideology that saw the West as the centre of the world often impels organizations to regard Western management practices as a universal norm, and to judge non-Western managerial practices against such a norm, with attendant consequences for the identities of Western and non-Western managers and employees. The remainder of this chapter will explore some concrete organizational sites in which postcolonialism can serve as an effective lens for understanding relationships around the structuring of otherness and identity.

Postcolonialism and identities of otherness in organizations

Implications of postcolonialism for understanding identity and otherness in organizations are immense. Postcolonialism alerts us to the lingering effects of colonial discourses on workplace practices and organizational arrangements. In particular, postcolonialism emphasizes the potency of representation as a social practice. Representation is one of the foundational concepts of postcolonialism. In conventional and everyday language, the term 'representation' usually refers to *political* representation – whereby individuals are elected to stand for governmental positions by the broader populace and are held accountable to their constituents. Within postcolonial thinking, representation also refers to the process whereby things, people and cultures are symbolically constituted or represented (Mitchell, 1995) in a multitude of venues, including art, literature, history, film, annual reports, advertisements, policy statements, and so on. Here, representation refers to ways in which any form of cultural expression stands for an aspect of reality, be it persons, things or practices (Gidley, 1992). Obviously such representations can never be divorced from political and ideological relationships involving global hegemonies, colonial histories and geopolitical moves (Gidley, 1992). It is primarily through such representational acts that the identities of both self and other are repeatedly constituted and reproduced (Hallam and Street, 2000).

Our main contention here is that these acts of representation are not only profoundly significant; they are also substantially organizational and institutional. In other words, representations of otherness take place within organizational milieus and are sustained through a nexus of institutional structures and arrangements. The classic example of organizational/institutional representations of otherness is, of course, orientalism itself. Said (1979), who gave the term 'orientalism' a new postcolonial sense, sees it as holding multiple meanings. The more conventional meaning of orientalism is an academic one denoting a scholarly field of study in which an orientalist is an expert on certain aspects of oriental society and culture. Orientalism also refers to a school of painting in which the subjects were always oriental and exotic in nature, typically being sultans and their palaces, harems and bazaars (Richon, 1985). For Said, orientalism is also 'a style of thought based upon an ontological and epistemological distinction made between "the orient" and (most of the time) "the occident"' (1979: 2). And, finally, orientalism is also the entire network of institutional interests that come together in discursively producing and having authority over the so-called Orient. As Said most effectively demonstrates, orientalist representations of the other were accomplished within an institutionalized system of scholarship and cultural production that repeatedly constituted Islamic cultures and people of the Near East as barbaric, exotic, licentious and cunning others (Richon, 1985). Orientalism, in fact, eventually emerged as a highly respected institutional field (DiMaggio and Powell, 1983) promoting legitimate scholarship, art and literature that was systematically engaged in studying and representing the other to the West.

For our purposes, what is important here are two things. First, that neo-colonial and neo-imperial discourses of otherness continue to be prevalent in diverse organizational settings; second, that these discourses are produced both *within* and *by* organizations. This implies that critically oriented scholarship on otherness in organizations needs to take some specific directions. postcolonialism suggests that organizational mechanisms for constituting otherness are predominantly *discursive* rather than taking place mainly at the level of individual beliefs and behaviours. This is not intended to deny the role of individuals and local groups in constituting otherness. Rather, it is an attempt to steer attention away from reductionist psychologistic explanations involving attitudes, mindsets and behaviours in favour of wider and more contextualized ones that recognize the role of organizational practices, professional vocabularies and structural arrangements (i.e. discourses) in manufacturing otherness. To illustrate these phenomena we will briefly examine three different organizational and institutional fields in which identities of otherness are produced. They are (a) organizational training programmes, (b) the tourism industry, and (c) museums and the art industry.

Training programmes

A variety of training programmes across many North American and Western European organizations ostensibly intended to make organization members more appreciative of internal and external cultural differences, somewhat ironically turn into sites for the systematic and problematic production of otherness.

These include programmes designed to (a) promote internal organizational sensitivity towards workplace diversity, (b) provide expatriate managers with desirable managerial skills in cross-cultural business encounters, and (c) train non-Western managers (in Eastern Europe and South Asia) in Western managerial practices. All these socialization venues become (perhaps inadvertently) organizational locations for the constitution of otherness through the systematic transmission of images about self and other that markedly echo the legacy of colonialist discourses.

Different ethnic minorities, women and Eastern European managers are regularly constituted as exotic, inadequate or underdeveloped others who need help, tolerance and acceptance from the dominant majority (Western) groups (Kostera, 1995; Prasad, 2000). While the intentions of these programmes appear (and may well be) progressive in their objectives, their actual effects can still continue to reproduce older imperial-style relationships between the West and the non-West other. Kostera's (1995) work on managerial training programmes conducted by Western-based companies and consultants in the erstwhile Soviet bloc countries provides an interesting analysis of ways in which Eastern European managers are repeatedly constituted as lagging behind their Western counterparts both economically and culturally. In her depiction, the Eastern European managers come very close to resembling the 'natives' of colonialist discourses, lacking the skills of advanced civilization and needing to be 'saved' or 'rescued' by Western managers, who in turn are recast as the missionaries of former centuries (Cannizo, 1998; Kostera, 1995). The problem with this model is that a specific pattern of cultural hierarchies and binaries are once again reproduced, albeit as 'help' being offered to the less-developed managers. Like the missionaries who 'gathered souls' in their bids for conversion to Christianity (Cannizo, 1998), these modern crusaders are also collecting candidates for conversion to Western managerial dogma. Again like the missionaries of colonial times, they also rupture existing cultural identities and sometimes replace them with ones in which the 'converted' always remain beholden to and behind their teachers from the West.

For our purposes, the main point to be underlined here is that postcolonialism helps us pinpoint discourses of otherness in everyday organizational practices such as training that may well be designed to 'improve' workplace conditions and enhance organizational effectiveness.

The tourism industry

Tourism is increasingly recognized as an organizational field in which identities of otherness (sexual, racial, ethnic, etc.) are constantly produced in order to cater to the Western consumption of difference (Britton, 1979; Enloe, 1989). The promotion and practice of tourism involves an active effort on the part of multiple organizations (e.g. travel agencies, tour operators, hotels, cruise lines, etc.) in taking up and commodifying other cultures. These organizations primarily sell images of the past as well as images of difference in ways that render otherness less frightening and easily available for consumption (Root, 1996). In this process, cultural distances between Western and non-Western cultures in particular may actually be widened, despite increased physical contact between them (Britton, 1979).

While tourist organizations constitute non-Western cultural identities in seemingly attractive and 'exotic' ways they nevertheless continue to reproduce old colonial relationships of dominance and subjugation in unexpected new ways. Let us take the case of the Caribbean – an area that is often hailed as an outstanding success in tourism marketing. Crick (1989) argues that in systematically constituting countries of the Caribbean as earthly paradises, their inhabitants are reduced to playing subordinate, sexualized and servile positions in the drama of Western consumption. In constituting the Caribbean as a tourist 'garden of Eden', tourists are fully encouraged to enjoy the 'sun, sand, sex and the sea', while local inhabitants are forced (at both symbolic and material levels) into playing servile roles that entirely cater to tourist demands (Crick, 1989; Taylor, 1973). As Crick points out, these images of 'leisure imperialism' (Britton, 1983) have real consequences for locals, who are often evacuated from tourist paradises and are enrolled in 'courtesy campaigns' designed to inculcate the right amount of deference and servility. Needless to say, over time these tourism discourses influence overall relationships between the West and the Caribbean, both within the domain of tourism itself as well as in other cross-cultural encounters. The problem, of course, is that these pervasive representations create fixed identities (Root, 1996) for both sets of players that are strongly reminiscent of the colonial binaries indicated in Table 4.1.

Tourist and travel organizations also explicitly promote and glamorize the so-called 'primitive' elements of non-Western cultures as a way of making their otherness starker and more attractive. This can take place both in the Third World or within Western countries themselves. In British Columbia, for example, a number of tourist organizations present native aboriginal cultures as one of the most promising experiences that the province can offer. The native identities offered for tourist consumption, however, are completely decontextualized from past histories and present political realities (Root, 1996). These native identities are significantly over-aestheticized, turning the spotlight on traditional crafts, colourful costumes, ceremonial dances and totem poles (Crosby, 1991). Urgent controversial issues such as land rights activism among these native groups is given no place for public representation in this discourse, and the native other continues to be appreciated solely with reference to his/her past with no active role visible in the present or the future. Postcolonialism helps us uncover the diverse organizational networks engaged in producing these identities, and some of their immediate consequences.

Museums and the art industry

Few institutional fields are as closely connected to the process and legacy of imperialism as museums. Yet, in many quarters, museums continue to be regarded as dispassionate and disinterested organizations engaged in recording histories and preserving cultures. The recent influences of postcolonialism have triggered considerable scholarly interest in understanding museums as pivotal cultural institutions engaged in the neo-imperial task of 'displaying cultures' and constituting identities of otherness in this process (Hallam and Street, 2000; Richards, 1993). Museums' connections with colonialism and imperialism are, moreover, no longer seen as exclusively belonging to the past. Museums continue to engage in practices of orientalism and exoticization in two prominent ways. The first is through the display and representation of non-Western art in the major art museums of the world (Clifford, 1988; Barringer, 1998), and the second is through the exhibition of non-Western cultures in ethnographic and folk museums (Clifford, 1988; Shelton, 2000).

Like the tourism industry, museums also decontextualize the subjects they represent by displaying specific cultural objects (such as masks or pieces of pottery) out of their context and turning them into abstract representations of entire complex cultural systems (Clifford, 1988). Museums also tend to gloss over internal cultural contradictions and present them instead as largely undifferentiated entities. As Hallam and Street (2000: 6–7) observe, the ideological work of museums has been 'to translate social and cultural heterogeneity into homogeneous unity and to emphasize boundaries which map zones of inclusion and exclusion'.

In sum, therefore, museums create overly simplified images of otherness which are easy to interpret as picturesquely primitive and in need of cultural protection by the West. This once again calls to mind the colonial project of 'rescuing' the other and asserting the West's authority over it. According to Barringer (1998), the historical role of museums as institutions responsible for the removal of objects and treasures from a colonial periphery to an imperial centre is one that has lasting impacts on contemporary orientations towards cultural objects from different societies. Examining the Victoria and Albert Museum in London (formerly the South Kensington Museum), Barrringer argues that the museum's constitution around its imperial legacy through the display of colonized peoples' possessions and gifts to the Empire firmly established the museum as the *custodian* of non-Western treasures, an identity that is hard to break away from even today. As a result, Western museums have a hard time relinquishing their possession and authority over important artefacts and often stand in the way of returning them to their earlier cultural homes (Root, 1996). Such examinations of museum's past and current roles are vital given ongoing discussions regarding the sovereignty over specific cultural artefacts such as the Parthenon marbles (formerly known as the Elgin marbles) or sacred objects confiscated from native potlatch ceremonies by the Royal Canadian Mounted Police. In this case, the constitution of otherness by museums may well have implications that could backfire on their own institutional identities.

Ethnographic museums also continue to reproduce old colonial oppositions, notably between civilized and 'savage' societies in their display of so-called primitive art and artefacts from countries such as Papua/New Guinea and other Pacific islands. Exhibitions of contemporary Third World societies in the Tropean Museum at Amsterdam also create a strong feeling of cultural inertia and passivity from which its inhabitants cannot escape (Root, 1996).

Discussion

Any serious attempt to understand questions of organizational culture and identity must necessarily examine the series of symbolic classifications demarcating self from other, typically formed around binary oppositions. For the most part, organizational scholars have been preoccupied with gender as the fulcrum around which crucial organizational identities are formed, and around which zones of inclusion and exclusion are drawn. In this chapter we have argued that (a) gender itself intersects substantially with race, ethnicity, religion, national origin, etc. to constitute a spectrum of 'other' identity categories, and (b) that colonialism (alongside patriarchy) remains one of the more compelling global experiences and world-views shaping the formation of identities in organizations all over the world. Otherness in organizations, therefore, is structured by more than gender, though gender remains an inescapable element of otherness.

We have also tried to emphasize the institutional nature of identity formation over the individual and group cognitive elements that usually receive attention in organization studies. We agree with Fabian (1991: 208) that 'the other is never simply given, never just found or encountered, but *made*' [emphasis added]. This making of otherness is to us a primarily institutional act in which multiple organizations and their players are simultaneously involved. postcolonialism can bring a historical analysis of the process of cultural othering to contemporary institutional efforts to study organizational boundary making. Institutionalists like Beisel (1992) have examined the work of organizations in constructing boundaries between obscenity and literature, while DiMaggio (1992) has looked at organizational stratification techniques that have created entire domains of 'high' and 'low' culture in American theatre, opera and art. Few institutional studies, however, have looked at the production of racial, ethnic and sexual identities in and by organizations operating under the legacies of colonialism and imperialism. Our chapter is an attempt to forge an intellectual venture between postcolonialism and institutional theory. Such a project can only contribute towards an enhanced understanding of organizational culture and identity under conditions of globalization.

References

Achebe, C. (1989). *Hopes and Impediments*. New York, NY: Doubleday.

Ashcroft, B., Griffiths, G. and Tiffin, H. (1995). *The Postcolonial Studies Reader*. London: Routledge.

Barringer, T. (1998). The South Kensington Museum and the Colonialist Project. In T. Barringer and T. Flynn (eds), *Colonialism and the Object: Empire, Material Culture and the Museum* (pp. 11–27). London: Routledge.

Beisel, N. (1992). Constructing a shifting moral boundary: Literature and obscenity in nineteenth century America. In M. Lamont and M. Fournier (eds), *Cultivating Differences: Symbolic Boundaries and the Making of Inequality* (pp. 104–128). Chicago, IL: University of Chicago Press.

Britton, R.A. (1979). The image of the Third World in tourism marketing. *Annals of Tourism Research*, 6: 18–28.

Britton, R.A. (1983). *Tourism and Underdevelopment in Fiji*. Canberra: Development Studies Monograph No. 31.

Bulbeck, C. (1998). *Re-Orienting Western Feminisms: Women's Diversity in a Postcolonial World*. Cambridge: Cambridge University Press.

Cannizo, J. (1998). Gathering souls and objects: missionary collections. In T. Barringer and T. Flynn (eds), *Colonialism and the Object: Empire, Material Culture and the Museum* (pp. 153–166). London: Routledge.

Carby, H.V. (1982). 'White woman listen! black feminism and the boundaries of sisterhood. In The Centre for Contemporary Studies (ed.), *The Empire Strikes Back: Race and Racism in 70's Britain*. London: Hutchinson.

Clifford, J. (1988). *The Predicament of Culture: Twentieth Century Ethnography, Literature and Art*. Cambridge, MA: Harvard University Press.

Cox, T. (1993). *Cultural Diversity in Organizations*. San Francisco: Berrett-Koehler.

Crick, M. (1989). Representations of international tourism in the social sciences: sun, sex, sights, savings and servility. *Annual Review of Anthropology*, 18: 307–344.

Crosby, M. (1991). Construction of the imaginary Indian. In S. Douglas (ed.), *Vancouver Anthology: The Institutional Politics of Art* (pp. 267–294). Vancouver: Talon Books.

Davies, M. (1983). *Third World – Second Sex: Women's Struggles and National Liberation*. London: Zed Books.

DiMaggio, P. (1992). Cultural boundaries and structural change: the extension of the high culture model to theater, opera and dance, 1900–1940. In M. Lamont and M. Fournier (eds), *Cultivating Differences: Symbolic Boundaries and the Making of Inequality* (pp. 21–57). Chicago, IL: University of Chicago Press.

DiMaggio, P. and Powell, W. (1983). The iron cage revisited: institutional isomorphism and collective rationality in organizational fields. *American Sociological Review*, 48: 147–160.

Emberly, J.V. (1993). *Thresholds of Difference: Feminist Critique, Native Women's Writings, Postcolonial Theory*. Toronto: University of Toronto Press.

Enloe, C. (1989). *Bananas, Beaches and Bases: Making Feminist Sense of International Politics*. London: Pandora.

Fabian, J. (1991). *Time and the Work of Anthropology: Critical Essays, 1971–1991*. Chur, Switzerland: Harwood Academic Publishers.

Ferguson, K. (1984). *The Feminist Case Against Bureaucracy*. Philadelphia, PA: Temple University Press.

Friedman, J. (1995). Global system, globalization and the parameters of modernity. In M. Featherstone, S. Lash and R. Robertson (eds), *Global Modernities* (pp. 69–90). London: Sage Publications.

Gandhi, L. (1998). *Postcolonial Theory: A Critical Introduction*. New York, NY: Columbia University Press.

Gidley, M. (1992). *Representing Others: White Views of Indigenous Peoples*. Exeter: University of Exeter Press.

Hall, C. (1996). Histories, empires and the post-colonial moment. In I. Chambers and L. Curti (eds), *The Post-Colonial Question: Common Skies, Divided Horizons* (pp. 65–77). London: Routledge.

Hall, S., Held, D. and McGraw, T. (1992). *Modernity and its Futures*. Cambridge: Open University Press.

Hallam, E. and Street, B.V. (2000). Introduction. In E. Hallam and B.V. Street (eds), *Cultural Encounters: Representing 'Otherness'* (pp. 1–10). London: Routledge.

Hulme, P. (1985). Polytropic man: tropes of sexuality and mobility in early colonialist discourse. In F. Barker, P. Hulme, M. Iverson and D. Loxley (eds), *Europe and Its Others* (Vol. 2: pp. 17–32). Colchester: University of Essex Press.

Irwin, K. (1991). Towards theories of Maori feminisms. In R. du Plessis (ed.), *Feminist Voices: Women's Studies Texts for Aotearoa/New Zealand* (pp. 63–74). Auckland: Oxford University Press.

Kostera, M. (1995). The modern crusade: the missionaries of management come to Eastern Europe. *Management Learning*, 3: 331–352.

Larrain, J. (1994). *Ideology and Cultural Identity: Modernity and the Third World Presence*. Cambridge: Polity Press.

Loomba, A. (1998). *Colonialism/Postcolonialism*. London: Routledge.

Lugones, M.C. and Spelman, E. (1990). Have we got a theory for you?: feminist theory, cultural imperialism and the demand for 'the woman's voice'. In Y. Al-Hibri and M.A. Simon (eds), *Hypatia Reborn: Essays in Feminist Philosophy*. Bloomington: Indiana University Press.

Maier, M. (1997). We have to make a MANagement decision: challenger and the dysfunctions of corporate masculinity. In P. Prasad, A. Mills, M.B. Elmes and A. Prasad (eds), *Managing the Organizational Melting Pot: Dilemmas of Workplace Diversity* (pp. 226–254). Thousand Oaks, CA: Sage Publications.

Martin, J. (1992). The suppression of gender conflicts in organizations. In D. Kolb and J. Bartunek (eds), *Hidden Conflict in Organizations: Uncovering Behind-the-Scenes Disputes*. Newbury Park, CA: Sage Publications.

Mascia-Lees, F.E. (1989). The postmodern turn in anthropology: cautions from a feminist perspective. *Signs*, 15: 7–33.

Mighty, J. (1997). Triple jeopardy: immigrant women of color in the labor force. In P. Prasad, A. Mills, M. Elmes and A. Prasad (eds), *Managing the Organizational Melting Pot: Dilemmas of Workplace Diversity* (pp. 312–339). Thousand Oaks, CA: Sage Publications.

Mills, A.J. (1988). Organization, gender and culture. *Organization Studies*, 9: 351–369.

Mitchell, W.J.T. (1995). Representation. In F. Lentricchia and T. McLaughlin (eds), *Critical Terms for Literary Study* (pp. 11–22). Chicago, IL: University of Chicago Press.

Mohanty, C.T. (1988). Under Western eyes: feminist scholarship and colonial discourses. *Feminist Review*, 30: 242–269.

Moore, H. (1994). *A Passion for Difference*. Cambridge: Polity Press.

Nandy, A. (1983). *The Intimate Enemy*. Delhi: Oxford University Press.

Oseen, C. (1997). The sexually specific subject and the dilemma of difference: rethinking the different in the construction of the nonhierarchical workplace. In P. Prasad, A. Mills, M. Elmes and A. Prasad (eds), *Managing the Organizational Melting Pot: Dilemmas of Workplace Diversity* (pp. 54–79). Thousand Oaks, CA: Sage Publications.

Pieterse, J.N. (1995). Globalization as hybridization. In M. Featherstone, S. Lash and R. Robertson (eds), *Global Modernities* (pp. 45–68). London: Sage Publications.

Prasad, A. (1997a). Provincializing Europe: towards a postcolonial reconstruction. *Studies in Cultures, Organizations and Societies*, 3: 91–117.

Prasad, A. (1997b). The colonizing consciousness and representations of the other: a postcolonial critique of the discourse of oil. In P. Prasad, A. Mills, M. Elmes and A. Prasad (eds), *Managing the Organizational Melting Pot: Dilemmas of Workplace Diversity* (pp. 285–311). Thousand Oaks, CA: Sage Publications.

Prasad, P. (2000). Promising Rainbows: An Institutionalist Analysis of Diversity Management. Paper presented at the Annual Meetings of the Academy of Management, Toronto, August.

Prasad, P. and Mills, A. (1997). From showcase to shadow: understanding the dilemmas of managing workplace diversity. In P. Prasad, A. Mills, M. Elmes and A. Prasad (eds), *Managing the Organizational Melting Pot: Dilemmas of Workplace Diversity* (pp. 3–27). Thousand Oaks, CA: Sage Publications.

Priyadarshini, E. (2000). A Critical Ethnography of the Production of the Indian MBA Discourse. Unpublished doctoral dissertation, School of Management, Lancaster University, Lancaster, United Kingdom.

Richards, T. (1993). *The Imperial Archive. Knowledge and the Fantasy of Empire*. London: Verso.

Richon, O. (1985). Representation, the despot and the harem: some questions around an academic orientalist painting by Lecomte-Du-Nouy. In F. Barker, P. Hulme,

M. Iverson and D. Loxley (eds), *Europe and its Others* (Vol. 1: pp. 1–13). Colchester: University of Essex Press.

Robertson, R. (1992). *Globalization: Social Theory and Global Culture.* London: Sage Publications.

Root, D. (1996). *Cannibal Culture: Art, Appropriation and the Commodification of Difference.* Boulder, CO: Westview Press.

Said, E. (1979). *Orientalism.* New York, NY: Viking.

Shelton, A.A. (2000). Museum ethnography: an imperial science. In E. Hallam and B.V. Street (eds), *Cultural Encounters: Representing 'Otherness'* (pp. 155–193). London: Routledge.

Smith, D.E. (1987). *The Everyday World as Problematic: A Feminist Sociology.* Milton Keynes: Open University Press.

Spurr, D. (1993). *The Rhetoric of Empire.* Durham, N.C.: Duke University Press.

Stoler, A.L. (1997). Making empire respectable: the politics of race and sexual morality in twentieth century colonial cultures. In A. McClintock, A. Mufti and E. Shohat (eds), *Dangerous Liaisons: Gender, Nation and Postcolonial Perspectives* (pp. 344–373). Minneapolis, MN: University of Minnesota Press.

Taylor, F.F. (1973). The tourist industry in Jamaica. *Social Economic Studies*, 22: 205–228.

Thomas, V.C. (1994). The downside of diversity. *Training and Development*, 48: 60–62.

5 Beyond body-counting

A discussion of the social construction of gender at work

Mats Alvesson and Yvonne Due Billing

Introduction

This chapter addresses gender in two crucial dimensions – men/women and forms of masculinity/femininity – and looks at both of them in general terms and specifically in relation to public organizations in Scandinavia. The main thesis is that, as a workplace, the public sector represents a prominent institution that contributes to the construction of gender. This large female workplace[1] is not regarded here primarily as an expression and manifestation of the interests of women; rather, women – in the social sense – are seen as being created by the public sector, thus reproducing existing gender relations. This thesis holds above all for Scandinavia, but we believe it also applies to those welfare states which have a high proportion of women in public organizations.

In order not to make the presentation too long, we shall abstain from demonstrating corresponding constructions of men, and in some parts of the text we just use woman/women as examples. Naturally this does not mean that we equate gender with woman. Since what distinguishes women/femininity can only be understood in relation to men/masculinity, statements about one sex mean that implicitly something is also being said about the other (see also Connell, 1995).

The chapter opens with a general discussion of the nature of gender and a brief survey of developments in this field of research. The tendency to set great store by body-counting is criticized, and the idea is challenged that the distribution of men and women in particular spheres helps us in any significant way to understand gender relations in a society. In order to understand gender construction at work we suggest that four elements should be studied: (1) the percentage share of the two sexes; (2) the gender aura or image of the activity (that is the ideas that people in the surroundings of the activity hold about the workplace); (3) the values and ideas that dominate the activity; (4) the form in which the activity is conducted (is it, for example, public or private, exposed to competition or 'protected'). We will elaborate on this 'model' on pp. 81–86. Thus we suggest that it is meaningful to examine cultural notions of masculinity and femininity and their concomitant dominance relationships. Masculinity and femininity are then not seen as essences or psychological traits, but as cultural ideas carried by a specific group about what is assumed to be typical or natural for men or women in terms of acting, thinking and/or valuing. This argument will be explored by reference to public organizations, which will be considered in light of the tension or friction between cultural ideas about the masculine and feminine. Large sections of the public sector (especially in Scandinavia) can be said to be marked not only by a preponderance of women but also by a pronounced feminine identity. It is not only the gender distribution in the public organizations but also the (constructed) conditions of work and the ideologies of these organizations that contribute to the creation of 'women' – and thus, indirectly, of 'men' – as social beings. Hence, the transformation of gender relations is at least partly a question of transforming public organizations.

What is gender?

Research in the social sciences emphasizes how men and women come into being and evolve in social and cultural contexts. Men and women in different cultures develop different customs and orientations; they are active in different spheres. The perception of certain occupations as feminine or masculine, and primarily dominated by one sex, is mainly the expression of social conditions, which in turn can be maintained if the gender segregation is regarded as normal and springs from women's and men's own 'natural' characteristics and 'true' preferences. But perceptions of the gender orientation of an occupation can be transformed over time, as the classical example of office work has shown; or an occupation can acquire a gender-neutral image, as personnel management has done. Biological differences are not regarded by many as the ultimate determinant of the way men and women act or of how work is divided between them, but opinions do differ as to whether or not biology plays some part in this. Some feminists believe we should neither exaggerate nor deny the importance of biological differences (e.g. Cockburn, 1991). Bearing and nursing children, according to some researchers, does give women a certain orientation that is quite distinct from men's (Chodorow, 1978; Hartsock, 1987). While admitting that childcare arrangements are affected by cultural conditions, these researchers point out that women have historically been predominant in this sphere, and that they still are. Others claim that gender – men/women, masculinity/ femininity – can be explained almost exclusively by reference to social processes, irrespective of biological gender differences. What may look like gender-specific inclinations or orientations can be better explained in terms of the positions and external social conditions in which men and women find themselves (Kanter, 1977). According to this view there are no feminine orientations linked to the female sex as such; there are simply orientations that reflect the conditions, work situations and career prospects that are typical of a particular group of people (i.e. women and men under similar circumstances). Rationality of caring often attributed to women could thus best be explained as an expression of the fact that the women in question work in one of the caring occupations, and under the conditions that are typical of such fields. From this would follow that women who do not work in these occupations should not exhibit any particular inclination for caring, unlike men who are involved in nursing or childcare. According to this view, there is thus no 'essence' which distinguishes the two sexes from one another.

However, even researchers who are not prepared to ascribe the possible characteristics of a group of members of a particular sex to their immediate social and material life situation, and who set great store by early psychological development and socialization instead, do generally maintain that, however slowly, gender is socially changeable. Historically, then, current gender patterns are a transient phenomenon. Gender today and gender the day after tomorrow are to a certain extent different things. In order to underline this point a distinction is often made between (biological) sex and (social) gender. The distinction has been exposed to a good deal of criticism, partly because it ignores the fact that the meaning or implication of biological sex is also socially defined (i.e. is a cultural phenomenon) (cf. Hallberg, 1992). As we shall see below, there is a tendency to start from biological definitions of men and women even among those who declare their interest in gender as a social construction – a situation which leads to some confusion.

A definition of social gender – in contrast to biological sex, which is determined by the chromosome constellation and is manifest in the sexual organs, the internal reproduction organs and hormones – can run along the following lines:

'Gender, in contrast, refers to a classification that societies construct to exaggerate the differences between females and males and to maintain sex inequality' (Reskin and Padavic, 1994: 3). Here gender suggests something 'wrong' or 'distorted', thus promoting the notion of something illegitimate. In this way gender almost begins to resemble a false ideology, not creating but distorting conditions as they are. The result is to women's disadvantage. Women do receive lower wages, are promoted less often, are sometimes exposed to sexual abuse, and have to do more housework. Without denying that such is the case, it can be claimed that gender is the result of an active process. Reskin and Padavic seem to be saying that beyond gender there is something objective, which has been exposed to a process of distortion that exaggerates the differences. They claim that in fact no significant differences exist between men and women. Instead, perhaps, gender in the sense of ideas about men, women and the relations between them, through social practices, actually *creates* men and women in the socialization processes and ongoing social constructions of social life. Acker (1992: 250) is saying much the same thing when she declares that gender 'refers to patterned, socially produced, distinctions between female and male, feminine and masculine'. Gender is something that we *produce*, not only in early childhood but when we participate in work organizations and other contexts.

Although it is difficult to adopt a process perspective, it is nonetheless more fruitful to try to understand gender as an organizing process than to refer to it as a fixed system (like patriarchy, gender system) or a distorting classification system. Gender is more usefully understood as a number of dynamic, ambiguous and varying phenomena rather than abstract, static and unequivocal ones. This applies particularly to present-day Western society. Rather than a single-gender order, we find a multiplicity of gendering.[2] It seems to us that the important thing is to look critically at the use, the meaning, the organization and the effects of distinctions between women and men, the feminine and masculine, and at the relations that precede and succeed them. In our view this is the very kernel of gender research (see Alvesson and Billing, 1997).

An important element in all social science is to deal with the tension or friction between challenging and reproducing the dominating ideas and attitudes. It could be claimed that in virtually every aspect of research work, particularly perhaps in writing, researchers are either preserving or challenging concepts and ideas.[3] In the present context it should be emphasized that the complex political character of the whole question of gender motivates paying great attention to the way it is handled. Otherwise there is a risk that in certain important respects we encourage the preservation of the status quo, running counter to our own ambitions regarding change.

A critique of the body-counting approach

It seems that the dominant approach is to treat gender as a variable to be studied in relation to other variables, starting from people's biological sex. This last is generally an unequivocal condition, although there are exceptions. It is this very simplicity in describing people as 'women' or 'men' that explains why the distinction is so basic, not only in everyday life but also in gender research. It appeals to common sense and political rhetoric and provides that lack of ambiguity in the material which fits so well into statistical processing and even into the sorting of qualitative data.

However, the focus on 'body counting' has recently met with growing criticism (Alvesson and Billing, 1997; Cálas and Smircich, 1996). When people are defined on a basis of certain bodily characteristics, the implication is that an individual's bodily equipment says something essential – perhaps even the most crucial thing – about them. Statistics, as well as statements which define the individual as 'man' or 'woman', without really considering how far the definition says anything relevant, thus create or recreate the idea that the body is crucial to an understanding of gender. The social and biological tend to be linked together, even though gender researchers generally claim to be interested in gender as a social construction; that is, not in any biological sex difference but in the social and cultural processes whereby 'men' and 'women' are formed as social beings. This is worth noting in view of the fact that the intention of most feminism is to abolish the importance of sex and sex-based ideas on gender in the sense of avoiding biological sex as a basic condition for the division of labour on the labour market or in the home, and for various kinds of differential treatment.

To a gynaecologist the distinction between man and woman on a basis of bodily criteria is relevant and important. To a social scientist it is not necessarily so. It is of course possible to envisage gender constructions whereby women identify themselves with the traditional mother, experience a special sort of individuation process and become/are defined as care-oriented, empathetic, relation-oriented, assume the main responsibility for their children and for the home, develop a mother-orientation as a primary identity, are valued primarily on a basis of sexual attractiveness, perceive themselves regularly and unequivocally as 'women', land in a woman's job, are discriminated at work by people who also define them as 'women', are subordinated to men in the world they live in, and are confined by themselves and/or by others within a female role.

Such gender-construction processes do of course occur. Many gender researchers even assume that they predominate. Different researchers emphasize different elements in the argument. For some, segregation and subordination are central elements in the social construction of women; for others the care orientation is what distinguishes woman. One possibility is to define woman in the gender sense (i.e. not sex) on a basis of the aspects listed above. A socially constructed woman would then exhibit most of the above-mentioned characteristics. However, these hardly apply to all or even to most women.[4] Some women tend to be more masculine-identified than feminine;[5] thus not all women develop 'highly feminine' orientations of the caring type, as not all give birth to babies; of those who do, many share at least part of the work in the family with their husbands (at least in our part of the world), and so on. If strong requirements are imposed on the definition of the social woman, only a minority of all 'bio-women' can be defined as women in the sense that is of primary interest to a social-science gender researcher. Even under less strong requirements, a number of bio-women will still hardly qualify as 'women' in this sense (cf. the derogatory designation 'social men' used about some women who are thought to distinguish themselves too little from men). If, for example, giving birth to children and caring for them are regarded as distinguishing features of women's experience and as generating a certain inclination or orientation, as many feminists do (e.g. Cockburn, 1991; Hartsock, 1987), then some bio-women never become 'women'. Of a particular group such as the employees in an organization, several will not have become 'women' at a particular time. On the basis of this concept of 'women', perhaps at the age of thirty half the public sector's bio-women have not yet become 'women'.[6]

Specific constructions of gender such as occur in a variety of processes are more interesting, however, than rigid generalized designations. From this perspective it is not a question of some essence in women's biology that appears during early psychological development and socialization, and/or that is established in connection with life events such as giving birth or caring for children; rather, gender is one element in various dynamic processes. Here we could say that men and women are constructed – sometimes by others and sometimes by themselves – in terms of gender; for example, in sex-focused behaviour such as flirting or partaking in some sex-stereotyped activity like heavy drinking or sewing-bees, or making direct reference to a specific identity: 'As a woman it can be difficult to …' Of course both men and women can sometimes be constructed in other terms altogether. Any one person possesses a multiplicity of social identities. Gender is just one of them. It does not always dominate. Living, particularly in organizations, means that different identities alternate, sometimes one is accentuated and sometimes another. A specific individual can be 'defined' in innumerable ways; that is to say, she perceives herself and is defined by others as being manager, subordinate, woman, economist, Swedish, middle-aged, divorced, mother, religious, colleague, friend, and so on and so on. The identities can converge or be decoupled at different times (i.e. woman manager, or manager rather than woman). This dynamic view can also embrace life histories and the advent of definitive or defining situations: having small children can mean that a confirmation of the woman identity occurs more often and the perception or attribution of the female identity becomes more intense. It probably often declines once the children are older and more self-propelling.

This leads to quite a different sort of understanding than if individuals are defined by gender-specific bodily attributes and an intimately related essence – 'femininity'/'masculinity' as a psychological set of traits. In the normal case the bodily attributes making the distinction male/female possible are relatively constant. Identities are typically less so in contemporary society.

In defence of body-counting feminism, it can be pointed out that the body is certainly one source from which certain cultural and social processes can flow or be targeted at, whereby the possessors of female and male bodies develop differently or are treated differently. If the possessor of a certain kind of body is ascribed to have a particular essence (masculine or feminine qualities), this will obviously have certain consequences; this is clearly shown by statistics of women and men at work. In Scandinavia, almost three-quarters of the public-sector employees and the great majority of nursing assistants, nurses, elementary school teachers, cleaners and home-helpers are women. In certain respects the body is obviously an important fixed point in our understanding of gender and gender constructions in society. It provides a point of departure for collective action and for raising political demands.

How can the empirical value of certain pieces of information about individual people's bodies – in relation to wages, positions, occupational groups and so on – be balanced against the theoretical emphasis on social constructions in gender research? Weighing the usefulness of body-counting against its problems might mean that we note the bodily differences and use certain statistics as input in our own reflections and analyses, subordinating the interest in sex-distinct bodies to a more comprehensive focus on subjectivities, orientations, cultural meanings, social practices, etc. In brief, the number of managers who have a certain (e.g. 'feminine') management style is more interesting than the number of managers who have female sexual organs. Since the relation between a person's work as a manager and their biological sex is rather weak, the latter tells us very little about the former.[7]

We suggest that designations such as 'men' and 'women' should be used with restraint in social science research; perhaps they should simply be reserved for the subjects and contexts in which they are constructed as such, in a physiological and social sense; in other words, when it is necessary to investigate whether someone is a 'man' or a 'woman' in a particular sense that goes beyond the chromosomal dimension. The meaning which is intended can then be suitably specified (e.g. a care-oriented person, a masculinist, a victim of discrimination, a person marked by motherhood, age, and so on). In addition it can be helpful to study ideas and statements that tend to contribute to the forming of 'men' and 'women'. Otherwise designations such as bio-man and bio-woman can be used in limited contexts referring exclusively to matters concerning the chromosomes or sexual organs.

On masculinity and femininity

A possible path in gender research involves exploring cultural forms of masculinity and femininity.[8] A central task is to study the way behaviour, work area, feelings, attitudes, priorities, and so on, in a particular culture, society, class, organization, profession, etc. are regarded as masculine or feminine.[9] The study of cultural meanings, and of how different forms of masculinity (and more seldom femininity) dominate in companies, technologies, sciences, politics, organization management, etc. provides the major alternative to gender-as-a-variable/body-counting research.

Ideas about masculinity and femininity certainly affect the way people reward or punish each other, often in subtle ways, for acting or not acting 'correctly' in gender terms. But it is also a question of how people develop, maintain and restructure an identity in accordance with their own (group) version of masculinity and femininity, which includes what is regarded as reasonable in freeing ourselves from these categories. Gender identities today are hardly likely to be constructed simply on a basis of old gender stereotypes. In this context it could be suitable to take a look at recent power theory.

Power can be said to consist of the processes and mechanisms that shape our ideas, values, will and identity.[10] Power is then related to discourses (ways of determining and discussing reality associated with a particular idiom), indicating what is normal and natural. Among other things power 'orders' us in terms of masculine and feminine; it prescribes a certain masculinity in business management contexts, for example, and a more pronounced femininity in modern childcare. According to Foucault (1980, 1982) and modern power researchers, power is a question of disciplining people by indicating what is normal, using knowledge among other things in doing so. In this way, subjects are created. In many spheres such as education, therapy, management theory, the upbringing and teaching of children, consumption, and so on, modern power discourses order and regulate individuals, claiming at the same time to be 'improving' them. They indicate norms for the way we should *be*, and – when power is effectively exercised – persuade us to scrutinize ourselves critically so that we try to develop ourselves in such a way as to live up to what has been defined as normal, neutral, true, good or aggressive. Thus power is not simply good or bad: given the open-ended and uncertain nature of our human possibilities, power subordinates or qualifies us with the help of a variety of institutional arrangements. Different forms of power, or the different ideas and social practices based on these, point us in different directions.

In many parts of our own society, men who are strikingly masculine (or feminine) or women strikingly feminine (or masculine), according to the definitions above, are to some extent looked down on; phrases like 'a Rambo type' and 'prisoners of their sex roles' help to point up the norms. The status of roughnecks and housewives is equally low, at least in Scandinavia. (Pub brawls and housebound women used to be more readily accepted. Nowadays the first suggests a need for the law or the social authorities to intervene, while the second might provoke some sort of consciousness-raising intervention.) Equality is the mark of those who keep up with the times. Women and men who live in pair relationships are often *almost* equal; in Sweden today this state of affairs is probably not unusual among many younger people. It may mean that both assume responsibility for home and children, but that the woman gives these things slightly higher priority (i.e. the man rates them slightly lower). In career terms the man is perhaps a little ahead of the woman. Among men the elements of masculinity are perhaps less pronounced than they used to be and many women do regard their professional careers as important, but both parenthood and professional careers are assigned a certain gender meaning, which gives (slightly) different weights to family and work as areas of activity and sources of identity. This difference in weighting can be seen as an expression of modern power: discourses relating to equality and meritocracy give greater emphasis to the parenting norm in men and the professional-career norm in women, while traditional ideas and practices underpin segregation and the subordination of women in organizations. How these and other forms of power support or contradict each other varies a great deal between and within groups, which means that restraint is called for when it comes to making generalizations.

The masculinity and femininity issue (MaF) can be approached in a great variety of ways. Many researchers link the concepts very closely to biology. Masculinity then designates the meaning of being a man. Although the content of masculinity can vary over time, or between classes and cultures, it is still related to the bio-man. Others detach MaF from the biological sexes, and regard MaF as cultural aspects of all sorts of different phenomena. MaF can pursue a fairly free existence *vis-à-vis* biology. Bio-men may be – or may be regarded as or see themselves as – relation-oriented and child-oriented; bio-women may like hunting, nuclear energy, drinking whisky, and may be competitive and career-minded. Men are generally regarded as primarily representing masculine ways of thinking and behaving, and women as representing feminine ways of thinking and behaving. The borderline between what is 'true' and what is stereotype in these perceptions is, to say the least, unclear. Moreover, things change over time and across situations.

Sometimes MaF are regarded as more or less a question of attributes or orientations, generally in the sense that everybody is said to exhibit something of each 'pole' – for example a combination of male and female traits or attitudes (e.g. Marshall, 1993). In men, masculinity generally dominates and femininity is less pronounced. The opposite should then apply to women.

We suggest that concepts such as masculinity and femininity should be used to describe the cultural and symbolical meaning with which people in a particular cultural group (society, class, organization) endow various phenomena. By defining phenomena in these terms, we order our world: bio-men and bio-women are given certain instructions about the natural way to feel, think, believe, desire and behave, on a basis of their definition as 'men' or 'women'. The world is divided into spheres, the masculine and the feminine. Values are divided into the 'male' and the 'female'. (Naturally not everything can be subsumed under such classifications: to watch the TV news, to work as a high-school teacher in biology, to vote for the social democrats or to play badminton are hardly gender-specific. In fact it can perhaps be claimed that nowadays many, or at least more, aspects of life can avoid being ascribed any direct masculine or feminine content.)

It is often asserted in a feminist perspective that the masculine is ranked above the feminine, and in many respects this is still the case. Perhaps today, though, this is too categorical a claim, at least in modern societies, where masculine institutions such as heavy industry and the military have lost a certain amount of ground, while 'soft' themes such as ecology and psychotherapy command more attention than before. In the business world the service sector is becoming increasingly dominant. In certain respects the transformation of industry can be described in terms of de-masculinization. Vast, rigid hierarchical bureaucracies enjoy less status than more organic, decentralized organizations. While traditional bureaucratic and rationalistic organization principles are often judged to be masculine (e.g. Ferguson, 1984), words such as 'corporate culture' and 'network' send signals about the importance of feelings, community, social relations and teams which are more in accord with femininity (Blomqvist, 1994; Gherardi, 1995). Contemporary popular management literature expresses leadership ideals which harmonize with constructions of femininity – even though the authors do not explicitly make the association (Fondas, 1997). In using terms like 'masculinity' and 'femininity', we should be careful not to do so in too general or unequivocal a way.

In the process of constructing and recreating meanings with gender implications we are also creating men and women. It is important here not to forget the local and diverse nature of cultural definitions. In some gender research there is a tendency to start from the standard definitions of masculinity and femininity which appear in the international literature, but which say very little about the way people locally (i.e. in a specific group) perceive their own social reality in terms of masculinity and femininity. As examples of such universalizing definitions, mention can be made of Hines (1992: 328) who suggests that masculinity emphasizes qualities such as 'hard, dry, impersonal, objective, explicit, outer-focused, action-oriented, analytic, dualistic, quantitative, linear, rationalist, reductionist and materialist', and Marshall (1993: 124) who stresses self-sufficiency, separation, independence, control, competition, focusing, rationality and analysis. For Kerfoot and Knights (1996: 79) the core of masculinity is 'a preoccupation with a particular instrumental form of "rational control"'. Femininity, on the other hand, implies an emphasis on feelings and recognizing the importance of the imaginative and creative (Hines, 1992: 314), and of inter-dependence, co-operation, receptivity, merging, acceptance, awareness of patterns, wholes and contexts, emotional tone, personalistic perception, being, intuition, and synthesizing (Marshall, 1993: 124).

These authors represent the view of masculinity and femininity that prevails in (part of) the research community. It is a view that certainly overlaps to some extent with ideas held more generally by the public at large. At the same time big variations are obviously likely within a community, and naturally also between several different communities. Groups may differ, not only in what they think is meant by 'masculine' and 'feminine' but also in the strength of their tendency to construct the world in such terms. A tendency *not* to take part in the gender construction is perhaps what equality is all about, although somewhat paradoxically the means employed often involve emphasizing bio-gender and focusing on body-counting as part of a policy to accomplish reductions in sexual divisions of labour (Deetz, 1992).

To acquire 'genuine' knowledge about local constructions of MaF is a difficult and time-consuming business. Instead, phenomena are often ascribed masculine and feminine orientations 'from a distance'. Distanced attributions tend to fall in with various totalizing concepts and with the researcher's a priori or elitist definitions of what should be counted as masculinity and femininity etc. (Alvesson and Billing, 1997). A definite set of principles, values or attributes is then regarded as 'masculine' or 'feminine'. A different picture emerges if we take account of the multiplicity of diverging and to some extent competing masculinities and femininities and try to discover which phenomena are regarded as masculine or feminine or gender-neutral by different people. Manual labourers, accountants, commandos and feminists, for example, may have conflicting ideas about what is masculine and what is feminine.

A 'model' for understanding gender constructions at work

Gender is a consequence of social construction processes. But how are woman and man constructed? Most obviously, and in terms of direct and indirect consequences, they are constructed in the shapes of biological women/men who dominate in 'feminine/masculine' activities conducted according to 'feminine/masculine' values and in 'feminine/masculine' forms. Here the form can refer among other things to the intensity of competition, which is usually defined as masculine. We are *not* using the expressions 'feminine' and 'masculine' in a tautological manner equal to the characteristics of the biological sexes but suggest that femininity and masculinity refer to four distinct elements in the gender construction:

1 The percentage share of the two bio-sexes.
2 The gender aura or image of the activity (i.e. the ideas that people in the surroundings of the activity have about the work).
3 The values and ideas that dominate the activity (within the work area).
4 The form, in which the activity is conducted (e.g. is it private or public, exposed to competition or 'protected').

We could perhaps envisage each one of these elements as diverging from the others in terms of MaF. A study of an advertising agency showed the agency to be powerfully dominated by men (1) who constructed the work (3) in feminine terms (intuitive, emotional, relation-oriented, etc.) – i.e. in terms agreeing with what is regarded as feminine, according to gender research (Alvesson and Köping, 1993). In this case elements (1) and (3) thus pull in different 'MaF directions'. The construction of women becomes stronger and more clear-cut the greater the multiplicity of femininities in a particular woman-dominated activity. For example, if childcare in a specific country is carried out almost exclusively by women (1); if the activity is generally regarded as feminine (2); if the primary values of the staff are clearly care-oriented in character (3); and if the activity is conducted in what is regarded as the maternal bosom of the public sector (4) – then all this will underpin a general tendency in that society to construct women as distinct from men. Thus, indirectly, men are being constructed too. It is after all the relation between men and women that is interesting. Every statement or idea about women has implications for an understanding of men, and vice versa. The categories only make sense in relation to each other. The women working in the field learn first of all that they are constructed and/or to construct themselves as distinctively non-masculine; but even broader cultural gender constructions which project themselves on women in general are influenced by the character of this sector. Hence there is a tendency for large parts of the public sector, and for women more generally, to be defined in terms of one another: the public sector is feminine, and the public sector is seen as a natural abode for women's occupational work.[11]

Similarly, if export industry for instance is led exclusively by men (1); if the activity is perceived by the general public as extremely masculine (2); if leading values are characterized by hierarchy and a strong emphasis on results, etc. (3); if it is claimed that the survival of the fittest applies under 'murderous competition'(4) – then all this powerfully underpins the construction of men and masculinity as radically different from women and femininity. If we were to imagine that the proportion of the underrepresented sex increased in the respective sectors (i.e. there were more 'soft' men and 'tough' women), this in itself would produce only a slight modification of the gender construction. Or if the aura and/or the leading values in the fields were to be changed – e.g. away from motherly care and towards professional teaching in childcare, and away from large-scale conquest and towards small-scale, decentralized, knowledge-based, creative problem-solving business centred around 'cultural meetings' and 'relational work' in export industry – then a similar gender effect (that is, a modest de-femininization and de-masculinization respectively) could be envisaged, even though the bio-gender composition had not altered. It would be the same if the general conditions were to be changed. For example, if childcare were made competitive so that nurseries receiving poor parent ratings dropped out, or if trade barriers, monopolizing tendencies or a general boom reduced the intensive competition in export companies, then here, too, childcare would be somewhat de-feminized, export industry would not carry quite such a masculine connotation and the bio-gender associated with it would be constructed less definitively. Also rationalizations based upon cut-backs would make it hard to keep up service orientation and care standards and would eventually dissolve the feminine character of the area. It may be seen as more instrumental and 'industry-like', thus being less strongly constructed in feminine terms.

The public sector as masculine and/or feminine

The public sector in Scandinavia powerfully underpins a very clear gender construction, since the private and public sectors are so manifestly bio-gendered. Moreover, big sections of the public sector are especially dominated by bio-women and are also usually constructed as markedly feminine. Childcare, the care of the elderly, and to some extent schools and health care, become *over-determinative in feminine terms*, which creates a strong feminine identity in the sector and probably also in the bio-women who work there. Non-feminine elements (i.e. elements that are so regarded) such as a business and/or market orientation, entrepreneurship, competition, and so on, are all regarded as odd and negative and threatening to the sector's strong, consistent identity (cf. Sundin, 1997). Westerberg (1997) noted that she was given access to a study of the public sector because she was a *woman* economist, which illustrates the insistence on the 'female'.

Thus, on various counts, the public sector is of central importance to the construction of gender. In our own society this sector is itself gendered as feminine, weak and protected, compared with industry which is masculine, productive and muscular.[12] There seems to be an idea that it is natural for women to work in the public sector. Many people claim that this serves women's interests, not least because most of them do work there. 'For women the public sector is of crucial importance. They strongly depend on it because of the hundred of thousands of jobs it offers ... and also because of the care it provides' (Davies, 1996). Others see women's close connection with the public sector as a historical coincidence, and as regrettably conservative. Södersten (1996) says that Sweden is unique in that the increase in female employment has taken place exclusively in the public sector, and that many people have concluded from this that women can only be employed there. He sees this view as grossly sexist. Cuts in the public sector would open the way for new forms of female enterprise, with women finding secure jobs and receiving market-related wages, he says. Ahltorp and Franke (1991) oppose the view of the public sector as a protected workshop for women, and declare that the time is ripe for women to earn a living in the private market.

It is difficult to judge this. It is quite possible that the historically generated and well-ingrained construction of masculinity and femininity, of men and women, works to the disadvantage of women in identity terms in the context of competing on the private labour market. Moreover, discrimination tendencies in companies can make things difficult for women. Our interest here, however, concerns the way gender is constructed, not the consequences of the gendering in the shape of discrimination, disadvantages, etc. If a larger number of women joined private companies on a general basis, this would lead to a reconstruction of gender, the tendency to maintain the distinction between masculine and feminine would be reduced, and the classification of the human race into 'men' and 'women' would lose some of its significance in organizational and work contexts – all this, provided the change did not reinforce the gendered division of labour in private companies and sectors. This would be the case, for example, if all women were only hired in the lower echelons of the companies. If this were the case then the gender-reconstruction consequences would naturally be more limited, even though a redistribution of bio-women from the feminine public sector and into the masculine private sector might in itself have a certain effect on the construction of gender.

Researchers of a feminist bent who want to describe the change in the public sector sometimes refer to a tendency towards masculinization (e.g. Stivers, 1993). Prominent examples include various attempts at new types of economic control which involve privatization and market solutions (see e.g. Johansson, 1997; Westerberg, 1997). Writing about the American public administration, Stivers says that

> the images of expertise, leadership, and virtue that mark defences of administrative power contain dilemmas of gender. They not only have masculine features but help to keep in place or bestow political and economical privilege on the bearers of culturally masculine qualities at the expense of those who display culturally feminine ones.
>
> (Stivers, 1993: 4)

She points out, for example, that the idea of the public administrator as a professional expert, possessed of technical specialized knowledge, impartiality, objectiveness and an ability to act as an independent authority in various situations calling for the exercise of judgement, contrasts with social conceptions about women. Stivers also notes 'the suppressed femininity of important administrative canons like responsiveness, service and benevolence', and claims that the public administration in the USA 'as reflected in its images of leadership, expertise and virtue, is culturally masculine (although its masculinity is as yet unacknowledged), but that it also reflects a significant element of femininity (although consciousness of its femininity has yet to dawn)' (1993: 122). She introduces an idea about unacknowledged but none the less 'real' masculinities and femininities. That people do not recognize an instance of masculinity does not stop researchers from trying to prove that it is there. In fact the very lack of recognition may even motivate the critical scrutiny. Typical of Stivers's approach is that she does *not* refer to the ideas and meanings of the people working in the public administration about professionality, leadership, and so on, in relation to the work, or to the way in which they regard these things in terms of MaF. Instead she looks at ideas and practices in terms of her own views about masculinity and femininity. The possible differences between the researcher's constructions and those of the objects/subjects of study therefore never become addressed.

Like many others who deal with the subject of masculinity, Stivers sees masculinization, or its domination, as something negative, at least in large parts of the public sector. In view of the general predominance of masculine ideas and rationality in all its forms, it seems reasonable to suppose that these will also make themselves felt in feminine spheres, where they will often be met with some scepticism. The same seems to apply to operational or organizational modes which are generally regarded as masculine: the masculine aura surrounding privatization and entrepreneurship seems to support the negative reaction to these modes among women working in the public services (Sundin, 1997).

However, rather than starting from an assumption of the 'natural' female character of the caring services, as many of those working in the public sector and even some researchers do, it is possible to approach the question in a more open way. In research terms the idea is not to seek some sort of masculine or feminine 'essence' in a particular activity, but to study instead how the activity is socially constructed. Childcare, for example, has traditionally been extremely women-dominated, albeit perhaps more in the way it is constructed as feminine than in actual sex representation;[13] but we cannot assume that the same will apply in the future. The aim of much work on equality may be to 'de-feminize' childcare and to persuade men to take parental leave and to work in the childcare system, and also to work for the possibility of men to be given custody of children to an extent equal to that of women. It is possible to envisage a 'de-feminization' of childcare, which does not mean the same as masculinizing it, unless we are to accept a one-dimensional MaF classification, implying the less of F the more of M. Childcare as a public institution lends itself to a multiplicity of social constructions. It can be seen as a thoroughly 'pure' caring activity, in which tenderness and caring are the main ingredients; it can be regarded mainly as a pedagogical project whereby the child is exposed to a variety of interventions on the part of child experts with a view to promoting its development; or it can be seen mainly in terms of supervision and physical care, whereby the children's safety and physical needs are met. We imagine that the first variant would be perceived as highly feminine, the second as slightly less so, and the third as more gender-neutral. In this third case it is even possible to imagine that an emphasis on secure physical frames for children's play, and so on, would highlight creating order and setting rules, and that sort of technical playground expertise could mean that the childcare work is constructed here as 'masculine'. It is evident, however, that childcare is normally constructed as 'feminine', even though there is not necessarily any self-evident or natural reason why this should be so. The construction is thus culturally based. Among other things a pronounced feminine construction can give rise to problems for men working in the field: they may be suspected of shady intentions, or female staff and parents may regard them as being too masculine and insensitive to be able to take proper care of the young (Allan, 1993). A possible ideal for social science could perhaps be to constantly question the uncritical reproduction of these natural self-evident beliefs?

Like many other occupational groups, childcare workers have been professionalized as a work category. The question is whether or not this implies masculinization, either in that the practitioners construct themselves, or are constructed by others, in masculine terms or in that certain elements of masculinity operate unseen and are therefore only identifiable by smart researchers. The question is difficult to determine. Historically, research has shown that when hitherto taboo-laden feminine work areas were reconstructed as scientific (e.g. in the case of dairy work, see Davidoff, 1986; Sommestad, 1992) these areas became attractive to men. Also Bradley (1993: 16) has shown that men eventually took over female specialities like baking, brewing and spinning when new machines or technique provided the 'rationale for men to redefine an old female occupation as a man's occupation'.

It seems difficult to say anything definite about other aspects of a possible masculinization of (Scandinavian) public organizations, such as privatization and/or entrepreneurship, or the adoption of a market and economics-oriented terminology. Such moves may well meet resistance, and this does appear to be the dominating response in Sweden (see e.g. Johansson, 1997; Westerberg, 1997), but we can also envisage people in women-dominated sectors adopting the new forms of work and control. In what terms should we describe these responses to change: as masculine, as pro-feminine or should we leave these terms altogether? Any construction may be used dependent on local ideas. Once again there is no masculine or feminine essence: the military, for example, can be constructed in feminine terms as peacekeepers and conflict-resolvers.[14] Whereas aggressiveness and attack are generally ascribed a masculine meaning, defence can be seen as their opposite – which does not necessarily mean that it is feminine, at least not if defence is a resistance which involves fighting.

In some male sections of the public sector certain elements of the 'feminine' may be present, or rather some elements which are often understood as masculine may be absent – market competition for example, as in the military, the police and the central state administration. However, the general orientation of these activities, their image and leading values have traditionally favoured a masculine construction of their operations, which means that the effect is not the same as we have noted in the case of feminine activities; the general perception of the public sector as feminine as opposed to the masculine world of industry thus has little resonance here.

Without wanting to exaggerate the pressure of competition and the emphasis on performance and results as something that directly affects every unit and every employee in a private company, it can at least be said that public operations do tend to be less strongly imbued with these values. In many public organizations, such as human service organizations for example, results cannot provide the main benchmark simply because they are too difficult to measure.

Instead the emphasis is on avoiding conflict, making sure everything looks good and maximizing the flow of resources (Perrow, 1978). Those who like everything to be well-ordered and businesslike, and who see here what they regard as the inefficiency of the public sector, often start advocating privatization or the introduction of various market-like measures to provide some impetus. As regards gender construction, perhaps the somewhat weaker emphasis on results that tends to characterize public sector activities may make it possible for public service employees to arrange their work-time so it fits childcare arrangements better than those who work in industry can.[15] Thus, for example, a public sector employer is probably less likely to try to dissuade an employee from staying at home to look after a sick child or to take parental leave. We do not want to lump public sector employers into one group, however, and disregard the influence of different cultures and informal norms in different parts of the public sector. Holt's (1992) research on the work culture at a Danish police station and an intensive care department at a hospital showed that at the male-dominated workplace (the police station) child-caring problems remained private – family responsibilities were not regarded as an issue at the workplace – whereas at the intensive care department family responsibilities were much noted when future work schemes were planned.

In Denmark special regulations for leave have been introduced to enable more of the unemployed to enter the labour market on a temporary basis. The majority of those who took leave in connection with this arrangement were female public employees, mainly because it was more difficult or risky for (female) private employees to exploit the opportunity. In addition, the fact that private employees often earn more than those in the public sector certainly helps to preserve the gender patterns as regards parental and other types of leave.

Some concluding comments

In this chapter we have started from the assumption that gender is socially created. This is not unconventional; but we have taken this idea somewhat further than is common. Without denying that biological and psychological differences may have some importance, the historical and cultural variations in gender relations are so considerable that social institutions, ideas and practices can obviously be said to be 'producing' gender. Many gender researchers in the social sciences declare their support for the assumption that gender is socially constructed, but they do not always take the implications of this seriously. The static is often emphasized at the expense of the dynamic and processual: the ongoing construction and reconstruction of gender relations are not addressed. Further, men and women are typically defined in body terms, while social and cultural aspects associated with the meaning of gender receive less attention.

Rather than focusing on men and women defined as bodies, we have suggested in this chapter that the consideration of cultural forms of masculinity and femininity is a more fruitful approach. Concentration on body-counting can easily result in a misleading homogenization of 'men' and 'women', and the reproduction of a rather unfortunate idea – unfortunate, that is, in terms of equality – about the natural and essential nature of a distinction based on the body. Widespread perceptions of bio-gender as automatically accompanied by certain inclinations and orientations appear to be unfounded, and they risk adding further weight to the stereotypes. This is also the case when a subject with a particular biology is routinely ascribed a standard social construction of gender.

Instead of assuming that women's orientations and situations create the structure and activities of the public sector, it is claimed in this chapter that the public sector – at least in welfare societies such as the Scandinavian – creates gender, thus playing an important part in reproducing existing power relations. The problem of the hen and the egg is obviously relevant here. But, starting from the idea of gender as socially constructed, it seems reasonable to regard social institutions as a central factor in the creation of gender relations. We are certainly not denying that one may see the concentration of female labour to certain areas within the public sector as an outcome of socialization processes and the more or less 'free choice' of biological women. To only, or mainly, focus on this would deny the active gender construction powers of the public sector in Scandinavia. Naturally the chapter only offers a general idea of the gendering effect of the public organizations. A deeper understanding of these issues would call for more detailed studies of specific activities and gendering processes, with particular attention being paid to multiplicity and contradictions (Alvesson and Billing, 1997). The interrelatedness of discourses of public sector and women's work is not, of course, the only women-constituting power of significance. Still, amongst the 'agencies' accounting for how women become women, the discourse of the public sector as an employer of females is a central one, at least in Scandinavia.

What is the relation between the view of gender outlined here, on the one hand, and the politics of equality on the other? One way of achieving equality is to reduce or abolish the differences between bio-men and bio-women; that is to say, by minimizing or blurring social gender. This would yield what could be called the fifty-fifty solution. The aim would then be to achieve equal bio-gender distribution in government, parliament and managerial positions, in taking parental leave and in being granted disputed custody, in the military, in child-care and the care of the old, etc. This would presumably imply a gradual de-feminization of the female sectors and a de-masculinization of male spheres. In this connection the distillation of women's sectors in feminine terms and the rejection of de-feminizing processes would hardly do much good. Two examples of the tendency to de-masculinize are the military and the police, who, at least in some countries (e.g. Scandinavia), are no longer regarded solely as 'experts in violence' but also as 'peace-workers'. This may make it easier to recruit and assimilate more bio-women into these services, which could in turn promote further de-masculinization. However, as has been pointed out, there is no mechanical relationship between bio-gender and MaF. In the long run, categories such as masculinity and femininity would naturally become meaningless, and the men/women classification would lose a lot of its importance in most social contexts. Social differentiation and the division of labour would no longer revolve round gender relations. This idea is based on the supposition that the sexes are alike – or at least can be made alike with the help of policies favouring equality and the ongoing gender neutralizations of institutions.

Equality can perhaps also be achieved by trying to upgrade the undervalued sex and the undervalued areas. This is sometimes referred to as the attribution of equal value or equal worth. The point then is not to redefine what is culturally regarded as masculine and feminine, or the related male and female activities, with a view to achieving equal gender distribution. Rather, the idea is to try to counteract skewness in the values that attach to these definitions. This idea of value or worth, which stems from the historical and possible biological differences between the sexes, easily becomes rather vague. Sometimes a price ticket is attached to it, but socially defined value cannot be equated with the size of an individual's wages. It is often also extremely difficult to determine how something is valued; evaluations naturally often differ, so perhaps we should be asking ourselves the question equal value, for whom?

Goals – like the fifty-fifty and equal-value solutions – tend to become rather mechanical and vague. The first is too strongly focused on the body to capture the core of gender as a societal phenomenon. It is also static, indicating too determined a view of possible and/or desirable gender relations. Since gender is such a flexible, indeterminate phenomenon, our knowledge about it is always provisional and uncertain. In this chapter the suggested perspective is more in the nature of a process, which means that the final goals are less definite. The proposed perspective takes note of gendering and seeks to reduce the homogeneity which it implies, whereby the power implied by the regulative ideals of masculinities and femininities can also be weakened. Here we have discussed how the masculinization and feminization of activities are at the heart of the social construction of gender. In so far as we want to break the traditional gender patterns – which today probably involve not so much pure discrimination as the way in which together we culturally and continually create these patterns, including the conservation of gender identities – this will to a large extent be a question of de-feminizing the 'highly feminine' and of de-masculinizing the 'highly masculine'. Power operates in the shape of 'instructions' that bind men and women to certain ways of living their lives (identities) and regarding themselves in terms of the variants of the masculine and feminine that dominate in their particular cultural social fields. To launch cultural redefinition processes is a difficult undertaking, and one that is filled with conflict. The public sector is in essential respects a creator of women as a social gender. To alter this would accord with certain ambitions concerning equality, but would meet strong opposition from established gender identities and shortsighted interests associated with bio-gender, as currently created.

Notes

1 In Sweden 73 per cent of the employees in the public sector in 1996 were women (SOU, 1998: 6), and within traditional occupations like nurse, midwife etc. they comprise more than 90 per cent (SCB, 1998). In Denmark 70 per cent of the employees in the public sector in 1999 were women (Danmarks Statistik, 1999).

2 This idea has been pushed far by postmodernists (e.g. Fraser and Nicholson, 1988; Nicholson, 1990; Rosenau, 1992; Weedon, 1987). We find this orientation productive for the destabilization of notions of gender, but do not agree with its somewhat narrow focus on the text and its somewhat onesidedly negative view on the search for patterns and tendencies.

3 To detect this we can look at what they are focusing on, and what they are problematizing on, what is taken for given and what is then reproduced. Are the researchers

associating themselves with conventional common sense – which may appear neutral and objective but which often has a conservative effect – or have they succeeded in de-familiarizing their material; that is, regarding the existing state of affairs not as natural and self-evident but as remarkable, exotic and changeable (Alvesson and Deetz, 2000; Ehn and Löfgren, 1982)?

4 Wahl (1992) asked female MBAs and civil engineers whether they considered themselves, generally speaking, to be differently treated compared with their male colleagues. She got seven answers 'yes, to a great extent', 77 'yes to some extent' and 147 'no, not at all', which could mean that a great many of these women *do not* feel that they are noticeably defined as 'a woman' in the sense of being 'different from a man' by those around them.

5 This seems to apply – or at any rate to have applied – for example to many women managers at higher levels (Hennig and Jardim, 1977), as well as to women with a natural science education (Bengtsson, 1983).

6 For a further discussion of this point and ideas about how it can be handled in research, see Alvesson and Due Billing (1997).

7 Research results about gender and leadership vary. Some of the more journalistic or consultancy-based articles and reports emphasize differences, while the greater part of the extensive academic literature claims that there is little or no difference between men and women as leaders. Research overall indicates that the differences are minor, and that it is anyway impossible to say anything definite about a person's managerial behaviour on a basis of their biological sex (for a review, see Alvesson and Due Billing, 1997: chs 6–7). It should be added that due to changes regarding gender and gender relations, as well as organizational activity and leadership ideals, studies made at a certain point in time cannot necessarily tell us much about conditions several years later.

8 The concepts often overlap with the male and female. We make a distinction between masculinity/femininity and male/female, in that we regard the first pair as more abstract and detached from biological sex, while the second comes closer to what men and women actually do, what they work at, and so on.

9 See, for example, Brooks and MacDonald (2000) who show how different cultures are developed within nursing, where the night shift is associated with feminine and the day shift with masculine values (of managerialism).

10 For an overview of modern power theory, see e.g. Clegg (1989).

11 Obviously we can't lump the whole public sector in a country together. Here we are considering the heavily woman-dominated areas such as elementary school, health care, the care of children and the old, social work but not areas such as the military, the police and road maintenance. And of course even within the first-mentioned activities there are parts which are often regarded as masculine (e.g. surgery and maths teaching). Perhaps we should remind the reader that we are here – and throughout the chapter – primarily referring to Scandinavian conditions. Here the public sector – when thought about and referred to at the aggregate level – is broadly ascribed a feminine meaning. School, health care, child and elderly care are broadly seen as examples of the public sector.

12 On this point, as on so many others, we start from impressions of widely held ideas and attributions. Naturally the risk is considerable that we are victims of preconceptions, that we are generalizing on a basis of what we have heard and read in the media, etc. Naturally it is important to note variations, contradictions and changes in ideas and actions. Obviously one must avoid overgeneralization. This chapter addresses the public sector in Scandinavia at the end of the twentieth century, and says nothing about public sectors in other countries (where, sometimes, the creation of order and regulations dominates over grant-giving and service). (Cf. Walby, 1990.)

13 We cannot equate the proportion of female persons active in a field with a field's feminine character. An area can be dominated by women, without to any great extent being defined as feminine according to the above criteria (relation-oriented, intuitive, emotional, and so on). This applies, for instance, to cleaning and office jobs.

14 Recently there was a campaign for the Danish army, stating in the ad 'We don't want any Rambos'.

15 The possibility cannot be excluded that widely held views about the public sector compared with industry may be misleading. But, for the theme and theses of this chapter, how it 'really' is perhaps means less than the ideas people entertain about it.

References

Acker, J. (1992). Gendering organizational theory. In A. Mills and P. Tancred (eds), *Gendering Organizational Analysis*. London: Sage.

Ahltorp, B. and Franke, E. (1991). *Spelet i pyramiderna. Om kvinnor och män på jobbet*. Stockholm: Norstedts.

Allan, J. (1993). Male elementary teachers: experiences and perspectives. In C. Williams (ed.), *Doing 'Women's Work'. Men in Nontraditional Occupations*. Newbury Park, CA: Sage.

Alvesson, M. and Deetz, S. (2000). *Doing Critical Management Research*. London: Sage.

Alvesson, M. and Billing, Y. Due (1997). *Understanding Gender and Organization*. London: Sage.

Alvesson, M. and Köping, A.-S. (1993). *Med känslan som ledstjärna. En studie av reklamarbete och reklambyråer*. Lund: Studentlitteratur.

Bengtsson, M. (1983). Varför blir somliga kvinnor naturvetare och inte humanister? *Psykologi i tillämpning*. Lunds Universitet, 1(1).

Blomqvist, M. (1994). *Könshierarkier i gungning. Kvinnor i kunskapsföretag*. Studia Sociologica Upsaliensia 39. Uppsala: Acta Universitatis Upsaliensis.

Bradley, H. (1993). Across the great divide: the entry of men into women's jobs. In C. Williams (ed.), *Doing 'Women's Work'. Men in Nontraditional Occupations*. Newbury Park, CA: Sage.

Brooks, I. and MacDonald, S. (2000). Doing life: gender relations in a night nursing subculture. *Gender, Work and Organization*, 7(4): 221–229.

Calás, M. and Smircich, L. (1996). From the 'woman's' point of view. Feminist approaches to organization studies. In S. Clegg, C. Hardy and W. Nord (eds), *Handbook of Organization Studies*. London: Sage.

Chodorow, N. (1978). *Reproduction of Mothering*. Berkely, CA: University of California Press.

Clegg, S.R. (1989). *Frameworks of Power*. London: Sage.

Cockburn, C. (1991). *In the Way of Women*. London: Macmillan.

Connell, R.W. (1995). *Masculinities*. Oxford: Polity Press.

Davidoff, L. (1986). The role of gender in the 'first industrial nation': agriculture and England 1780–1850. In R. Crompton and M. Mann (eds), *Gender and Stratification*. Cambridge: Polity Press.

Davies, K. (1996). *Önskningar och realiteter*. Stockholm: Carlsson.

Deetz, S. (1992). Disciplinary power in the modern corporation. In M. Alvesson and H. Willmott (eds), *Critical Management Studies*. London: Sage.

Ehn, B. and Löfgren, O. (1982). *Kulturanalys*. Lund: Liber.

Ferguson, K. (1984). *The Feminist Case Against Bureaucracy*. Philadelphia, PA: Temple University Press.

Fondas, N. (1997). Feminization unveiled: management qualities in contemporary writings. *Academy of Management Review*, 22: 257–282.

Foucault, M. (1980). *Power/Knowledge*. New York, NY: Pantheon.

Foucault, M. (1982). The subject and power. *Critical Inquiry*, 8: 777–795.

Fraser, N. and Nicholson, L. (1988). Social criticism without philosophy: an encounter between feminism and postmodernism. *Theory, Culture and Society*, 5(2–3): 373–394.

Gherardi, S. (1995). *Gender, Symbolism and Organizational Cultures*. London: Sage.

Hallberg, M. (1992). *Kunskap och kön*. Göteborg: Daidalos.

Hartsock, N. (1987). The feminist standpoint: developing the ground for a specifically feminist historical materialism. In S. Harding (ed.), *Feminism and Methodology*. Milton Keynes: Open University Press.

Hennig, M. and Jardim, A. (1977). *The Managerial Woman*. New York, NY: Anchor Press.

Hines, R. (1992). Accounting: filling the negative space. *Accounting, Organization and Society*, 17(3–4): 314–341.

Holt, H. (1992). Arbejdspladskulturens indflydelse på familielivet. In S. Carlsen and J.E. Larsen (eds), *Den svære balance*. Copenhagen: Ligestillingsrådet.

Johansson, U. (1997). Den offentliga sektorns paradoxala maskuliniseringstendenser. In E. Sundin (ed.), *Om makt och kön i spåren av offentliga organisationers omvandling*. SOU, Vol. 83, Stockholm: Fritzes.

Kanter, R.M. (1977). *Men and Women of the Corporation*. New York, NY: Basic Books.

Kerfoot, D. and Knights, D. (1996). 'The best is yet to come?': the quest for embodiment in managerial work. In D. Collinson and J. Hearn (eds), *Men as Managers, Managers as Men*. London: Sage.

Marshall, J. (1993). Organizational communication from a feminist perspective. In S. Deetz (ed.), *Communication Yearbook*, Vol. 16. Newbury Park, CA: Sage.

Nicholson, L. (ed.) (1990). *Feminism/Postmodernism*. New York, NY: Routledge.

Perrow, C. (1978). Demystifying organizations. In R. Sarri and Y. Heskenfeld (eds), *The Management of Human Services*. New York, NY: Columbia University Press.

Reskin, B. and Padavic, I. (1994). *Women and Men at Work*. Thousand Oaks, CA: Pine Forge Press.

Rosenau, P.M. (1992). *Post-Modernism and the Social Sciences. Insights, Inroads, and Intrusions*. Princeton, NJ: Princeton University Press.

SCB Statistics Sweden (1998). *Women and Men in Sweden. Facts and Figures 1998*. Stockholm: Statistics Sweden.

Södersten, B. (1996). Nedskärningar bra för kvinnor. *Dagens Nyheter*, 13(7).

Sommestad, L. (1992). Från mejerska till mejerist. En studie av mejeriyrkets maskuliniserings process. Lund, Sweden. Arkiv.

SOU (1998). Vol. 6. Stockholm: Fritzes.

Stivers, C. (1993). *Gender Images in Public Administration*. Newbury Park, CA: Sage.

Sundin, E. (1997). Den offentliga sektorns omvandling och kvinnors och mäns företagande inom typiskt kvinnliga sektorer. In E. Sundin (ed.), *Om makt och kön i spåren av offentliga organisationers omvandling*. SOU, Vol. 83, Stockholm: Fritzes.

Wahl, A. (1992). *Kvinnliga civilekonomers och civilingenjörers karriärutveckling*. Stockholm: EFI.

Walby, S. (1990). *Theorizing Patriarchy*. Oxford: Basil Blackwell.

Weedon, C. (1987). *Feminist Practice & Poststructuralist Theory*. Oxford: Basil Blackwell.

Westerberg, L. (1997). Dubbla rationaliteter – en diskussion kring två studier av barnstugor med resultatansvar. In E. Sundin (ed.), *Om makt och kön i spåren av offentliga organisationers omvandling*. SOU, Vol. 83, Stockholm: Fritzes.

6 'Managing' diversity

Identity and power in organizations

Erica Gabrielle Foldy

[A]lthough modern organizations produce engine parts, meals, telecommunication services ... or whatever, they also contribute to the production of people, identified in particular ways.

(Jenkins, 1996)

Diversity ... [is] a site where the 'partial fixation' of political identity takes place.

(Cavanaugh, 1997)

Introduction

As identity in organizations becomes an increasingly common topic (e.g. Dutton *et al.*, 1994; Pratt and Rafaeli, 1997; Whetten and Godfrey, 1998), one salient point is often overlooked: identity is a contested site. 'Identity is something *over* which struggles take place and *with* which stratagems are advanced' (Jenkins, 1996: 25). Identities shape interests, loyalties, passions; they are a prized resource (Gamson, 1991; Hunt *et al.*, 1994).

Work organizations are a central arena for this contest, with practitioners and scholars alike recognizing the significance of identity. Recently, *Fortune* magazine trumpeted the importance of identity to organizations. Its article on 'The 100 best companies to work for in America' (Branch, 1999: 120) enthusiastically declared that these companies are 'not only offering a job and some knockout benefits; they're also selling an identity'. Researchers have demonstrated that employees' identities can affect their motivation, job satisfaction, performance, propensity to leave, and commitment to their employer (Ashforth and Mael, 1989; Dutton *et al.*, 1994; Mael and Ashforth, 1992; Whetten and Godfrey, 1998). A number of studies document how management, unions and other groupings attempt, implicitly and explicitly, to shape those identities (Covaleski *et al.*, 1998; Ezzamel and Willmott, 1998; Kondo, 1990; Kurtz, forthcoming; Leidner, 1993).

If identity is contested, it stands as a site where powerful forces clash. A basic assumption of this chapter is that power is inherent and central to identity: 'Social identities exist and are acquired, claimed and allocated within power relations' (Jenkins, 1996: 44). How one identifies – and with whom one identifies – has enormous consequences for how compliant or resistant one is to existing organizational arrangements (Clegg, 1994; Knights and Willmott, 1985, 1989). A strong organizational identification will bind an employee more closely to the organization (Dutton *et al.*, 1994; Whetten and Godfrey, 1998). A strong sub-group identification with a union, a department or a profession, may challenge that connection (Ezzamel and Willmott, 1998; Kurtz, forthcoming). Organizations and their leaders care about how employees identify because the salience and meaning of those identities can have an enormous influence on an employee's connection to the organization.

While this chapter assumes that power and identity are profoundly inter-twined in all organizations, it also recognizes that this interconnection operates differently depending on organizational context. For example, identity has become increasingly visible – and complicated – in many companies as diversity programmes have multiplied. (According to one estimate, in 1995, 70 per cent of *Fortune* 50 companies had some kind of diversity programme in place (Kelly and Dobbin, 1998). Smaller companies are following suit.) Implicit in diversity programmes is the company's recognition (however superficial) that their employees are not a homogeneous mass, united in their membership as company employees. Rather, their extra-organizational identities, such as gender or race, matter. But attention to these extra-organizational identities brings organizations into a whole new arena. Companies have long tried to influence their employees' identification with the organization. Addressing their gender or racial identifications is another matter. The very fact that an organization is deliberately trying to deal with diversity issues therefore shapes the relationship between power and identity in that workplace.

This chapter explores in more depth how power dynamics influence identity in the context of diversity programmes. I choose this context for three reasons. First, identity and diversity are fundamentally interwoven. An influential review of the organizational literature on diversity concludes, '[T]he concept of identity appears to be at the core of understanding diversity in organizations' (Nkomo and Cox, 1996: 339). Gender is one dimension of identity commonly addressed by diversity programmes; race is another. Other identities, such as sexual orientation, are increasingly being considered. Second, diversity programmes are widespread, but little studied and under-theorized (Comer and Soliman, 1996; Nkomo and Cox, 1996; Prasad and Mills, 1997). Finally, diversity programmes are clearly relevant to organizational culture. They have their most immediate impact on observable manifestations of the culture, including representation of different demographic groups and organizational policies. But to really change an organization, the programmes must reach to the less visible and more embedded aspects of culture: values and underlying assumptions (Schein, 1985). Few programmes reach this depth (Thomas and Ely, 1996).

'Managing diversity' is the most common label for diversity-related work in today's organizations (Litvin, 2000; Nkomo, 1997). *Webster's New World Dictionary* (1974: 859) defines 'manage' as 'to control the movement or behavior of ... manipulate; to have charge of'. If we understand identity as a valued, contested resource and we understand diversity initiatives as one site in which identity is shaped, then 'managing diversity' takes on a whole new meaning: a way of controlling the widespread, enormously varied, potentially revolutionary effects of multiple identities in the workplace; having charge of that multiplicity's enactment and influence. This chapter will add a power dimension to discussions of diversity and identity in organizations, a perspective largely lacking in the organizational studies literature on these issues, which tends towards an 'upbeat naiveté' (Prasad and Mills, 1997: 5). These authors continue:

> any framing of the notion of diversity needs to take into account the demographic characteristics of those in positions of power (white males), the often silenced voices of the Other (i.e. women, people of color, the aged, etc.) and the multitude of political interactions between dominant and non-dominant groups within organizations.
>
> (Prasad and Mills, 1997: 23)

Nkomo and Cox (1996: 349) also call for diversity researchers to attend to 'what sustains and maintains the pattern of power relations in organizations'. By theorizing at the intersection of diversity, identity and power, I hope to add to an understanding of all three concepts and their interrelationship.

But 'power' itself is a contested site; theorists from different fields and ideological persuasions understand it very differently. Hardy and Leiba-O'Sullivan (1998) propose a useful framework for theories of power, building off Lukes (1974), which I summarize very briefly here. The 'mainstream' approach, most common in management literature, focuses on who wins and who loses: whether A or B is more able to influence the other's behaviour. Power dynamics are present only in the context of observable conflict. Little attention is given to long-term structural power imbalances. The 'critical' perspective starts with these structural imbalances, asserting that they give dominant groups like management a great latitude of control over subordinate groups like workers. It analyses how hegemonic influences exact compliance, while still leaving room, outside of power's effects, for worker resistance. A Foucauldian approach, sometimes placed under the critical umbrella, asserts that power arises at innumerable points, not simply or even largely from dominant groups. Analyses of power must look at its capillary effects, its pervasive and ubiquitous presence, while recognizing that no place beyond the reach of power exists.

These different views of power have different consequences for how power and identity are intertwined. After describing each view in more depth I elaborate these implications, creating a framework for understanding the relationship between power and identity. I then apply this framework to a particular phenomenon: diversity programmes in organizations. I will demonstrate how each approach illuminates different facets of how power is inscribed and enacted through these initiatives. In summary, this chapter uses all three perspectives to present a theoretical model for understanding the intersection of power and identity issues in today's companies, focusing on the particular impact of diversity programmes.

Theorizing power

In this section, I briefly review three broad perspectives on power, building on the framework from Hardy and Leiba-O'Sullivan (1998). I will summarize and compare three analytically distinct approaches or lenses to theorizing power: mainstream, critical and Foucauldian.

The 'mainstream' view of power in organization studies is similar to the pluralist perspective found in political science and sociology. It defines power as some version of the following: the ability of A to get B to do something which otherwise B would not do (e.g. Dahl, 1957; Pfeffer and Salancik, 1978). This approach limits power's influence to a fairly bounded sphere: instances with observable conflict occurring within a decision-making process (Lukes, 1974). Inherent in this perspective is the assumption of a 'fair fight' among competing groups (Hardy and Clegg, 1996: 628). Ingrained resource imbalances or hierarchical authority play little role in these models. No single player dominates.

The mainstream view usefully draws attention to the concrete outcomes of contained, observable political battles: who wins and who loses reveals an enormous amount about relative power within a particular arena. It also attends to multiple actors and their multiple bases of power.

However, this view has drawn much criticism from those working within the 'critical' perspective, most often on two grounds. First, the mainstream approach tends to focus on explicit decision-making and observable conflict, implying that the lack of opposition equals consent. Second, many charge that this approach ignores historically and societally embedded power imbalances, taking a rather sanguine view of social conflict.

Lukes (1974) is perhaps the most influential voice regarding the first charge. The mainstream approach, he says, focuses on observable behaviour, decision-making, conflict and grievances. But, Lukes observes, what about those situations in which no group comes forward with an alternative agenda, when no overt or covert conflict exists? 'To put the matter sharply, A may exercise power over B by getting him to do what he does not want to do, but he also exercises power over him by influencing, shaping or determining his very wants' (Lukes, 1974: 23).

Lukes's work, and that of other critical theorists, is influenced broadly by Marxist theory and more particularly by Gramsci's theory of hegemony. According to Stuart Hall's (1996a) interpretation of Gramsci, a dominant group has hegemony when its interests co-ordinate with the interests of other groups and with the life of the state as a whole. It encompasses the notion that powerful interests can shape the way people think. In fact, hegemony infiltrates into every corner of political, economic, social, cultural and individual life. Gramsci goes on to suggest a mechanism for how consent and compliance are created: common sense or the 'practical consciousness of the masses of the people' (Hall, 1996a: 431). 'In order to consolidate their hegemony, ruling groups must elaborate and maintain a popular system of ideas and practices ... which he [Gramsci] called common sense' (Omi and Winant, 1994: 67). So, common sense is profoundly shaped, if not created, by ruling groups.

Embedded in the notion of hegemony is the second critique of the mainstream lens. Critical theorists reject the reassuring possibility that all kinds of groups and interests have roughly equivalent access to the decision-making machinery. The mainstream tradition 'misrepresents the balance of power. It attributes far too much power to subordinate groups' (Hardy and Clegg, 1996: 629). Critical theorists argue that management interests are likely to dominate in an organization, given their structural position in the power hierarchy. Critical theorists would further agree that the mainstream approach 'paints an ideologically conservative picture that implicitly advocates the status quo and hides the processes whereby organizational elites maintain their dominance' (Hardy and Clegg, 1996: 629).

But this dominance is incomplete. While debate rages among critical theorists about the possibility and extent of resistance (Braverman, 1974; Edwards, 1979; Goldman, 1983; Jermier *et al.*, 1994), it is generally agreed that some openings exist. For the most part, though, resistance is rarely successful; at best, it brings about ameliorative, as opposed to transformative, change.

For proponents of the critical lens, power manifests itself by shaping the desires and aspirations of a relatively compliant public. In fact, Gramsci, Lukes and others believe that power can actually distort perceptions so thoroughly that individuals cannot see their 'true' interests. This faith in objectivity, in an ability to break through a false consciousness, has been criticized by post-structuralist theorists. In her critique of Lukes, Fletcher (1992: 32) says, 'it is not possible to determine the "real interests" of any group – dominants or subordinates – without specifying the particular ideology framing the argument'. Our analyses of power are themselves infused with embedded assumptions which give us only a partial stance from which to critique. But how can we critique if we ourselves are implicated?

The third main approach to power, the Foucauldian lens, seems to offer a way out of this potential paralysis. The point is not to privilege one point of view over another, or identify objective reality, but to investigate these different power-inflected voices and their implications for how we live, think, feel and identify. Similarly to Gramsci and Lukes, Foucault theorizes power as pervasive and, often, unseen. In fact, for Foucault, 'power is everywhere' (Foucault, 1993: 518) and 'power is exercised from innumerable points' (ibid.: 519). He believes that power and knowledge mutually constitute each other. 'We are subjected to the production of truth through power and we cannot exercise power except through the production of truth' (Foucault, 1980: 93). It follows naturally that, for Foucault, power is implicated in how we make sense of the world and ourselves.

But while our sense-making may be fundamentally prescribed by structures of language, knowledge and power, there is no 'reality' hidden within. Any way of thinking, any ideology, can be mined for its distortions, assumptions, and implications. And all of us are influenced by many different, varied, and contradictory ways of thinking, some of which can bind us more firmly to the system while others undermine our attachment to it. For Foucault, the mechanism of 'common sense' is itself too hegemonic, too monolithic. His concept of discourses provides a mechanism for how power inscribes ways of thinking and acting on individuals, while allowing for multiplicity and variation. According to Weedon,

> discourses, in Foucault's work, are ways of constituting knowledge ... Discourses are more than ways of thinking and producing meaning. They constitute the 'nature' of the body, unconscious and conscious mind and emotional life of the subjects which they seek to govern.
>
> (Weedon, 1987: 108)

We are all subject to multiple discourses; discourses influence our every thought, every action.

Theorists and researchers influenced by Foucault also understand resistance somewhat differently than critical theorists. There is no separate space for 'resistance', for action that is somehow unoccupied and untainted by hegemonic forces. Many behaviours have multiple and contradictory consequences; resistance and compliance are often simultaneous. 'Resistance and consent are rarely polarized extremes on a continuum of possible worker discursive practices ... Resistance frequently contains elements of consent and consent often incorporates aspects of resistance' (Collinson, 1994: 29).

Foucault can be distinguished from the critical theorists in several important ways. (It is important to note, however, that many see the 'critical' label as broadly including Foucauldian approaches and would argue there is no bright line between them.) Most simply, critical theorists see external, dominant forces, acting from on high, inexorably shaping our consciousness, including our sense of self, and blinding us to our true interests. But for Foucault, power is not an external force acting on a being otherwise untouched by power. We are constituted through power; discourses are the substance from which we are constructed. By the same token, power doesn't come from on high; it is not only the property of certain dominant people or institutions. Everyone has power; power is everywhere. Their origins obscure and varied, discourses are ubiquitous. Theorizing power as a top-down pressure or force misses the multiple sources and enactments of power. Finally, since we are never outside power, never free of its discourses, we are never in a position to determine the state of nature outside power – and, therefore, never able to determine anyone's 'true' interests.

These, then, are three relatively distinct theoretical approaches to power: mainstream, critical and Foucauldian. Each has very different implications for understanding the relationship between power and identity. I explore these implications in the next section, constructing a framework which can then be applied to the impact of diversity programmes in the workplace.

Theorizing identity and power

Recent theorists in psychology, social psychology, sociology and cultural studies have challenged the notion, basic to modernist thought, of identity as a solid, coherent sense of self (Collinson, 1994; Hall, 1996a, 1996b; Jenkins, 1996; Kilduff *et al.*, 1997; Kondo, 1990; Nkomo and Cox, 1996; Schlenker, 1985).

Not surprisingly, for such an abstract and ambiguous concept, many definitions of identity exist, illuminating different facets. Schlenker provides a useful starting point:

> Identity can be regarded as a theory of self that is formed and maintained through actual or imagined interpersonal agreement about what the self is like. Analogous to a scientific theory, its contents must withstand the process of consensual agreement by informed, significant observers.
>
> (Schlenker, 1985: 67)

Identity must be continually reconstituted. 'Human beings are engaged in a process of constructing, sustaining, and restoring a sense of self-identity as a continuous reality in the face of circumstances ... that either confirm or pose a challenge to its narrative' (Ezzamel and Willmott, 1998: 364).

Nkomo and Cox (1996), in their overview of the diversity literature in organizational studies, suggest that identity is at the core of understanding diversity and propose an approach to theorizing identity that I rely on in this chapter. First, they argue, that since individuals have multiple identities, no single identity can be isolated or understood autonomously. Different identities interact in varied ways in various different contexts; those interactions say as much or more about identity than the 'pure' effects of only one identity.

Second, Nkomo and Cox continue, different kinds of identities have very different organizational and social consequences. Identities based on embedded social divisions like race or class will affect dynamics very differently from identities based on more contingent organizational groupings like work group or even profession. Equating these two very different kinds of identity ignores the role of systemic and institutionalized differential treatment based on race, gender and class. So, as a third point, specific identities must be understood in their cultural and historical context: the effects of race, for example, are different than the effects of class. Fourth, researchers must also be careful to avoid essentializing particular identities, assuming that a particular identity affects all those with that identity in the same way. The identity of 'woman' means very different things to different people.

Jenkins makes little distinction between identity and social identity. 'All human identities are in some sense – and usually a stronger rather than a weaker sense – *social identities*' (1996: 4). However, he goes on to define social identity as 'the systematic establishment and signification, between individuals, between collectivities, and between individuals and collectivities, of relationships of similarity and difference' (ibid.). Certain such identities, like gender and ethnicity, tend to be primary; but any number of identifications with various groupings are possible. Because organizations classify, categorize and distribute individuals and groups – as workers or managers, accountants or mechanics, occupants of cubicles or corner offices – they play a particularly important role in the social identification process.

Jenkins (1996) adds another point useful for our discussion: the internal–external dialectic of identification. He notes that how we self-identify is only part of the equation. How others identify and categorize us is at least as important, if not more important. 'It is not enough to assert an identity. That identity must also be validated (or not) by those with whom we have dealings' (Jenkins, 1996: 21). Ignoring the role that outsiders can play in shaping an individual's identity ignores the centrality of power in identity processes.

Identity and the three approaches to power

In this section, I construct a framework which suggests how each power lens views issues related to identity. However, the lines between the different frameworks are much less clear as we look at how each deals with identity. While there are broad differences, many theorists in each camp reside at the borders between the approaches.

For most mainstream theorists, identity simply isn't part of the picture. Focused as they are on decision-making and formal conflict, they tend to ignore less tangible factors or the dynamics that may be involved. However, one significant theoretical stream operating from the mainstream perspective has begun to address the question of identity. Resource mobilization theorists, seeking to understand collective action and social movements, focus on the resources – tangible and intangible – that parties are able to mobilize on behalf of their cause. Power is conceptualized as the amount of available resources, the ability to achieve goals, and access to the decision-making process.

For many years, the relationship between power and identity was ignored by resource mobilization scholars. More recently, however, collective identity is seen as both a requirement for collective action and an end in itself (Gamson, 1995; Gamson, 1992). Taylor and Whittier (1992: 105) define collective identity as 'the shared definition of a group that derives from members' common interests, experiences and solidarity'. According to Gamson, 'the construction of a collective identity is a negotiated process in which the "we" involved in collective action is elaborated and given meaning' (Gamson, 1991: 40).

Given the mainstream focus on the ability to dominate decision-making, what is the importance of collective identity? Collective identity is necessary for collective action (Gamson, 1995; Gamson, 1991; Kurtz, forthcoming). Collective actors, such as social movements or organizations, need some kind of shared identity as the basis for working together, identifying common interests, developing a shared strategy, and ultimately winning the battle. Further, as individuals and groups work together, they are continually re-enacting and reconstructing this shared identity. A broad collective identity is both a basis and an outcome of group action.

This, then, is the primary way in which the mainstream approach to power addresses questions of identity: the role of collective identity in collective action and social movements. The role of individual identity and its relationship to collective identity have not been well elaborated.

Critical theorists on power have addressed identity to a greater extent. In

Table 6.1 Power and identity

Power lens	Relationship between power and identity
Mainstream	Focuses on winners and losers of defined, observable conflict and therefore largely ignores identity. One sub-stream, resource mobilization theory, recognizes the importance of collective identity, the shared sense of a group based on its members' common interests and beliefs. Collective identity is both a basis for and an outcome of collective action.
Critical	Powerful forces can profoundly shape identity. Hegemonic influences affect the basic ways in which we make sense of the world and ourselves. Other entities, including social movements and organizations, also affect our identity through both deliberate and unconscious identity practices. Though identity is contested among varying forces, dominant influences are more powerful and likely to win.
Foucauldian	Rather than individuals being acted upon by power, manipulated by external forces, they are constructed through power relations. There is no pure, elemental essence that is corrupted by power. Power and identity constitute each other: particular, historical power relations create particular identities which then serve to maintain those power relations.

their picture, power relations have a profound effect on our 'common sense'. They shape our understanding of how the world works and where we fit in. Since power dynamics have such a profound effect on our sense-making, certainly they also dramatically influence our sense of who we are, our identity. Raymond Williams writes that hegemony is a 'saturation of the whole process of living – not only of political and economic activity ... but of the whole substance of lived identities and relationships' (1977: 110). That is, ruling groups have the power to reach all the way into our basic understanding of who we are and use that as a form of control. The critical view then goes beyond this assertion to argue that, given its importance, identity is contested. Individuals as well as broader interests and groupings see it as a valuable commodity. They battle for the ability to shape identity; to claim a foothold.

One researcher, writing about social movements and collective identity, has introduced a useful concept for thinking about identity battles more broadly. 'Collective identity... is not innate, essential, permanent, fixed. Rather it is a social construction. As a social construction, it is a matter in which movements can intervene' (Kurtz, forthcoming: 12). Kurtz goes on to theorize that there are tools movements can use that she calls 'identity practices'. Identity practices are 'a range of social practices by movements which can have significant collective identity implications' (Kurtz, forthcoming: 174). For social movement groups, these practices include things like what demands are made, what outside support is cultivated, and how the culture is formed. Kurtz notes that employers and other authorities use their own identity practices. Some practices are deliberate attempts to shape organizational identification, like orientations for new employees, training and team-building retreats, and large employee events filled with motivational speakers, games, awards and other ceremonial rituals. However, many other organizational policies and characteristics could be considered implicit identity practices. For example, an organization with an all-white, all-male leadership team is telegraphing what identities are valued in that environment.

So, for critical theorists, powerful forces can profoundly shape identity. Hegemonic influences affect the very basic ways in which we make sense of the world and ourselves. Other entities are not silent. Social movements and movement organizations, for example, also affect our sense of self through both deliberate and unconscious practices. But though identity is a battleground, dominant influences are seen as much more powerful and more likely to win.

The Foucauldian image of power focuses less on dominance and subordination. Rather than individuals being acted upon by power, manipulated by external forces, Foucault understands individuals as being constructed through power relations. There is no individual space outside the reach of power; there is no pure, elemental essence that is then corrupted by power. In this view, power and identity constitute each other: particular, historical power relations create particular identities which then serve to maintain those power relations. The process of identity formation is 'a medium as well as an outcome of the ... relations of power' (Knights and Willmott, 1985: 41).

Because individuals are constructed from cross-cutting discourses, identities are fragmented and inconsistent. Individuals' identities will be both compliant and resistant. Any one identity – a racial or gender identity, for example, can itself be internally contradictory, including elements of consent and opposition. Because of this, the process of identity formation is by no means monolithic or determined.[1]

> Almost invariably, the sense of subjectivity is internally contradictory: positive, enabling features of power relations may also be experienced as negating or constraining. In which case, the exercise of power may meet resistance despite the fact that subjects are practically tied to its confirmation by their identity.
>
> (Knights and Willmott, 1989: 537)

The yoke of power relations is enormously influential, but not deterministic. As Weeks (1993: 636) puts it: '[Identities] are self-creations, but they are creations on grounds not freely chosen but laid out by history.'

Foucault was less interested in developing theoretical models than in exploring 'how power seeps into the very grain of individuals' in concrete, exhaustive detail (Foucault, 1979: 28). From this work we can glean two primary mechanisms in which power affects identity: disciplinary power and pastoral power (Covaleski *et al.*, 1998; Marsden, 1997). The power of disciplines comes from their ability to formalize, standardize and regulate human activity. Developed originally in monasteries, disciplinary practices are found in most, if not all, organizations – armies, hospitals, bureaucracies, etc. Such practices define standards and measurements for behaviour, create hierarchies based on competence, and develop tools to exact compliance with the norm. While both disciplinary power and pastoral power bind internal, individual desires together with external forces, pastoral power focuses more on what Foucault called 'technologies of the self'. These 'require that the inner truths of one's self be both discovered through self-examination and expressed outwardly through speech so as to affirm and transform oneself' (Covaleski *et al.*, 1998: 297). An archetypal expression of pastoral power is the act of confession in religious settings. Through the workings of technologies of the self and of regulatory disciplines, identity and power are co-created and mutually reinforcing.

In summary, I suggest that each approach understands the relationship between power and identity in a different way. The mainstream perspective largely ignores identity, though social movement theorists are exploring the notion of collective identity as a requirement for and outcome of collective action. For critical theorists, identity is included in the hegemonic reach of dominant forces. Foucault theorizes identity and power as constructed through each other. Each of these lenses would then view the influence of diversity programmes in organizations very differently. In the next section, I briefly discuss the phenomenon of diversity programmes. I then apply this framework to elaborate how each lens illuminates different facets of identity and power relations found in efforts to manage diversity.

Power, identity and diversity programmes

Diversity programmes are becoming an accepted practice in workplaces across the United States, but approaches range widely (Cox, 1994; Fine, 1995; Jackson,

Table 6.2 Power, identity and diversity programmes

Diversity practice	Mainstream lens	Critical lens	Foucauldian lens
Overall diversity initiative	Diversity programmes have potential to level playing field for marginalized groups.	Diversity programmes are window dressing which will never address structurally embedded power differences.	By opening up the terrain of identity, a key site for the reproduction of power relations, diversity programmes invite the possibility of change and resistance. However, change will inevitably be incremental; transformational change is almost impossible.
Diversity training	Training can help members of marginalized groups succeed by adapting better to the organizational culture. It can also help members of dominant groups identify their prejudices and stereotypes.	Such training is likely to see the individual, rather than organizational structure and policy, as the locus of change. Therefore, it won't challenge dynamics of privilege and subordination. Training is often a substitute for real organizational change.	Training contains both disciplinary and pastoral mechanisms for inscribing power on individuals. Training disseminates and inculcates guidelines for 'correct' behaviour regarding marginalized groups; it also encourages participants to identify and reveal their own contributions to discrimination.
Affinity groups	These groupings allow marginalized groups greater access to resources and decision-making by creating a collective voice. They also help members acculturate and succeed through larger networks, help with learning the ropes, and give greater access to mentors.	These groups have no choice but to follow a management agenda; if they don't they will be dismantled. Simply by providing a space for oppressed groups to meet together, they can provide openings for resistance, but any substantial change efforts are doomed.	These groups are sites of both compliance and resistance. They do offer a semi-autonomous space to identify commonalities based on particular identities; however these commonalities may then be harnessed to the goals of the organization.
Mentoring programmes	Mentoring is an excellent way to help disadvantaged employees gain access to valuable resources like connections to senior management and sage career advice.	Mentoring is a way for protégés to learn how to work the system. Whatever radical potential protégés from marginalized groups might have had is replaced by a desire to assimilate and succeed.	Mentoring is a vehicle for pastoral power. Mentors and protégés use the intimacy of personal relationships to align the protégé's identity with the goals of the organization.

1992; Thomas and Ely, 1996; Thomas, 1999; Walker and Hanson, 1992). Initiatives can include a number of different components, including diversity training, identity-based affinity or support groups, mentoring programmes, changes in performance appraisal and compensation, and changes in human resource policies (Kossek and Lobel, 1996). I now apply the three-lens framework on power and identity to diversity programmes as a whole and to certain practices in particular.

Diversity initiatives

From a mainstream perspective, organizations are made up of a variety of different groupings – based on department, profession, rank, etc. – all jockeying for position. While in the short run certain groups will have the advantage, in the long run no particular set of individuals will dominate. Most mainstream power theorists pay little attention to groups based on demographic identities; they simply don't factor in. But some might acknowledge that certain groups – e.g. people of colour – face greater short-term barriers than other groups, and these disadvantages should be addressed. Diversity programmes have the potential to level the playing field for groups traditionally under-represented at mid- and upper-echelons in organizations. They can do so by transferring resources to members of marginalized groups, by helping them play the game better and be more successful, by enabling their access to decision-making processes, and by identifying biases and prejudices on the part of individual managers.

Critical theorists would have a much more jaundiced view of such initiatives. Hardy and Leiba-O'Sullivan's critical perspective on empowerment programmes is quite relevant here:

[E]mpowerment can be viewed as an exercise in the management of meaning to enhance the legitimacy of organizational goals and to influence behavior unobtrusively. By managing meaning and using power to create the perception that organizational and employee interests converge ... empowerment programs reduce the necessity of having to use more visible or coercive forms of power to ensure organizational goals are met and to quell resistance.

(Hardy and Leiba-O'Sullivan, 1998: 466)

Similarly, diversity programmes can increase the organizational commitment of members of marginalized groups, without actually making any organizational changes. If anything, diversity programmes might be considered even more insidious because they attempt to harness the very identities that could, from the critical perspective, be the basis for resistance, and recast them as the basis for compliance.

Unlike affirmative action, these theorists would argue, which at least acknowledged that current businesses have a social debt to particular groups, managing diversity initiatives are justified by reference to organizational productivity and profit. Haunted by the spectre of unions, diversity programmes almost never address class issues or structurally embedded power differences. Many diversity programmes will soft-pedal the entire notion of diversity, defining it as including any kind of difference, rather than highlighting group identities like race and gender. If race and gender do provide a focus, the theme will be integrating them into the current culture, rather than exploring structural changes. Further, such programmes will be construed as 'helping' the disadvantaged, rather than recognizing how dominant groups have a stake in acknowledging their own privilege. At best, they help women and people of colour adapt better to current organizational practices. At worst, they simply provide cover for management against charges of discrimination.

For those using a Foucauldian lens, all organizational practices are caught in a web of power relations that reproduce the status quo and prevent significant change. Similarly, diversity initiatives are created out of a particular set of organizational discourses, norms, characteristics and exigencies; those leading the initiative have little choice but to enact it in such a way that it reinforces the organization's operating procedures. Diversity programmes are particularly important because they directly address identity, and identity is a key site for the reproduction of power relations. However, reproduction is never complete or perfect; interstices are created. By opening up the terrain of identity, diversity programmes invite the possibility of creative change and resistance. Still, such change will almost inevitably be incremental and localized; transformational change is almost impossible.

Following from this overall argument, these theorists would attend to how particular discourses contribute to the maintenance of business as usual. For example, one scholar suggests that the 'business case' for diversity – the mantra that leveraging differences is good for the bottom line – 'serves as a powerful weapon in the hands of the defenders of the status quo' (Litvin, 1999: 21). By using profit-making as the justification for such programmes, businesses can ignore other imperatives, like the pursuit of fairness, and ignore persistent problems of discrimination and dominance. The particular discourse of the business case is one mechanism through which diversity programmes simply reproduce existing power relations.

Diversity training

Diversity training is the most common element of diversity initiatives. Such training can range from two-hour introductory workshops to intensive, experiential week-long retreats. In addition, the content and approach of such training varies widely (Fine, 1995; Kossek and Lobel, 1996; Nemetz and Christensen, 1996). Some introductory sessions provide information about changing labour and consumer markets and how attention to diversity issues will enhance the company's bottom-line. Many programmes tend to focus on interpersonal issues: they encourage participants to identify their own stereotypes and prejudices and learn more about other groups' cultural patterns. Such approaches see the individual as the locus of change. Some training, though it's much more rare, addresses societal-level dynamics like institutional racism and systemic sexism. I suggest that the reactions from the different camps of power theorists will depend on what kind of training is being offered.

For mainstream theorists, diversity training is a useful component of diversity programmes. Such training is central to evening the odds for marginalized groups. It can teach members of such groups to adapt better to the organizational culture – how to dress, speak, behave, socialize, etc. – and therefore garner greater success. It can also encourage members of dominant groups to ferret out any barriers they may unconsciously be placing before other people. Therefore, training addressing individual and interpersonal issues plays a key role in getting white women and people of colour better access to decision-making circles and greater resources. Training that addresses systemic factors like racism and sexism, however, is problematic. The system is not at fault. The system, given time, will work for white women and people of colour, as it has for generations of previous groups who overcame discrimination in employment. Workshops that target all members of dominant groups just blame the innocent and create a backlash. There are no pervasive imbalances of privilege and oppression that should be addressed.

Like all components of diversity programmes, training programmes will reflect and reinforce the interests of dominant groups in organizations, according to a critical perspective. Such trainings could be considered identity practices, an explicit attempt to shape how employees think about themselves. Training sessions will be constructed around the premise that diversity management is good for the organizational bottom-line – rather than a moral imperative for companies (and a larger capitalist system) that have systematically discriminated against particular social groups. Such sessions are likely to concentrate on the individual and interpersonal dynamics of prejudice, instead of tackling the embedded structures, both in the company and in its environment, that privilege the few at the expense of the many. In any case, critical theorists would continue, training is often a substitute for real organizational changes, like increasing representation of marginalized groups at higher levels or changing compensation systems.

A Foucauldian lens draws attention to the disciplinary and pastoral mechanisms of inscribing power. Diversity training might be construed as including both elements, depending on its approach. A common incantation of diversity programmes is the declaration of their intention to change behaviour, rather than attitudes. It is not our place to change how employees think or feel, goes the reasoning, but we can require certain types of conduct. Demanding particular actions or practices is an example of disciplinary coercion or pressure. Management identifies acceptable and unacceptable behaviours, develops a system of measurement, evaluates employees against these standards, and disciplines accordingly. Training plays an essential role in disseminating and inculcating the guidelines. Some training, however, does attempt to reach employees at a deeper, more personal, more vulnerable level. It encourages participants to reflect on their own prejudices, ferret out their contributions to discrimination, and proclaim these in some public setting. Here, pastoral mechanisms are at work. It is no surprise, therefore, that training programmes are such a popular component of diversity initiatives: their versatility makes them useful as transmitters of both overt and covert enforcement.

Affinity groups

Affinity groups are identity-based support groups, sometimes called employee network groups (Cox, 1994; Friedman *et al.*, 1998; Friedman, 1996; Friedman and Carter, 1993). These groups have four distinguishing characteristics. First, they are organized on the basis of some kind of social identity, like race or gender, in order to address the needs of that group. Second, the groups are intra-organizational. Third, they are organized by members, not by management. Fourth, they are formally recognized and acknowledged in some way by the larger organization; they are not an informal social group of some kind (Friedman, 1996). In a sample of Fortune and Service 500 companies, 29 per cent had network groups (Friedman and Carter, 1993). They have three basic purposes: (1) self-help – to develop friendship and professional ties among their members and help them negotiate the generally white- and male-dominated culture of their companies; (2) organizational change – to encourage the organization to become more welcoming through recruitment, mentoring programmes, etc.; (3) community involvement such as fundraisers for minority scholarships and the like.

From a mainstream perspective, such groupings allow disenfranchised groups to gain access to resources and decision-making in a pluralistic setting. Individual employees may be reluctant to speak up, for fear of some kind of retaliation, and a lone voice might be ignored. By combining voices and efforts, however, employees risk less and garner greater attention. These groups help their members acculturate and succeed, through larger networks, help with learning the ropes, and greater access to mentors. They also provide management with the organized perspective of marginalized groups and could lead to changes in how the organization recruits, promotes and rewards its employees. In fact, such groups could be seen as the private counterpart to politically organized ethnic groups vying for power in a pluralist electoral and legislative arena (Omi and Winant, 1994). Resource mobilization theorists, operating from a mainstream perspective, might see affinity groups as a forum for building collective identity among employees from similar backgrounds. Similarly to such processes outside companies, some minimal sense of collectivity would be a necessary precursor, but the organizing process itself would expand and enhance that group identity. That growing sense of solidarity could be a catalyst for more assertive collective action. In fact, some gay and lesbian groups have been successful in advocating for domestic partner benefits and other gay-friendly policies (Creed and Scully, 1998, 2000; Foldy and Creed, 1999).

Given the fundamental shape of power relations in American companies, critical theorists would be highly sceptical of the power of affinity groups. Any such groups have no choice, they would argue, but to acquiesce to a management agenda. There are few rights to freedom of association on private corporate terrain. Union organizers have some legal protection, though it can be quite flimsy, but members of affinity groups have no such externally recognized status to protect them from management authority. If such groups contribute to management's direction and strategy, they will be tolerated or even encouraged. If not, they'll be dismantled. Such groups allow management to harness a solidaristic energy to the benefit of the company – to make the 'extra-organizational', organizational.

However, critical theorists might acknowledge, the very fact that white women and people of colour are granted some freedom to meet privately and discuss issues could provide potential openings for resistance. In fact, such groups are an alternative source of organized identity practices within companies. Some individual members may try to use the group as a forum for more radical consciousness-raising. However such efforts are doomed, more than likely. Only unions can provide any real challenge to management authority. Acutely aware of this, management makes it clear that such groups do not have the authority of unions and cannot act like unions. One study of such groups begins by saying that these groups 'are not the kind of union-like, antagonistic, anti-company entities that are feared by many managers. If anything, most groups are concerned with helping members achieve their companies' business goals. The tone of these groups is, for the most part, very positive' (Friedman and Carter, 1993: 1).

A Foucauldian approach might view affinity groups as a fascinating paradox. Extra-organizational identities like race or gender are often seen as a source of potential resistance to existing power relations (Clegg, 1994; Hardy and Clegg, 1996). Yet, here are business leaders around the country endorsing and even initiating groups which deliberately highlight such an identity. Apparently, they see such groups as a potential source of energy and commitment to organizational goals. Most likely, from a Foucauldian perspective, they are sites of both compliance and resistance, of cross-cutting discourses. These groups do offer a semi-autonomous space in which to explore issues that would be difficult to do otherwise. This space can act as an interstice through which resistant thinking and actions find an opening. On the other hand, that space is shot through with exigencies and restrictions allowing minimal freedom of movement. Not only that, but the individuals in the group are so identified with and through the current set of power relations that an autonomous space bringing them together has limited value.

Mentoring programmes

Some companies have initiated mentoring programmes in response to data indicating that mentoring relationships play a crucial role in career development (Kram and Hall, 1996). While some programmes are designed to help all employees, others concentrate on white women and people of colour. Generally, these latter programmes match up senior white men (and some women) with lower-level employees from marginalized groups. Such programmes may include help with cross-racial and cross-gender relationships, and suggestions for coaching and counselling people from backgrounds different from one's own.

From a mainstream viewpoint, such programmes are an excellent way to help disadvantaged employees gain access to such valuable resources as connections to senior management and sage career advice. Such resources can then give such employees a seat at the decision-making table. The critical approach would not be so benign. Mentoring is a way for protégés to learn how to work the system, how to be successful within the existing paradigm. Whatever radical potential a protégé might have had – because of alienation from a white male-dominated system – is replaced with a desire to assimilate in order to get ahead. Mentoring facilitates the alignment of employee identity with the organization. Finally, mentoring relationships are very imbalanced: mentors have all the power; protégés are quite dependent on them. Foucauldian theorists might agree in part. Mentoring has been identified by other researchers as a vehicle for pastoral power, 'a technique by which junior members absorb, imbibe and interiorize the more subtle, tacit, and noncodifiable aspects of an organization's goals' (Covaleski *et al.*, 1998: 302). These authors saw mentoring as a primary method of aligning identity and organization. But the power dynamics are not so simple. Mentors may be judged by the success of their protégés: upward-moving protégés provide a career boost; problematic protégés can be an obstacle to further growth. Particularly in turbulent environments, when the rules change quickly, mentors may be able to learn as much from their protégés as the reverse (Kram and Hall, 1996). Assuming a simplistic, top-down power vector (as critical theorists are prone to do) conceals more intricate, contradictory and subtle power dynamics present in all situations.

In this section, I have suggested how different views of power and differing understandings of the relationship between power and identity could produce very different commentaries on the effects of diversity programmes in organizations. The three lenses illuminate varied faces, facets, dynamics, and consequences of attempts to manage diversity. Through this exercise, I hope I have illustrated the benefits of using multiple lenses when analysing organizations. Relying on one lens alone, I would argue, can impoverish understanding of complex phenomena; accepting the potential wisdom of varying approaches adds richness and depth to exploration.

Conclusion

In this chapter I have created a framework that links power and identity. I then applied that framework to organizational efforts to manage diversity. The chapter suggests, most simply, that managing diversity means managing identity. By attending to multiple facets of their employees, employers are inescapably involved in shaping how they define and understand themselves.

In addition to exploring the intersection of power, identity, diversity and organizations, I hope this theory will have fruitful consequences for how we understand all four concepts individually. Such an approach could enrich current notions of power by extending it into the micro-dynamics of personal identity. It provides several answers to the question: how are power and identity connected? This approach could also help change the way the organization studies literature thinks about identity. Rather than seeing it as internally generated or simply linked to referent groups, my theoretical model sees identity as constituted, in different ways, by force relations. This approach could advance understanding of diversity issues in organizations by acknowledging that genuine attempts to address diversity issues will pose inherent challenges to existing power relations; it is not possible to address diversity without addressing power. Finally, this approach could add to our understanding of organizations by contending that power is present even at the most micro levels of analysis. It also points to the role organizational culture plays in constructing identity. Diversity policies are observable cultural artefacts which can act as identity practices. Values and underlying assumptions also, surreptitiously, shape employee sense-making about the self. Diversity programmes, therefore, are one important link between organizational culture and gender or racial identity.

What implications does this framework hold for the practice of addressing diversity and multiculturalism in organizations? Most simply, it argues for entering the fray, but with awareness and acknowledgement of the complex power dynamics at play. Diversity programmes that downplay or ignore issues of dominance and subordination cannot succeed in making even superficial changes in organizations; they are sidestepping the elephant in the room. Such programmes will likely lead to cynicism among all employees, both from dominant and marginalized groups, and contribute to the general pessimism about the effectiveness of these initiatives. But blanket criticism from the left, what this chapter terms the critical approach, ironically can play into the hands of right-wing critics of such programmes. Both groups may be equally condemnatory of such programmes, but because the dominant discourse tends to be conservative, particularly in the business arena, left critics may simply add ammunition to conservative arguments. Further, by dismissing any effort as inevitably co-opted and corrupt, left critics abandon diversity practice to individuals and groups who have no interest in significant challenges to the status quo. Finally, an ongoing critique of Foucauldian approaches suggests that they abdicate responsibility for organizational or social change by their pessimistic determinism. Ironically, holding the contradictory messages from each of the three perspectives might enable an aware, complex, multifaceted, flexible and responsive approach that makes inroads where other attempts fall short. I hope this effort contributes to that difficult, but very important work.

Note

1 Foucault's interpreters disagree on how much room he left for individual agency in his understanding of the web of power relations. This is partly due to the fact that his own view seems to have changed over the course of his work. Hall (1996b) and Knights (1992) both argue that Foucault gave greater room to human agency in his later work.

References

Ashforth, B.E. and Mael, F. (1989). Social identity theory and the organization. *Academy of Management Review*, 14(1): 20–39.

Branch, S. (1999). The 100 best companies to work for in America. *Fortune*, 163: 118–144.

Braverman, H. (1974). *Labor and Monopoly Capital*. New York, NY: Monthly Review.

Cavanaugh, J.M. (1997). (In)corporating the other? Managing the politics of workplace difference. In P. Prasad, A.J. Mills, M. Elmes and A. Prasad (eds), *Managing the Organizational Melting Pot: Dilemmas of Workplace Difference* (pp. 31–53). Thousand Oaks, CA: Sage Publications.

Clegg, S. (1994). Power relations and the constitution of the resistant subject. In J.M. Jermier, D. Knights and W.R. Nord (eds), *Resistance and Power in Organizations* (pp. 274–325). London: Routledge.

Collinson, D. (1994). Strategies of resistance: power, knowledge and subjectivity in the workplace. In J.M. Jermier, D. Knights and W.R. Nord (eds), *Resistance and Power in Organizations* (pp. 25–68). London: Routledge.

Comer, D.R. and Soliman, C.E. (1996). Organizational efforts to manage diversity: do they really work? *Journal of Managerial Issues*, 8(4): 470–483.

Covaleski, M.A., Dirsmith, M.W., Heian, J.B. and Samuel, S. (1998). The calculated and the avowed: techniques of discipline and struggles over identity in Big Six public accounting firms. *Administrative Science Quarterly*, 43: 293–327.

Cox, T., Jr. (1994). *Cultural Diversity in Organizations: Theory, Research and Practice*. San Francisco, CA: Berrett-Koehler Publishers.

Creed, W.E.D. and Scully, M. (1998). Switchpersons on the tracks of history: situated agency and contested legitimacy in the diffusion of domestic partner benefits. *Academy of Management*. San Diego, CA: 7–12 August.

Creed, W.E.D. and Scully, M. (2000). Songs of ourselves: employees' deployment of social identity in workplace encounters. *Journal of Management Inquiry*, 9(4): 391–412.

Dahl, R.A. (1957). The concept of power. *Behavioral Science*, 2: 201–205.

Dutton, J.E., Dukerich, J.M. and Harquail, C.V. (1994). Organizational images and member identification. *Administrative Science Quarterly*, 39: 239–263.

Edwards, R. (1979). *Contested Terrain: The Transformation of the Workplace in the Twentieth Century*. New York, NY: Basic Books, Inc.

Ezzamel, M. and Willmott, H. (1998). Accounting for teamwork: a critical study of group-based systems of organizational control. *Administrative Science Quarterly*, 43: 358–396.

Fine, M.G. (1995). *Building Successful Multicultural Organizations*. Westport, CT: Quorum Books.

Fletcher, J.K. (1992). A poststructuralist perspective on the third dimension of power. *Journal of Organizational Change Management*, 5(1): 31–38.

Foldy, E.G. and Creed, W.E.D. (1999). Action learning, fragmentation, and the interaction of single-, double-, and triple-loop change: a case of gay and lesbian workplace advocacy. *Journal of Applied Behavioral Science*, 35(2): 207–227.

Foucault, M. (1979). *Discipline and Punish*. Hammondsworth: Penguin.

Foucault, M. (1980). Two lectures. In C. Gordon (ed.), *Power/Knowledge: Selected Interviews and Other Writings, 1972–1977* (pp. 78–108). New York, NY: Pantheon.

Foucault, M. (1993). Power and knowledge. In C. Lemert (ed.), *Social Theory* (pp. 517–524). Boulder, CO: Westview Press.

Friedman, R., Kane, M. and Cornfield, D.B. (1998). Social support and career optimism: examining the effectiveness of network groups among black managers. *Human Relations*, 51(9): 1155–1177.

Friedman, R.A. (1996). Defining the scope and logic of minority and female network groups: can separation enhance integration? *Research in Personnel and Human Resources Management*, 14: 307–349.

Friedman, R.A. and Carter, D. (1993). African American Network Groups: Their Impact and Effectiveness. Report. Washington, DC: Executive Leadership Council.

Gamson, J. (1995). Must identity movements self-destruct? A queer dilemma. *Social Problems*, 42(3): 101–118.

Gamson, W.A. (1991). Commitment and agency in social movements. *Sociological Forum*, 6(1): 27–50.

Gamson, W.A. (1992). The social psychology of collective action. In A.D. Morris and C.M. Mueller (eds), *Frontiers in Social Movement Theory* (pp. 53–76). New Haven, CT: Yale University Press.

Goldman, P. (1983). The labor process and the sociology of organizations. *Research in the Sociology of Organizations*, 2: 49–81.

Hall, S. (1996a). Gramsci's relevance for the study of race and ethnicity. In D. Morley and K.-H. Chen (eds), *Stuart Hall: Critical Dialogues in Cultural Studies* (pp. 411–440). London: Routledge.

Hall, S. (1996b). Introduction: who needs identity? In S. Hall and P. de Gay (eds), *Questions of Cultural Identity* (pp. 1–17). London: Sage Publications.

Hardy, C. and Clegg, S.R. (1996). Some dare call it power. In S.R. Clegg, C. Hardy and W. Nord (eds), *Handbook of Organization Studies* (pp. 622–641). London: Sage Publications.

Hardy, C. and Leiba-O'Sullivan, S. (1998). The power behind empowerment: implications for research and practice. *Human Relations*, 51(4): 451–483.

Hunt, S.A., Benford, R.D. and Snow, D.A. (1994). Identity fields: framing processes and the social construction of movement identities. In E. Larana, H. Johnston and J.R. Gusfield (eds), *New Social Movements: From Ideology to Identity* (pp. 185–208). Philadelphia, PA: Temple University Press.

Jackson, S.E. (1992). *Diversity in the Workplace: Human Resources Initiatives*. New York, NY: Guilford Press.

Jenkins, R. (1996). *Social Identity*. London: Routledge.

Jermier, J.M., Knights, D. and Nord, W.R. (1994). *Resistance and Power in Organizations*. London: Routledge.

Kelly, E. and Dobbin, F. (1998). How affirmative action became diversity management. *American Behavioral Scientist*, 41(7): 960–984.

Kilduff, M., Funk, J.L. and Mehra, A. (1997). Engineering identity in a Japanese factory. *Organization Science*, 8(8): 579–592.

Knights, D. (1992). Changing spaces: the disruptive impact of a new epistemological location for the study of management. *Academy of Management Review*, 17(3): 514–536.

Knights, D. and Willmott, H. (1985). Power and identity in theory and practice. *Sociological Review*, 33(1): 22–46.

Knights, D. and Willmott, H. (1989). Power and subjectivity at work: from degradation to subjugation in social relations. *Sociology*, 23(4): 535–558.

Kondo, D.K. (1990). *Crafting Selves*. Chicago, IL: University of Chicago Press.

Kossek, E.E. and Lobel, S.A. (1996). *Managing Diversity: Human Resource Strategies for Transforming the Workplace*. Cambridge, MA: Blackwell.

Kram, K.E. and Hall, D.T. (1996). Mentoring in a context of diversity and turbulence. In E.E. Kossek and S.A. Lobel (eds), *Managing Diversity: Human Resource Strategies for Transforming the Workplace* (pp. 108–136). Cambridge, MA: Blackwell Publishers, Inc.

Kurtz, S.R. (1994). *All Kinds of Justice: Labor and Identity Politics*. Dissertation, Boston College.

Leidner, R. (1993). *Fast Food, Fast Talk*. Berkeley, CA: University of California Press.

Litvin, D.R. (2000). Defamiliarizing diversity: a cultural studies analysis. Dissertation, University of Massachusetts.

Litvin, D.R. (1999). The Business Case for Diversity and the 'Iron Cage'. Paper presented at the International Conference on Language in Organizational Change and Transformation, Columbus, Ohio.

Lukes, S. (1974). *Power: A Radical View*. London: Macmillan.

Mael, F. and Ashforth, B.E. (1992). Alumni and their alma mater: a partial test of the reformulated model of organizational identification. *Journal of Organizational Behavior*, 13: 103–123.

Marsden, R. (1997). Class discipline: IR/HR and the normalization of the workforce. In P. Prasad, A. Mills, M.B. Elmes and A. Prasad (eds), *Managing the Organizational Melting Pot: Dilemmas of Workplace Diversity* (pp. 107–127). Thousand Oaks, CA: Sage Publications.

Nemetz, P.L. and Christensen, S.L. (1996). The challenge of cultural diversity: harnessing a diversity of views to understand multiculturalism. *Academy of Management Review*, 21(2): 434–462.

Nkomo, S.M. (1997). The ideology of managing diversity. In Paper presented at Academy of Management. Boston, MA. 8–13 August.

Nkomo, S.M. and Cox, T., Jr. (1996). Diverse identities in organizations. In S.R. Clegg, C. Hardy and W. Nord (eds), *Handbook of Organization Studies* (pp. 338–356). London: Sage Publications.

Omi, M. and Winant, H. (1994). *Racial Formation in the United States*. New York, NY: Routledge.

Pfeffer, J. and Salancik, G.R. (1978). *The External Control of Organizations: A Resource Dependence Perspective*. New York, NY: Harper & Row.

Prasad, P. and Mills, A. (1997). From showcase to shadow: understanding the dilemmas of managing workplace diversity. In P. Prasad, A. Mills, M.B. Elmes and A. Prasad (eds), *Managing the Organizational Melting Pot: Dilemmas of Workplace Diversity* (pp. 3–27). Thousand Oaks, CA: Sage Publications.

Pratt, M.G. and Rafaeli, A. (1997). Organizational dress as a symbol of multilayered social identities. *Academy of Management Journal*, 40(4): 862–898.

Schein, E. (1985). *Organizational Culture and Leadership*. San Francisco, CA: Jossey-Bass.

Schlenker, B.R. (1985). Identity and self-identification. In B.R. Schlenker (ed.), *The Self and Social Life* (pp. 65–99). New York, NY: McGraw-Hill Book Company.

Taylor, V. and Whittier, N.E. (1992). Collective identity in social movement communities: lesbian feminist mobilization. In A.D. Morris and C.M. Mueller (eds), *Frontiers in Social Movement Theory* (pp. 104–129). New Haven, CT: Yale University Press.

Thomas, D.A. and Ely, R.J. (1996). Making differences matter: a new paradigm for managing diversity. *Harvard Business Review*, 74 (September–October): 79–90.

Thomas, R.R., Jr. (1999). Diversity management: some measurement criteria. *Employment Relations Today*, Winter: 49–62.

Walker, B.A. and Hanson, W.C. (1992). Valuing differences at Digital Equipment Corporation. In S.E. Jackson (ed.), *Diversity in the Workplace: Human Resources Initiatives* (pp. 119–137). New York, NY: Guilford Press.

Weedon, C. (1987). *Feminist Practice and Poststructuralist Theory*. Cambridge, MA: Blackwell.

Weeks, J. (1993). Sexual identification is a strange thing. In C. Lemert (ed.), *Social Theory*. Boulder, CO: Westview Press.

Whetten, D.A. and Godfrey, P.C. (1998). *Identity in Organizations: Building Theory Through Conversations*. Thousand Oaks, CA: Sage Publications.

Williams, R. (1977). *Marxism and Literature*. Oxford: Oxford University Press.

Part III

Methods

Beyond explorations

7 History/herstory

An introduction to the problems of studying the gendering of organizational culture over time

Albert J. Mills

Introduction

Rowlinson and Procter (1999: 369–370) contend that the utilization of an organizational culture perspective can provide 'theoretical relevance for business history' but conclude that this potential 'has not been fulfilled' due, in large part, to the 'conventions that divide business history from organizational culture studies'. The chosen approach, they continue, 'is not a function of what is being studied but *represents the preferences of the researcher for how research should be done*' (Rowlinson and Procter, 1999: 389, emphasis in the original). This problem is magnified when we consider the issues and concerns that divide feminists from business historians and mainstream approaches to organizational culture. This chapter reviews some of the key problems involved in developing a study of the gendering of organizational culture over time. The chapter begins by making the argument for why feminists should study the cultures of organizations. It then moves on to consider the problem of developing an appropriate theoretical framework – examining issues of focus, terms, assumptions, methods of study, and feminist divides. Finally it considers some of the problems involved in studying organizational culture over time, including questions of feminist historiography, the selection of a particular organizational culture, time, progress versus change, corporate histories and archival materials, and creating a sense of organization over time. Some of the problems are illustrated through reference to an ongoing study of the gendering of British Airways.

Should feminists study the cultures of organizations?

The idea of organizational culture has captured the imagination of management theorists and practitioners for the past quarter of a century. Although interest peaked in the late 1980s (Kieser, 1997) there are signs of renewed interest from a new generation of researchers (see Ashkanasy *et al.*, 2000). With its focus on 'norms, values, beliefs and ways of behaving' (Eldridge and Crombie, 1974: 89), some feminists have argued that organizational culture is an important heuristic for studying workplace discrimination (Gherardi, 1995; Mills, 1988; Morgan, 1988; Smircich, 1985). This viewpoint has strengthened in recent years, as is witnessed by a growing number of socio-legal and organizational studies that have explored the links between organizational culture and discriminatory practices (Aaltio-Marjosola, 1994; Aaltio-Marjosola and Lehtinen, 1998; Abella, 1984;

Alvesson and Due Billing, 1997; Helms Mills and Mills, 2000; Korvajarvi, 1998; Mills and Murgatroyd, 1991; Wilson, 1997, 2001).

While mainstream accounts of organizational culture have generally ignored gender, legal developments in the field of employment equity, particularly in North America, have shifted emphasis away from individual *intent* towards a study of the relationship between discriminatory *outcomes* and combinations of organizational processes and practices. In the United States, for instance, the landmark *Griggs* v. *Duke Power Co.* [1971] case held that, 'If an employment practice which operates to exclude [minorities] cannot be shown to be related to job performance, the practice is prohibited' (quoted in Abella, 1984: 201). In Canada the 1984 Royal Commission on Equality in Employment characterized the root cause of workplace inequities as 'systemic discrimination'. The Commission argued that the problem of workplace discrimination lay with 'the structure of systems designed for [white able-bodied males]', and 'practices based on white able-bodied males' perceptions of everyone else' (Abella, 1984: 9–10). In more recent times an interest in 'diversity management' has encouraged mainstream research into the links between organizational culture and exclusionary practices (see Foldy, Chapter 6 this volume).

Growing interest in organizational culture notwithstanding, the question remains 'Why should feminists study the cultures of organizations?' The answer I would give is that:

- much of feminist theory takes as its starting point Oakley's (1972) notion of gender as 'culturally specific patterns of behaviour which may be attached to the sexes';
- numerous feminist studies have explored the relationship between aspects of culture, the social construction of gender and discrimination, focusing on such things as language, attitudes, patterns of behaviour, symbolism, dress, patterns of belief, value systems, stories, rites, rituals, ceremonies, and physical artefacts;
- feminist studies of the relationship between cultural milieu and gendered outcomes (see Ginsburg and Lowenhaupt Tsing, 1990) suggest a framework for an integrated, holistic approach that facilitates understanding of how various cultural factors may work together to create a particular outcome; and
- organizational cultures can be viewed as 'miniature societies with unique configurations of people, myths, beliefs and values' (Brown, 1998: 5).

This last point is particularly contentious. There are those feminist studies of organization which argue that organizational arrangements provide unique settings in which gendered practices develop (see Ferguson, 1984; Kanter, 1977), and there are those who contend that organizational forms are shaped by patriarchal power relations which strongly influence how gender is understood within organizational settings (see Witz and Savage, 1992; Wolff, 1977). There is merit in both viewpoints. It would be hard to contend that such things as familial relationships did not influence how members of an organization viewed 'men' and 'women' (Eldridge and Crombie, 1974; Pollert, 1981). On the other hand, it seems equally hard to avoid the notion that organizations are local sites where sexuality is constructed (Burrell, 1992). This chapter emphasizes the latter view, arguing that the social construction of gender takes place in several locations, and that organizations have been central aspects of human experience since at least the eighteenth century and are, thus, important places where gender is defined.

Study of organizational culture provides a holistic approach to various aspects of organizational life, including language and communication (Tannen, 1994), structure (Savage and Witz, 1992), dress (Rafaeli *et al.*, 1997), organizational discourse (Burrell, 1992), sexuality (Hearn *et al.*, 1989), and symbols, images and forms of consciousness (Acker, 1992). An organizational culture framework, thus, is not in opposition to studies of specific aspects of organizational life but provides a heuristic for studying those cultural factors *in combination*.

The value of a culture approach can be illustrated through the example of weight requirements for female flight attendants. When Hochschild (1983) studied emotional labour in US airlines in the early 1980s she found discriminatory 'weight standards' for female flight attendants. Maximum weights were around 135 lb. Those who exceeded that weight were not hired and recruits who met the requirement were constantly weighed to ensure that they did not gain weight. Those who did were fired. The same was true in Britain where British European Airways (BEA) and British Overseas Airways Corporation (BOAC) had maximum weight limits of between 120 and 140 lb. On the surface we need not know anything of an airline's culture to realize that such weight requirements are discriminatory. In the words of one flight attendant: 'Passengers aren't weighed, pilots aren't weighed, in-flight service supervisors aren't weighed. We're the only ones they weigh. You can't tell me it's not because most of us are women' (quoted in Hochschild, 1983: 102). The remedy is fairly simple, change or eliminate the weight requirement. On the other hand, if we want to understand how we can inhibit some discriminatory practices and change others we may need to understand how they develop and are maintained. Indeed, in the case of weight standards unions representing the flight attendants lost several 'heated battles' in the US courts (ibid.).

In the airline industry the issue of weight has been a concern from the beginning of commercial air travel. If an aircraft is too heavy it won't achieve the required lift for take-off. The weight also has to be balanced throughout the aircraft to ensure it is stable in flight. Weight limits were set for luggage, and in the mid-1920s airlines started the practice of weighing the passengers. There was a maximum weight for each passenger and his or her luggage combined (Hudson and Pettifer, 1979). When airlines began to hire flight attendants they imposed a height and weight requirement on recruits. The first generation of flight attendants was men, hired by a number of European airlines and called 'stewards'. The British airline Imperial Airways was one of the first to hire stewards and used the weight and height restrictions as a selling feature of their service, describing the stewards as 'small, agile, quick-moving men' (see Mills, 1998). When Imperial Airways' successors, BOAC and BEA, first began to hire female 'stewardesses' in 1946 they continued the practice of weight and height restrictions. These women were to be British, 'preferably light-weight', and aged between 23 to 30 years (Edwards and Edwards, 1990: 59). At this point in time within BOAC and BEA gendered notions of a female's weight was largely confined to expectations that the average women would/should be lighter than the average man of similar height. Indeed, both airlines were anxious to distance themselves from the promotion of sexuality based on bodily appearance (Mills, 1997). Nonetheless, weight had been established as a factor of control, whose power lay in reference not only to official rules and regulations but to the discourse of aircraft safety. Thus, with changing mores inside and outside of the airline industry in the 1960s it was relatively easy to shift the meaning of weight restrictions to concerns with the stewardesses' physical appearance while appearing to ground those concerns in established safety issues.

Accepting the argument that an organizational culture lens is a valuable heuristic for the study of organizational gendering, there are then a number of epistemological and methodological problems to be confronted in developing a study of the culture of a particular organization. Some of those issues and problems are dealt with elsewhere in this book and include questions about the 'subject' of study (see Part II), the self and gender work (see Bruni and Gherardi, Chapter 2; Katila and Meriläinen, Chapter 10), and how to study organizational cultures through a value survey instrument, content analysis, and interviewing (see, respectively, Wicks and Bradshaw, Chapter 8; Benschop and Meihuizen, Chapter 9; and Aaltio, Chapter 11). This chapter focuses specifically on historiography and the problem of developing an understanding of organizational culture over time. But first there is the issue of definitions, understandings, or models of organizational culture.

Adopting, adapting or developing a framework of analysis

As we have seen from Parts I and II of this book, there are numerous, often conflicting, definitions of organizational culture. The debate on organizational culture is well known (see Martin, 1992; Martin and Frost, 1996) and will not be revisited here, except to draw out some implications for feminist research. The question is, can existing understandings of organizational culture be adapted to feminist research or do we need to develop new concepts? The absence of gender within mainstream accounts of organizational culture, for instance, encourages scepticism about the models on which they are based. Deal and Kennedy's (1982) notion of 'strong' and 'weak' cultures, for example, references masculine values of what is good ('strong') and what is bad ('weak'). Similarly their fourfold typology of organizational cultures involves 'an unselfconscious use of language which carries gendered implications' (Wilson, 2001: 172), with references to the 'tough guy/macho', 'work hard/play hard', 'bet the company' and 'process' cultures.

The problem of adopting or adapting existing theoretical frameworks is not new to feminist research (see Gilligan, 1982; Harding, 1991; Squire, 1989) but it is always important to remind ourselves of the gendered nature of the process. Within the field of organizational analysis a classic example of feminist adaptation is that of Ferguson's (1984) 'strategic use of Foucault's notion of discourse'. Within the debate around the gendering of organizational culture itself, Wilson (1997, 2001) adapts the work of Schein (1992). She argues that there are three ways in which the relevance of gender can be examined in Schein's work. First, he makes overt references to gender as significant features of culture. Second, there are aspects of his theorizing that can be extended and extrapolated to explain gendered phenomena. Third, there are gendered assumptions that are not critically examined.

(Wilson, 2001: 173)

Deconstructing the gendered aspects of Schein's work is only the first step for Wilson; she then goes on to reframe the work from a 'symbolic perspective' which, she argues, 'is more sympathetic to a gendered perspective, and more easily incorporates gender as one of many aspects of reality' (Wilson, 2001: 185). In contrast to what she sees as the inherent functionalism in Schein's approach, Wilson (2001: 170) argues that while symbolism also views culture as an integrated pattern 'it is more sympathetic to the local creation of meaning' which may lead to shared and non-shared webs of meaning. Within Wilson's (1997, 2001) work the notion of organizational culture is implied rather than defined. It is a root metaphor for capturing sets or patterns of shared meanings that impact on how masculinity and femininity are understood in a given setting.

Perhaps the best known and now classic study of organizational culture from a feminist symbolic approach is Silvia Gherardi's (1995) *Gender, Symbolism and Organizational Cultures*. Within the symbolist framework she has little difficulty adopting Antonio Strati's definition of organizational culture as consisting of 'the symbols, beliefs and patterns of behaviour learned, produced and created by the people who devote their energies and labour to the life of an organization' (quoted in Gherardi, 1995: 13). Gherardi (1995: 20) sees her approach as involving 'a performative definition of organizational culture as the system of meanings produced and reproduced when people interact. An organizational culture is the end-product of a process which involves producers, consumers and researchers. Thus the construction of meaning is purposive, reflexive and indexical.' Nonetheless, in outlining her definition of organizational culture Gherardi makes it clear that she does not wish 'to enter into polemic with other points of view' but rather to merely point out her preference for 'an interpretative definition' (1995: 13). Indeed, not all feminist approaches study organizational culture from an interpretative or symbolic point of view (see, for example, Chapter 8 by Wicks and Bradshaw in this volume), and it is not the purpose of this chapter to pose one approach against another. Also, it is not always the case that interpretative or symbolic accounts lend themselves to gendered analysis of organizational culture (Calás and Smircich, 1996; Clegg and Dunkerley, 1980).

My own theoretical preference – grounded in a materialist approach – led me to a reworking of Clegg's (1981) rules theory (Helms Mills and Mills, 2000; Mills, 1988, 1989; Mills and Murgatroyd, 1991), defining organizational culture as 'a particular configuration of "rules," enactment and resistance, within which gendered relationships are embedded and manifest' (Mills, 1988: 367).

Adapting, adopting and developing appropriate theoretical frameworks depend on such things as focus, terms, assumptions and methods. Each has embedded within it gendered notions that shape the outcomes of the study of a particular organizational culture.

Focus

For the most part studies of organizational culture have focused on manage-ment-defined outcomes of productivity, growth, profits, etc. There are three main ways that this can encourage a neglect of gender. First, there is the approach characterized by Deal and Kennedy (1982) that culture may be seen as something to manipulate in the service of management. There are several layers of problem here, including the notion that people's feelings and values can be shaped in the service of management. Arguably, this downgrading of human feelings and emotions is more likely to obscure than illuminate gender concerns. Second, aspects of a culture not thought to contribute to the desired outcomes may be ignored. Peters and Waterman (1982), for example, focus on factors that contribute to efficiency and economic success. Excellent companies are characterized as those which provide clear guidance and strategies to employees and which encourage them to feel committed to the company. In this case not only were discriminatory practices ignored but the problem was com-pounded by a failure to consider the impact of strategy (Morgan and Knights, 1991) and organizational commitment practices (Crompton and Jones, 1984) on gendered selves. In recent years a number of studies within the 'diversity man-agement' framework have argued that a lack of effectiveness may be linked to discriminatory practices. These studies, despite a number of criticisms that may be levelled at them (Prasad and Mills, 1997), have raised the profile of dealing with gender discrimination as an important aspect of 'improving' an organi-zational culture. Third, a focus on productivity and efficiency may help to repro-duce the status quo. Deal and Kennedy (1982), for example, value as 'strong' cultures those which are characterized as having a system of informal rules that are rooted in superordinate beliefs. This can encourage approval of existing cul-tures – such as the 'tough guy/macho' culture – which overly emphasis mascu-line values to the detriment of female employees. The status quo may also be reinforced where there is an emphasis on the unifying aspects of organizational culture. From this perspective organizational culture is seen as a unifying force, the all-embracing social glue. However, this has been criticized for ignoring gender (and race) differences (Wilson, 2001: 176).

Terms

Certain descriptions of cultures or aspects of culture may serve to reinforce rather than address gendered practices within a particular culture. Deal and Kennedy's (1982) use of the terms 'strong' and 'weak' cultures is a case in point. Here the terms reference a deeper gendered discourse of strength as masculine and weakness as feminine.

Assumptions

Underlying gendered assumptions influence the way that certain models con-ceptualize organizational culture, which in turn reinforces the gendered charac-ter of the organization. Wilson's (2001) critique of Handy's (1985) fourfold typology of organizational cultures provides a telling example. According to

Wilson (2001: 171), while Handy evaluates each culture type in terms of its ability to carry out the overt functions of the organization, he ignores the covert agendas within organizations, 'particularly those of people in powerful positions. Reference is made to power in each culture type ... but not to the gendered nature of that power, concentrated generally in the hands of white, heterosexual, able-bodied males'. Wilson (2001) goes on to criticize Handy's job category assumptions, taking it for granted that secretarial and clerical jobs are women's work.

Methods of study

The purposes that inform a particular approach to organizational culture can have an important impact on creating or addressing gendered outcomes. Schein (1992), for instance, contends that there are two main approaches to the study of organizational culture – clinical and ethnographic. The clinical approach is generated by the interests of organizational 'stakeholders' to solve a particular problem. When, for example, Nova Scotia Power Corporation hired a consultant to 'take a snap-shot' of its organizational culture the company was interested in discovering the extent to which its culture change programme was working. Senior management were interested in the extent to which employee attitudes and morale was 'improving' (Helms Hatfield, 1994). The ethnographic approach is generated by 'broader' concerns to contribute to the study of organizations. When Nicole Morgan (1988) studied the culture of the Canadian Public Service, for example, she was interested in shedding light on how organizational cultures become gendered and how they change over time. The clinical approach, favoured by Schein (1992), is problematic for feminist research in that it relies on the access requirements and restrictions of organizations under study, and limits study to those companies providing access. Helms Hatfield (Helms Hatfield, 1994; Helms Hatfield and Mills, 1997), for example, gained unlimited access to Nova Scotia Power to 'assist' the company to develop a survey on employee attitudes to culture change, but her access was restricted when, at a later date, she attempted an ethnographic study of the impact of re-engineering on employees' attitudes. At this latter stage the consultants were concerned that Helms Hatfield's study might say something unfavourable about their re-engineering programme. There is no knowing how the company would have reacted to the more sensitive issue of discriminatory practices. On the other hand, access is a serious problem for ethnographic studies of organization. Often ethnographic studies may address broader issues of gender discrimination, which are either of no direct interest or are highly controversial to the specific organization under study. Morgan's (1988) study, for instance, although useful to those interested in change in the Canadian Public Service, was nonetheless a damming indictment of those in charge over the years. In recent years, especially with a growing corporate interest in employment equity and diversity management, a number of feminist researchers have managed to achieve a balance between clinical and ethnographic practice – gaining access by offering insights into corporate problems while negotiating space to research and address broader issues of gender discrimination. Current interest in postmodernism and post-feminism has, to some extent, seen a merging of interest between companies and researchers in 'local' practices. For the companies involved this type of research can provide insights into their own employment practices. For the post-feminist researcher the research can generate insights into localized sites of gender construction.

'Women', 'men', and feminist organizational analysis

A particularly critical question for feminist study is the role of the researcher in the process (Kirby and McKenna, 1989; Stanley and Wise, 1983). In particular the role of the male researcher has been dramatically brought to the fore in Acker and van Houten's (1974) analysis of the Hawthorne Studies and the role of 'sex based power differentials'. Essentially, they argue that in a company where female subordinates were under the control of male managers 'the paternalistic attitudes and manipulation' by the male researchers added to female subordination and influenced the outcomes of the research. The situation was exacerbated by the fact that the Hawthorne Studies involved clinical research (Schein, 1992), with work being undertaken to solve management problems of productivity and morale.

In recent years there have been further reflections within the framework of feminist organizational analysis on the role of men. Nonetheless, this has yet to reach the level of debate witnessed in other fields, such as that of literary criticism where concerns have been raised about the potential for male research to dominate 'feminist writing' while failing to reflect adequately the basic oppression of women (Jardine and Smith, 1987).

More than most Jeff Hearn and Wendy Parkin have brought this issue to the fore, arguing that 'just as there are questions about the police investigating themselves and the unlikelihood of outcomes being free of bias, similarly there are questions of in-built bias in research done by men in organizations and by women who suffer least from discrimination' (Hearn and Parkin, 1992: 64). To get around this problem they argue for strategies to facilitate and encourage more women – particularly those most disadvantaged – to research organizations, and for men 'concerned about sexism' to play a role in unearthing the ways in which men control organizations (see Hearn and Parkin, 1987, 1991; Hearn *et al.*, 1989). In recent years Hearn has developed a focus on men and masculinities which is intended to continue to raise questions about 'men's work' in feminist research but also the problem of male authority in feminist writing (Collinson and Hearn, 1994, 1996; Hearn, 1992). (See also Chapter 3 in this volume.)

Hearn's reflections have led him to describe his work as 'profeminist' (Hearn *et al.*, 1989) to capture the relationship of support (the 'feminist' project) and unintended distance ('pro'). Steeped in similar concerns I describe my own work as 'aspirational feminist' (Mills, 1994b) to capture the idea that the research and the reflections are ongoing. The debate, however, is far from closed and requires careful and constant reflection.

Studying organizational culture over time

In applying the culture metaphor to the study of organizational realities some scholars tend towards analysis based on a reading of contemporary events while others argue for analysis of the long term. Schein (1992), for example, argues for a 'clinical approach' which focuses on short-term problem-solving. Pettigrew (1979), on the other hand, contends that a focus on culture over time is a better way to understand patterns of change than getting a snapshot at one point in time. Similar approaches can be found in feminist studies of organizational culture. Wilson's (1997, 2001) studies of Finco, for example, examined aspects of culture over a relatively short period of time, while Morgan's (1988) study of the Canadian Public Service looked at the impact of culture over a considerable number of years. Neither approach is more valid than the other. Short-term studies provide an understanding of existing organizational cultures and their established practices, and help us to gauge the type, range, and localization of discriminatory practices at a given point. Longitudinal studies, on the other hand, allow us to assess how discriminatory practices come into being, are maintained, and changed/or can be changed over time. In the remainder of the chapter we shall explore some of problems involved.

Feminism and historiography

To study an organizational culture over time involves the construction of a history of sorts, and there are different feminist approaches to the study of history. Humphreys (1994), for example, argues that there are three main forms of feminist historiography – history by women, history about women, and history written from a feminist point of view. In a similar vein, Scott argues that

> [o]pinions differ on how History should be rewritten and on the ultimate purpose of women's history. For some scholars, rewriting is inevitable once the terms of women's experience have been documented; for others, the exposure of the profound differences between women and men – the delineation of some inherent sexual difference – is the real aim of historical inquiry; for a third group ... there is a need to redefine the terms of traditional analysis.
>
> (Scott, 1987: 22)

Following Humphreys (1994: 87), the first approach focuses on bringing 'a woman's point of view' to the analysis of history. It is an approach that is closely linked to the consciousness-raising polemics of the women's movement. In Humphreys' (1994: 87) view, 'there are now signs of increasing awareness that history written exclusively about, by and for women can never achieve more than ghetto significance'. While this viewpoint is echoed within feminist study of organizations (Calás and Smircich, 1996), the approach retains strong adherents. The Women in Management (WIM) school of thought, for instance, has successfully argued for years that female researchers need to study the impact of organizations, including organizational culture, on women. This has generated a number of studies that not only identify specific areas of workplace discrimination but also the 'special' or 'unique' qualities that women bring to the workplace. The work of Judi Marshall (1994) exemplifies this approach. Her now classic study of women managers involves what she calls two strands: 'One strand is the "public" issue of the movement of women into management jobs;

the other is the relevance to me personally of looking at women's issues' (Marshall, 1994: 1). Here women's voice is to the fore and permeates each and every level of the book. Elsewhere Marshall has gone on to apply this approach to the study of women and organizational culture, studying such things as how women experience organizational cultures as high context, preprogrammed with male values (1993c); helping women managers to use an awareness of cultural patterns as coping strategies (1993b), and exploring the dynamics of resilience as a guide to women managers (1993a). As Marshall (1993a) expresses it, it is not the business of women alone to address gender issues in organization – but neither can they wait for men to be major initiators, as this reinforces the latter's power and privilege to define meaning.

The second approach focuses on 'including women in the historical record' (see, for example, Davis, 1994: 85). Again this has its critics. Humphreys (1994: 87) argues that women's history 'faces the challenge of showing that it can transform and enrich the mainstream historical tradition which it accuses of bias, rather than merely filling in some intestinal gaps in the picture'. This is a perspective shared by Scott, who contends that, first,

> women's history will always remain separate, a subdepartment of History, unless its practitioners are able to point out its relationship to History or the rewriting of History. Second, a separate women's history tends to confirm the notion that women belong in a separate sphere. This underscores, indeed legitimizes, the existing lines of sexual difference – and the inequality associated with them.
>
> (Scott, 1987: 22)

Nonetheless, there have been a number of interesting and valuable studies of organizational culture from this perspective. In particular Susan Porter Benson (1978, 1981, 1986) has explored the contribution of women to the development of work cultures in the US sales industry. Likewise, Nicole Morgan's (1988) study of women in the Canadian federal public service exposes discriminatory practices over time while bringing to the fore the voices of some of the women who experienced the culture first-hand. Commenting on the book, Sylvia Gold, then president of the Canadian Advisory Council on the Status of Women (CACSW), states that:

> listening to women's voices, past and present, to tell of their experiences is essential to an understanding of women's search for respect and equality. Through these voices, we learn not only of indignities suffered, but of progress made through the confluence of public debate spurred on by women's groups, of politicians responding to an articulate and vocal female electorate, and of government officials carrying out the political will.
>
> (Morgan, 1988: i)

The third approach sees the subject-matter of women's history as 'the history of conceptions of gender (i.e. of "men" and "women" as social, not natural beings) and of the social relationships and experiences to which gender ideologies are tied, rather than as the history of "women" in isolation' (Humphreys, 1994: 87).

This ranges from social constructionist to post-feminist approaches. Mills and Murgatroyd (1991), for example, explore how organizational rules provide a context (and contest) of meaning in which 'men' and 'women' gain a gendered sense of self. Gherardi's (1995: 19) 'cultural approach to organizational culture investigates how the symbolic construction of gender comes about, how it varies from one culture to another, and how the preferences system sustains social thought on gender'. While Czarniawska and Calás (1997: 327) contend that 'gendering may have become an important outcome of modernization processes for contemporary notions of gender identity might be associated with westernization, internationalization, and transnationalization activities worldwide'.

Choosing an organization to study

Having adopted an appropriate feminist historiography, the first practical issue to confront you will be the type or types of organizational that you are going to study. The problem, naturally enough, is that your choice of organization will be shaped by what aspects of gendering you are trying to illuminate and/or by your access opportunities. If, for example, you are interested in the impact of re-engineering on the gendered self that will clearly limit your study to those organizations that have experienced a process of re-engineering (Fondas, 1997). If, on the other hand, you are interested in the relationship between 'emotion work' and gendering then you will need to study appropriate organizations (see Hochschild, 1983). Equally the type of access available to you may decide your mind. Ely and Meyerson (2000: 592), for example, were contacted by the chief executive of a manufacturing and retail company to pursue a study of gender and organizational change.

The choice of organization will almost certainly be compounded by the problem of attempting to study a company over time. For one thing it is important that the organization *has* a history (i.e. that it has been in operation for a lengthy period of time). Here there are some good rules of thumb that may be useful.

First, it is a good idea to find an organization that is still in operation. It may increase the apparent relevance of the study if you can reference events in an ongoing concern; there will still be people actively involved in the process who can provide insights into current and past events; and there will be potential for the observation of various aspects of cultural manifestations. Furthermore, though not strictly essential, it can add to interest in the study where the organization has attained a certain level of recognition. Mark Maier's work on the impact of masculinity on organizational outcomes (Maier, 1993, 1997; Maier and Messerschmidt, 1998) was, arguably, all the more poignant because it was focused on the Challenger space shuttle disaster. My own work is focused on British Airways and, more recently, Air Canada, because, in part, of the prominence of certain airlines in a nation's economy and sense of identity (Mills, 1994a; Mills and Hatfield, 1998). More than most, airline companies have had a profound influence on popular culture providing, among other things, prominent and enduring images of idealized masculinity (i.e. 'the pilot', 'the engineer') and femininity (i.e. 'the stewardess').

Second, for purposes of tracking events over time it is essential that the organization has been in operation long enough for certain practices to develop, become established and then change. My own preference is to study companies that have been in continuous operation for a period of fifty years or more. This allows me to compare the impact of major changes within the company (e.g. personnel turnover, restructuring, leadership changes, merger, change of owner- ship, etc.) and the socio-political context. However, the period of time is arbi- trary and will depend on the specific aims of the project. What may be a deciding factor in the timescale is an ability to trace the origins of the company. In order to trace the origins of an organization's culture it is important to choose an organization where it is possible to trace how it came into being. The older the company, the more problematic this issue becomes (e.g. key people may have died, memories fade, documents are lost). Some solution to the problem may be found where the company has an established archive and where there has been much already written on the company (advice given to me by the feminist historian Barbara Roberts).

Third, find a company with an established archive. This can serve two useful functions. It can provide documentation that helps the researcher gain an understanding of key events, people and activities over time, and it can provide an important form of access to the company. British Airways (BA) proved useful in this regard. The company maintains an archive at London's Heathrow Airport where it has collected together a wealth of material. The archive is run by an archivist and a number of volunteers and is sometimes made available to 'bona fide researchers'. Air Canada has also maintained an archive, which has recently been deposited with the National Aviation Museum in Ottawa. Given that it is housed in a government agency whose mandate requires it to assist avi- ation research, the Air Canada archive is even more accessible than BA's.

Fourth, find a company that has already been the subject of written histories. As noted later, there are problems with this but it does reduce the time needed to gain a sense of some of the key events, persons and activities over time. Both British Airways and Air Canada and their predecessors, for example, have several histories written about them (see, for example, Bao, 1989; Collins, 1978; Jackson, 1995; Penrose, 1980; Pudney, 1959; Smith, 1986; Stroud, 1987).

A question of time

Time is something that dogs historical analysis. For one thing it takes consider- ably time to study an organizational culture over the life of an organization. More importantly there is the theoretical question of time itself. Bluedorn (2000: 118) has drawn attention to the fact that 'time' is an issue within the study of organizational culture 'yet so few studies have been conducted about time as an organizational culture phenomenon'. But what I want to draw attention to is the issue of cause and effect over time. For a number of studies of organi- zational culture time is presented – either implicitly or explicitly – as a progres- sive series of events and incidents whose influence can be found in current aspects of the culture. This is seen most clearly in discussions of the role of 'the founder' in the development of an organization's culture (see Deal and Kennedy, 1982; Peters and Waterman, 1982). Postmodernist and symbolic accounts, on the other hand, argue that to understand an organizational culture we need to know something about what it *means* to those involved (see Gherardi, 1995; Alvesson and Due Billing, 1997). To return to the example of airline weight restrictions. The recruitment of 'small, light-weight' flight attendants was part of British Airways' culture for the better part of sixty years yet its meaning for those involved changed drastically over those years – from issues of safety in the 1920s to concern with bodily attraction in the 1960s.

My own approach to this problem – arising out of a rules approach – has been to argue that time should not be studied as a continuous process but as a series of junctures, or 'concurrence of events which create a moment in time – a series of images, impressions and experiences which act to give the appearance of a coherent whole and which influence how [an] organization is understood' (Mills, 1994b: 2). That is, that the history of a given organization should not be seen as a series of progressively changing events but as a series of key time-frames which shape how things were viewed at a given period of time. To understand a particular time-frame we need to piece together the various factors – rules, actors, discourses, and formative contexts – which shaped the world-view of organizational members at the time (Helms Mills and Mills, 2000). In brief, while a particular set of factors may come together to create particular ways of viewing the world a change in those factors can lead to a change in the subjectivity of those involved – creating different ways of viewing the world over time. To understand a particular period (or 'juncture') we need to understand not only the main features involved but also the particular subjectivity of the time. Arguably, through longitudinal study of an organization it is possible to understand not only how its culture becomes discriminatory but how it changes or can be changed. The research question here is: What specific cultural differences can be noted over time and what configuration of social and organizational factors appear to be associated with each difference (i.e. what distinct junctures can be identified)?

Progress vs. change

This raises the issue of progress. A key problem to be addressed in reading the cultural history of an organization is the overwhelming modernist tendency to present history as a progressive unfolding of events. Feminist researchers are not immune to the problem and there is no shortage of accounts that suggest a progressive advancement of women over time (Calás and Smircich, 1996). Yet, even if a standard of female advancement could be agreed, there is evidence that the history of female employment has not followed a path of linear development (see Ehrenreich and English, 1974). Higonnet *et al.* (1987: 4) argue that 'gender systems are not fixed, but respond and contribute to change' and, as such, may, from the perspective of 'women's rights', be characterized as going through a paradoxical process of progress and regress. Higonnet and Higonnet (1987) refer to this process as 'the double helix'. An example of this can be drawn from study of the British airline industry in the period 1945–1960. When BEA and BOAC began to employ female stewardesses in the late 1940s both airlines were at pains to stress that the women would be equal to their male counterparts, 'part of a hard working crew'. Associations of 'glamour' with the new female flight attendants were frowned upon, and the airlines went to great length to 'desexualize' the image of the female 'steward'. In its stead an equity image was developed. Female flight attendants wore a similar-styled uniform to that of their male counterparts, received an equal rate of pay, and were referred to as 'stewards'. This was a tremendous advance on the airlines' previous recruitment policies. Yet, within fifteen years BEA and BOAC – along with most major world airlines – had developed training practices, styles of dress and appearance, and marketing strategies based on eroticized images of the female flight attendant or 'hostess' (see Mills, 1997). The feminist researcher may be better served avoiding a search for cues that support a notion of progress over time, instead examining events to see what they tell us about the development and eradication of specific forms or processes of discrimination.

Corporate histories and documentation

Corporate histories are useful in providing a number of clues as to key personnel, events and incidents in a company over time; but they are also problematic. Clearly, the intent of the corporate historian differs significantly from that of the feminist researcher. The focus of the feminist researcher is on a company as 'a site of sexual construction' (Burrell, 1992); that is, a particular set of social arrangements that influence how people come to view themselves as men and women. The company historian, on the other hand, focuses on a selected company in terms of its stated purposes (e.g. the provision of an airline service), setting out to document how well it met its objectives over time. This 'systematic study of individual firms on the basis of their business records' (Tosh, 1991, quoted in Rowlinson and Procter, 1999: 380) serves to highlight some factors to the exclusion of others. This often means that not only is gender ignored but that the problem of gender is compounded where associations between masculinity and business are naturalized.

To take the example of British Airways. Accounts of the founding of the airline in 1919 focus on warfare (the role of the war in encouraging aviation), technology (advances in airplane development), government (aviation policy), and the various exploits of the men who came to found, run, and fly for the new airline. Masculinity is embedded in each layer – warfare and technology, for example, reference the activities of specific groups of men. The reader is left with the unassailable impression that commercial aviation is quite naturally a male business. Indeed, some commentators argue that it is hardly unexpected that women were not involved in aviation at this time when they were not part of a number of other industrial groupings. But that doesn't take some important factors into account. To begin with there were a number of prominent female flyers in 1919, but none was hired as commercial airline pilots. In 1918 the Women's Royal Air Force (WRAF) made history by being the first ever female military organization to be established on the same day as its male counterpart (RAF). More than twenty-five thousand women – some of them officers, a few of them involved in aircraft maintenance – served in the WRAF between 1918 and 1919; none was employed in commercial aviation. During the war tens of thousands of women served in aircraft production and manufacturing factories, some of which were converted into the very aerodromes that served the new commercial airlines, yet none of these women was hired. Indeed, between 1919 and 1924 of the over three hundred employees in British commercial airlines less than a handful were women – all in secretarial and clerical jobs (Mills, 1994a). It is only through the problematization of masculinity that we can begin to make sense of how and why these various women were excluded from commercial aviation.

As we shall see, the cues that corporate historians rely on to construct the history of a selected organization are linked to ongoing debates within capitalism concerning property rights, efficiency, and the political economy of organizational success. As such they have varying links to ongoing discourse on the nature of masculinity and femininity. This influences the sense of continuity that gives an organization a history, and it decides which voices are heard and which are not.

In a similar vein corporate archives tend to contain selective documents and other artefacts that highlight some voices at the expense of others. Those documents themselves are problematic in that they were likely developed by those in privileged positions (e.g. managers, editors, corporate accountants, marketing personnel, film producers) for specific ends. To that end, Douglas cautions:

> when we look closely at the construction of past time, we find the process has very little to do with the past at all and everything to do with the present. Institutions create shadowed places in which nothing can be seen and no questions asked. They make other areas show finely discriminated detail, which is closely scrutinized and ordered. History emerges in an unintended shape as a result of practices directed to immediate, practical ends.
>
> (Douglas, 1986: 69–70)

The BA archive, for example, consists of a large number of documents that include numerous in-house newsletters. Until quite recently much of the copy (text, photographs) concerned the activities of male employees and senior managers. There was relatively little on the abilities and activities of female employees (Mills, 1995). Douglas (1986: 70) goes on to suggest that, 'to watch these practices establish selective principles that highlight some kind of events and obscure others is to inspect the social order operating on individual minds'. That is true to a certain extent. Corporate images are often powerful in their impact and may not only reflect but create an organization's discourse. To that end, the study of corporate culture can draw on corporate materials to reveal a powerful element of the imaging process to which people were exposed over time. However, a note of caution is required:

> We cannot simply accept at face value the written records or people's memories; we cannot assume that women's experience lies outside officially constructed contexts, as a definably separate, 'purer' commentary on politics. Instead we must read the evidence we accumulate for what it reveals about how people appropriate and use political discourse, how they are shaped by it and in turn redefine its meaning.
>
> (Scott, 1987: 29)

Constructing a sense of organization over time

In the late 1990s a former Nazi concentration camp victim sued the German drug company, Beyer, claiming that it had been complicit in medical experiments on her while she was a prisoner. Not unexpectedly the company argued it had no association with the wartime Beyer. The previous company of that name had been dismantled after the war and a new company established. Not one of the company's many employees had worked for the old Beyer. In a similar fashion, a new book on IBM argues that the company worked closely with the German National Socialist Party during the Second World War (Black, 2001). In reply IBM contends that the Nazi Party took over the company's German assets during the period, so it was not really the same IBM. These cases highlight some of the problems of tracing events, people, and artefacts over time to come up with a meaningful study of an organization's culture.

When developing a corporate history a number of enacted cues (Weick, 1995) are used to create a sense of organization over time. These include such things as legal status, acquisitions and mergers, economic prominence and sociopolitical status, organizational memory and coherence of key personnel across time.

The fact that a company has been legally constituted, and has more or less operated under those terms for a period of time, provides a useful starting point for a corporate history. Yet it was on the point of legal ownership and constitution that both Beyer and IBM have questioned claims to a historical legacy that neither company wants to be associated with. Similar problems can be found with the less controversial corporate histories. Although British Airways claims to be one of the world's oldest commercial airlines it does so by laying claim to several predecessor companies that differed in terms of ownership and structure. For example, BA's predecessor companies include Instone Airline Ltd (a privately owned company in the hands of the Instone brothers that operated prior to 1924), Imperial Airways (a government-subsidized organization that was in operation between 1924 and 1939), and the British Overseas Airways Corporation (a nationalized airline which operated in various forms from 1940 until 1974).

A major strategy for organizational growth and competitiveness is one of acquisition and mergers, and this means that 'successful' companies change over time. This can be specifically problematic for the study of gender and organizational culture – for wherein lies the culture? Where are the organizational boundaries? If we trace British Airways back in time we find 57 different predecessor companies. The BA of today is very different from the BA of 1994, which in turn is very different from the BA of 1974. In 1974 BA was established from a merger of BOAC and BEA. Since that time the company acquired Dan Air, and Brymon Airways. Following 1994 it has since acquired Caledonian Airways. Most histories of British Airways have little to say about events or people in the acquired companies. Their histories, and associated voices are lost in the focus on something called 'British Airways' (i.e. locations and leaders associated with the 'main' company). Of those companies who merged to form Imperial Airways, British Airways Ltd (an airline that operated for a short time in the 1930s) and BOAC only the more prominent (in terms of relative size and/or financial standing) receive attention in histories of BA. This is influenced by corporate memory.

In the construction of corporate histories accounts inevitably draw upon 'memories' or 'traces' from a variety of sources, including corporate documents (e.g. internal memoranda, annual reports advertisements, press statements, in-flight magazines, in-house journals and newsletters), films, artefacts (e.g. physical structures, stories, language), and 'informants' (e.g. interviews, observations, letters, biographies). These accounts are usually framed within the context of organizational memories in which some 'memories' are privileged over others; that is, they are selected representations of events that have been given prominence by more powerful members of the organization (from editors to executives). In the process, not only women's voices but many of the male voices from the merged or acquired companies are excluded from memory. Reviewing sources from Imperial Airways, BOAC, BEA and British Airways archival material it is clear that some airlines are more central to the 'collective memory' than others. By and large, the five 'founding airlines', Instone, AT&T, Supermarine, Daimler and HPT, plus Imperial Airways, BOAC and BEA, take centre-stage in corporate recollections and histories. Little or no references are made to any of the other 49 predecessor airlines.

Although it is difficult to construct a coherent sense of organization over time there are a number of feminist strategies for dealing with the problems involved. To begin with, it is less important for feminist research than it is for corporate history to focus on a particular company over time: an organization's legal boundaries and its culture are often two different things. While the corporate historian is concerned to document how particular legal boundaries were established and maintained, feminist study of organizational culture is concerned to understand how particular social arrangements impact on people's understandings of gender. This suggests that it is more important to focus on a particular set of regularized social interactions and follow them through several periods of development and change. This means that a particular aspect of an organization should be studied and traced over time. In the British Airways case, for example, I have tried to trace particular sets of relationships that constituted core aspects of an organization over time. This meant focusing on such things as piloting, stewarding and selected administrative relationships in Imperial Airways and studying the impact on those relationships of merger with British Airways Ltd in 1939. Similarly, those same sets of relationships – identified through specific but changing personnel – were followed through BOAC and the new BA. Less important were relationships within the various merged or acquired companies, except in their impact on the culture under study. Thus, company names – such as Imperial Airways, BOAC and BA – were less important for the boundaries that they delineated as for the meanings they bestowed on selected sets of relationships.

Summary

Study of the gendering of organizational culture is a difficult but exciting process and in this chapter I have tried to give something of the flavour of both. Most of the examples were taken from my own studies of British Airways and reflect my own peculiar approach (i.e. rules, junctures). Other approaches will naturally differ depending on the theoretical frameworks adopted and I have attempted to give some indication of the different approaches and the implications for study. The inevitable space and time constraints have meant that there is much that I have left out. Some of this I have taken up elsewhere (Mills, 2000, 2002). Issues around content analysis and interviewing have been discussed elsewhere in this book (see Chapters 9 and 11 respectively). On gender issues and field research a good starting place is Warren (1988); on the study of life histories and archival research see, respectively Plummer (1983) and Webb *et al.* (1984); on the relationship between history, theory and social context the collection on 'Making Histories' by the Centre for Contemporary Cultural Studies (1982) is an excellent read; and, finally, on feminist research methods three of the best works in my opinion remain Stanley and Wise (1983), Roberts (1981), and the lesser-known but excellent Canadian work by Kirby and McKenna (1989).

References

Aaltio-Marjosola, I. (1994). Gender stereotypes as cultural products of the organization. *Scandanavian Journal of Management*, 10(2): 147–162.

Aaltio-Marjosola, I. and Lehtinen, J. (1998). Male managers as fathers? Contrasting management, fatherhood and masculinity. *Human Relations*, 51(2): 121–136.

Abella, R.S. (1984). *Equity in Employment. A Royal Commission Report*. Ottawa: Ministry of Supply and Services Canada.

Acker, J. (1992). Gendering organizational theory. In A.J. Mills and P. Tancred (eds), *Gendering Organizational Analysis* (pp. 248–260). Newbury Park, CA: Sage.

Acker, J. and van Houten, D.R. (1974). Differential recruitment and control: the sex structuring of organizations. *Administrative Science Quarterly*, 9(2): 152–163.

Alvesson, M. and Due Billing, Y. (1997). *Understanding Gender and Organizations*. London: Sage.

Ashkanasy, N., Wilderom, C. and Peterson, M. (eds) (2000). *Handbook of Organizational Culture and Climate*. Thousand Oaks, CA: Sage.

Bao, P.L. (1989). *An Illustrated History of British European Airways*. Feltham, Middlesex: Browcom Group Plc.

Benson, S.P. (1978). 'The clerking sisterhood'. Rationalization and the work culture of saleswomen in American department stores, 1890–1960. *Radical America*, 12: 41–55.

Benson, S.P. (1981). The Cinderella of occupations: managing the work of department store saleswomen, 1900–1940. *Business History Review*, LV(1): 1–25.

Benson, S.P. (1986). *Counter Cultures: Saleswomen, Managers, and Customers in American Department Stores, 1890–1940*. Urbana, IL: University of Illinois Press.

Black, E. (2001). *IBM and the Holocaust: The Strategic Alliance Between Nazi Germany and America's Most Powerful Corporation*. New York, NY: Crown.

Bluedorn, A.C. (2000). Time and organizational culture. In N.M. Ashkanasy., C.P.M. Wilderom and M.F. Peterson (eds), *Handbook of Organizational Culture and Climate* (pp. 117–128). Thousand Oaks, CA: Sage.

Brown, A. (1998). *Organisational Culture*. London: Financial Times/Pitman Publishing.

Burrell, G. (1992). Sex and organizational analysis. In A.J. Mills and P. Tancred (eds), *Gendering Organizational Analysis* (pp. 71–92). Newbury Park, CA: Sage.

Calás, M.B. and Smircich, L. (1996). From 'the woman's' point of view: feminist approaches to organization studies. In S.R. Clegg, C. Hardy and W.R. Nord (eds), *Handbook of Organization Studies* (pp. 218–257). London: Sage.

Centre for Contemporary Cultural Studies (ed.) (1982). *Making Histories. Studies in History-Writing and Politics*. London: Hutchinson.

Clegg, S. (1981). Organization and control. *Administrative Sciences Quarterly*, 26: 532–45.

Clegg, S. and Dunkerley, D. (1980). *Organization, Class and Control*. London: Routledge & Kegan Paul.

Collins, D.H. (1978). *Wings Across Time. The Story of Air Canada*. Toronto: Griffin House.

Collinson, D. and Hearn, J. (1994). Naming men as men: implications for work, organization and management. *Gender, Work and Organization*, 1(1): 2–22.

Collinson, D.L. and Hearn, J. (eds) (1996). *Men as Managers, Managers as Men*. London: Sage.

Crompton, R. and Jones, G. (1984). *White-Collar Proletariat: Deskilling and Gender in Clerical Work*. London: Macmillan.

Czarniawska, B. and Calás, M.B. (1997). Another country: explaining gender discrimination with 'culture'. *Hallinnon* [Finnish Journal of Administrative Studies], 4: 326–341.

Davis, N.Z. (1994). What is women's history? In J. Gardiner (ed.), *What Is History Today?* (pp. 85–87). London: Macmillan.

Deal, T.E. and Kennedy, A.A. (1982). *Corporate Cultures*. Reading, MA: Addison-Wesley.

Douglas, M. (1986). *How Organizations Think*. Syracuse, NY: Syracuse University Press.

Edwards, M. and Edwards, E. (1990). *The Aircraft Cabin*. Aldershot: Gower Technical.

Ehrenreich, B. and English, D. (1974). *Witches, Midwives, and Nurses: A History of Women Healers*. New York, NY: The Feminist Press.

Eldridge, J.E.T. and Crombie, A.D. (1974). *The Sociology of Organisations*. London: George Allen & Unwin Ltd.

Ely, R.J. and Meyerson, D.E. (2000). Advancing gender equity in organizations: the challenge and importance of maintaining a gender narrative. *Organization*, 7(4): 589–608.

Ferguson, K.E. (1984). *The Feminist Case Against Bureaucracy*. Philadelphia, PA: Temple University Press.

Fondas, N. (1997). Feminization unveiled: management qualities in contemporary writings. *The Academy of Management Review*, 22(1): 257–282.

Gherardi, S. (1995). *Gender, Symbolism, and Organizational Cultures*. London: Sage.

Gilligan, C. (1982). *In A Different Voice: Psychological Theory and Women's Development*. Cambridge, MA: Harvard University Press.

Ginsburg, F. and Lowenhaupt Tsing, A. (eds) (1990). *Uncertain Terms: Negotiating Gender in American Culture*. Boston, MA: Beacon Press.

Handy, C. (1985). *Understanding Organizations* (3rd edn). Harmondsworth: Penguin.

Harding, S.G. (1991). *Whose Science? Whose Knowledge?: Thinking from Women's Lives*. Ithaca, NY: Cornell University Press.

Hearn, J. (1992). *Men in the Public Eye: The Construction and Deconstruction of Public Men and Public Patriarchies*. London: Routledge.

Hearn, J. and Parkin, P.W. (1987). *'Sex' at 'Work' – The Power and Paradox of Organizational Sexuality*. Brighton: Wheatsheaf.

Hearn, J. and Parkin, P.W. (1991). Women, men and leadership: a critical review of assumptions, practices and changes in the industrialized nations. In N.J. Adler and D. Izraeli (eds), *Women in Management Worldwide*. New York, NY: M.E. Sharpe.

Hearn, J. and Parkin, P.W. (1992). Gender and organizations: a selective review and a critique of a neglected area. In A.J. Mills and P. Tancred (eds), *Gendering Organizational Analysis* (pp. 46–66). Newbury Park, CA: Sage.

Hearn, J., Sheppard, D., Tancred-Sheriff, P. and Burrell, G. (eds) (1989). *The Sexuality of Organization*. London: Sage.

Helms Hatfield, J.C. (1994). Implementation and results of a planned culture change in a public utility. In *The Proceedings of the Annual Conference of the Administrative Sciences of Canada*, 15 (pp. 102–111). Halifax, Nova Scotia.

Helms Hatfield, J.C. and Mills, A.J. (1997). Guiding Lights and Power Sources: Consultants Plug into the Management of Meaning in an Electrical Company. Paper presented at the Colloquium of European Group for Organizational Studies, Budapest.

Helms Mills, J.C. and Mills, A.J. (2000). Rules, sensemaking, formative contexts and discourse in the gendering of organizational culture. In N. Ashkanasy, C. Wilderom and M. Peterson (eds), *Handbook of Organizational Climate and Culture*. Thousand Oaks, CA: Sage.

Higonnet, M.R. and Higonnet, P.L.R. (1987). The double helix. In M.R. Higonnet, J. Jenson, S. Michel and M.C. Weitz (eds), *Behind the Lines. Gender and the Two World Wars* (pp. 31–47). London: Yale University Press.

Higonnet, M.R., Jenson, J., Michel, S. and Weitz, M.C. (eds) (1987). *Behind the Lines. Gender and the Two World Wars*. London: Yale University Press.

Hochschild, A.R. (1983). *The Managed Heart*. Berkeley, CA: University of California Press.

Hudson, K. and Pettifer, J. (1979). *Diamonds in the Sky. A Social History of Air Travel*. London: Bodley Head/BBC Publications.

Humphreys, S. (1994). What is women's history? In J. Gardiner (ed.), *What is History Today?* (pp. 87–89). London: Macmillan.

Jackson, A.S. (1995). *Imperial Airways and the First British Airlines 1919–40*. Lavenham: Terence Dalton.

Jardine, A. and Smith, P. (eds) (1987). *Men in Feminism*. London: Methuen.

Kanter, R.M. (1977). *Men and Women of the Corporation*. New York, NY: Basic Books.

Kieser, A. (1997). Rhetoric and myth in management fashion. *Organization*, 4(1): 49–74.

Kirby, S. and McKenna, K. (1989). *Experience, Research, Social Change. Methods from the Margins*. Toronto: Garamond.

Korvajarvi, P. (1998). *Gendering Dynamics in White-Collar Work Organizations*. Tampere, Finland: University of Tampere.

Maier, M. (1993). 'Am I the only one who wants to launch?' Corporate masculinity and the space shuttle Challenger disaster. *Masculinities*, 1(2): 34–45.

Maier, M. (1997). 'We have to make a management decision': Challenger and the dysfunctions of corporate masculinity. In P. Prasad, A.J. Mills, M. Elmes and A. Prasad (eds), *Managing the Organizational Melting Pot: Dilemmas of Workplace Diversity* (pp. 226–254). Newbury Park, CA: Sage.

Maier, M. and Messerschmidt, J.W. (1998). Commonalities, conflicts and contradictions in organizational masculinities: exploring the gendered genesis of the Challenger disaster. *The Canadian Review of Sociology and Anthropology*, 35: 325–344.

Marshall, J. (1993a). Organizational cultures and women managers: exploring the dynamics of resilience. *Applied Psychology: An International Review*, 42(4): 313–322.

Marshall, J. (1993b). Patterns of cultural awareness as coping strategies for women managers. In S.E. Kahn and B.C. Long (eds), *Work, Women and Coping: A Multidisciplinary Approach to Workplace Stress* (pp. 90–110). Montreal: McGill-Queen's University Press.

Marshall, J. (1993c). Viewing organizational communication from a feminist perspective: a critique and some offerings. In S. Deetz (ed.), *Communication Yearbook* (pp. 122–143). Newbury Park, CA: Sage.

Marshall, J. (1994). *Women Managers: Travellers in a Male World*. Chichester: John Wiley & Sons.

Martin, J. (1992). *Cultures in Organizations: Three Perspectives*. Oxford: Oxford University Press.

Martin, J. and Frost, P. (1996). The organizational culture war games: a struggle for intellectual dominance. In S.R. Clegg, C. Hardy and W.R. Nord (eds), *Handbook of Organization Studies* (pp. 599–621). London: Sage.

Mills, A.J. (1988). Organization, gender and culture. *Organization Studies*, 9(3): 351–369.

Mills, A.J. (1989). Gender, sexuality and organization theory. In J. Hearn, D.L. Sheppard, P. Tancred-Sheriff and G. Burrell (eds), *The Sexuality of Organization* (pp. 29–44). London: Sage.

Mills, A.J. (1994a). The gendering of organizational culture: social and organizational discourses in the making of British Airways. In M. DesRosiers (ed.), *Proceedings of the Administrative Sciences Association of Canada, Women in Management Division*, 15 (pp. 11–20). Halifax, Nova Scotia: ASAC.

Mills, A.J. (1994b). No Sex Please, We're British Airways: A Model for Uncovering the Symbols of Gender in British Airways' Culture, 1919–1991. Paper presented at the 12th annual conference of the Standing Conference on Organizational Symbolism (SCOS), Calgary, Alberta.

Mills, A.J. (1995). Man/aging subjectivity, silencing diversity: organizational imagery in the airline industry – the case of British Airways. *Organization*, 2(2): 243–269.

Mills, A.J. (1997). Duelling discourses – desexualization versus eroticism in the corporate framing of female sexuality in the British airline industry, 1945–60. In P. Prasad, A.J. Mills, M. Elmes and A. Prasad (eds), *Managing The Organizational Melting Pot: Dilemmas of Workplace Diversity*. Newbury Park, CA: Sage.

Mills, A.J. (1998). Cockpits, hangars, boys and galleys: corporate masculinities and the development of British Airways. *Gender, Work and Organization*, 5(3): 172–188.

Mills, A.J. (2000). Cultural traces and traces of culture: problems of studying corporate culture over time. In R. Sexty (ed.), *Proceedings of the Business History Division of the Administrative Sciences Association of Canada, Annual Conference*. Montreal, 8–11 July. Montreal: Administrative Sciences Association of Canada.

Mills, A.J. (2002). Studying the gendering of organizational culture over time: concerns, issues and strategies. *Gender, Work and Organization*, 9(3): 286–307.

Mills, A.J. and Hatfield, J.C.H. (1998). Air Canada vs. Canadi>n: competition and merger in the framing of airline culture. *Studies in Cultures, Organizations and Societies*, 4(1): 1–32.

Mills, A.J. and Murgatroyd, S.J. (1991). *Organizational Rules: A Framework for Understanding Organizations*. Milton Keynes: Open University Press.

Morgan, G. and Knights, D. (1991). Gendering jobs: corporate strategies, managerial control and dynamics of job segregation. *Work, Employment and Society*, 5(2): 181–200.

Morgan, N. (1988). *The Equality Game: Women in the Federal Public Service (1908–1987)*. Ottawa: Canadian Advisory Council on the Status of Women.

Oakley, A. (1972). *Sex, Gender and Society*. London: Temple Smith.

Penrose, H. (1980). *Wings Across the World. An Illustrated History of British Airways*. London: Cassell.

Peters, T. and Waterman, R. (1982). *In Search of Excellence – Lessons from America's Best Run Companies*. New York, NY: Warner Communications.

Pettigrew, A. (1979). On studying organizational cultures. *Administrative Science Quarterly*, 24: 570–581.

Plummer, K. (1983). *Documents of Life*. London: George Allen & Unwin.

Pollert, A. (1981). *Girls, Wives, Factory Lives*. London: Macmillan.

Prasad, P. and Mills, A.J. (1997). Managing the organizational melting pot: dilemmas of diversity at the workplace. In P. Prasad, A.J. Mills, M. Elmes and A. Prasad (eds), *Managing The Organizational Melting Pot: Dilemmas of Workplace Diversity* (pp. 3–27). Thousand Oaks, CA: Sage.

Pudney, J. (1959). *The Seven Skies.* London: Putnam.

Rafaeli, A., Dutton, J., Harquail, C.V. and Mackie-Lewis, S. (1997). Navigating by attire: the use of dress by female administrative employees. *The Academy of Management Journal,* 40(1): 9–45.

Roberts, H. (ed.) (1981). *Doing Feminist Research.* London: Routledge & Kegan Paul.

Rowlinson, M. and Procter, S. (1999). Organizational culture and business history. *Organization Studies,* 20(3): 369–396.

Savage, M. and Witz, A. (eds) (1992). *Gender and Bureaucracy.* Oxford: Blackwell.

Schein, E. (1992). *Organizational Culture and Leadership* (2nd edn). San Francisco, CA: Jossey-Bass.

Scott, J.W. (1987). Rewriting history. In M.R. Higonnet, J. Jenson, S. Michel and M.C. Weitz (eds), *Between the Lines. Gender and the Two World Wars.* London: Yale University Press.

Smircich, L. (1985). Is the concept of culture a paradigm for understanding organizations and ourselves? In P.J. Frost, L.F. Moore, M.R. Louis, C.C. Lundberg and J. Martin (eds), *Organizational Culture* (pp. 55–72). Beverly Hills, CA: Sage.

Smith, P. (1986). *It Seems Like Only Yesterday.* Toronto: McClelland & Stewart.

Squire, C. (1989). *Significant Differences – Feminism in Psychology.* London: Routledge.

Stanley, L. and Wise, S. (1983). *Breaking Out: Feminist Consciousness and Feminist Research.* London: Routledge & Kegan Paul.

Stroud, J. (1987). *Railway Air Services.* Shepperton, Surrey: Ian Allan.

Tannen, D. (1994). *Talking 9 to 5.* New York, NY: Morrow.

Warren, C.A.B. (1988). *Gender Issues in Field Research.* Newbury Park, CA: Sage.

Webb, E.J., Campbell, D.T., Schwartz, R.D. and Sechrest, L. (1984). The use of archival sources in social research. In M. Bulmer (ed.), *Sociological Research Methods* (pp. 113–130). London: Macmillan.

Weick, K. (1995). *Sensemaking in Organizations.* London: Sage.

Wilson, E.M. (1997). Exploring gendered cultures. *Hallinon Tutkimus,* 4: 289–303.

Wilson, E.M. (2001). Organizational culture. In E.M. Wilson (ed.), *Organizational Behaviour Reassessed. The Impact of Gender* (pp. 168–187). London: Sage.

Witz, A. and Savage, M. (1992). The gender of organizations. In M. Savage and A. Witz (eds), *Gender and Bureaucracy* (pp. 3–62). Oxford: Blackwell.

Wolff, J. (1977). Women in organizations. In S. Clegg and D. Dunkerley (eds), *Critical Issues in Organizations* (pp. 7–20). London: Routledge & Kegan Paul.

8 Investigating gender and organizational culture

Gendered value foundations that reproduce discrimination and inhibit organizational change

David Wicks and Pat Bradshaw

Introduction

Research in gender and organization is both plentiful and theoretically diverse, yet gender and organizational culture remains a topic which is ripe for study because of its prevalence in organizational settings, and the limited empirical research demonstrating the breadth of the gendered assumptions and values present in ostensibly gender-neutral environments. Organizational culture more broadly has been researched extensively since 1980 when it became a popular topic of study in organizational behaviour. The concept of organizational culture arises from viewing organizations less as machines and more as social entities, possessing socialization processes, social norms and structures. Organizational culture, therefore, can be viewed as a set of widely shared attitudes, values and assumptions that give rise to specific behaviours and physical manifestations which become entrenched in the minds and practices of organizational participants (Schein, 1991). Clearly a cultural approach to studying organization is much more than a passing fad, and can in fact reveal many aspects of organizational life ignored or undetected by other theories of, or perspectives on, organization (Trice and Beyer, 1993). Despite this acknowledged legitimacy of research on organizational culture, there remains a relative paucity of empirical research that specifically illustrates in what ways gender relations and organizational culture are connected.

The purpose of this chapter is to contribute to these emerging discussions about the gendered nature of organizational culture. Although theoretical work (Gherardi, 1994; Maier, 1991; Mills, 1988), discourse analysis (Mills, 1994) and deconstruction of texts (Calás and Smircich, 1991; Martin, 1990; Mumby and Putnam, 1992) indicate the dominance of a male ethos in organizations and a privileging of the masculine in organizational discourses, little empirical work has been done to reveal the breadth of these patterns, and the extent to which sexual discrimination has become embedded in the cultural values that form the basis of organizational cultures. Gherardi (1995: 12) criticizes those who still suggest that the linkages between gender and culture have yet to be properly developed, suggesting that 'common sense' will tell anybody that organizational cultures are 'strongly gendered' because organizations themselves are gendered. As a starting point in this research we build upon the works of Alvesson and

Due Billing (1992), Acker (1990, 1992) and Mills (1988) who so convincingly argue the importance of formal organizations in producing and reproducing gendered structures and processes. To say that cultures can be characterized as 'masculine' (i.e. individualistic, competitive and rational), or that organizations are becoming 'feminized' (i.e. collective, caring and connected), does not, however, clarify the extent to which organizations differentially encourage gender-specific attitudes and behaviours and subsequently hinder the accomplishment of a wide range of equity and anti-discrimination goals. These claims fail to clarify the specific behaviours and values that women and men are rewarded for showing, how organizations themselves socialize women and men differently, and thus help shape gender identities in society at large. In short, understanding the gendered nature of organizational culture requires a more in-depth analysis of specifically *what* types of behaviours and attitudes are produced and reproduced through organizational cultures and *how* embedded gender-based assumptions and values can both enable and constrain organizational members. This requires assessing the dualistic nature of gender and culture that examines not only the way cultures impose expectations on organizational members but also how organizations prescribe notions of 'proper' behaviours of women and men more broadly.

In the study described in this chapter we use a survey instrument to capture managers' perceptions of values that underlie individual thought and action in organizations. If organizational culture consists of the symbols, beliefs and patterns of behaviour that are learned and reproduced by organizational members (Strati, 1992), then inquiry at any level can provide insights into the aspects of an organization's culture. In fact, research on culture typically begins with a set of values and assumptions, whether conscious or unconscious, providing the explanation for observable norms, symbols and rituals, and the context within which they occur (O'Reilly *et al.*, 1991). Managers' perceptions of the values displayed by organizational members and rewarded by the organization can therefore be viewed as reflections of unconscious thoughts and feelings, or taken-for-granted beliefs which are a part of the ultimate source of these values, thus representative of the organization's culture(s) (Schein, 1991). And to the extent that a strong organizational culture can be a hindrance to change, revealing the discriminatory potential contained in an organization's culture can create the scrutiny necessary to suggest that habit, history and tradition may in fact be the primary obstacle to creating more equitable and tolerant workplaces.

In the remainder of this chapter we review literature on gender and organizational culture, report the results of a value survey of managers of Canadian work organizations that supports the claims contained in this literature, and finally explore some implications of these dynamics for organizational theory and change. In the following section we begin with a review of the mainstream organizational culture literature, highlighting the general absence of consideration of gender influences, and how gender can be used as an analytic perspective from which cultural phenomena can be studied. Upon conclusion of this section we hope to have documented the need for, and the benefits of broadening, the study of organizational culture to both identify and understand its gendered nature.

Theoretical background

The idea that organizations have culture borrows heavily from the works of cultural anthropologists over a long period of time, which in mainstream organizational literature often leads to culture being treated as an undefined, yet pervasive characteristic of society and organization. Allaire and Firsirotu (1984) make the distinction between culture as a socio-cultural versus an ideational system, of which the former views culture as meshed into the social system and manifested in ways-of-life and the latter as interrelated, but distinct from the social realm, located in the minds of culture bearers, in shared meanings and/or symbols. Similarly, Smircich (1983a) makes the distinction between culture as a root metaphor versus a variable. The former advocates exploring organizations as subjective experience and investigating the patterns which make organizational actions possible; the latter considers culture as a background factor, explanatory variable or framework influencing the development and reinforcement of beliefs. In either of these conceptualizations the opportunity exists to view culture, respectively, as either a fundamental characteristic of the organization or a type of structural contingency which can be managed to improve organizational outcomes. In mainstream organizational literature, the latter approach has been largely dominant (e.g. Crozier, 1964; Child, 1981; G.G. Gordon, 1991; Peters and Waterman, 1982; Pettigrew, 1979). This dominance is reflected in the way in which cultures are studied and in the prescriptions for change that may result. Therefore culture is typically seen as either an integrating mechanism that acts as a sort of social glue or an outcome of a variety of influence processes that struggle for dominance (Meyerson and Martin, 1987).

This chapter, rather than focusing attention on how to create or manage the 'right' sort of culture to improve effectiveness, directs attention to the privileging of certain values and ways of behaving that often create an unwelcome environment for individuals who do not fit with existing cultural beliefs and practices. Underlying our approach are the beliefs that there is not one type of organizational culture that is suitable for all organizations, and that organizational culture can be changed because it represents a particular set of conventions or rules, many of which are gender-based (Mills, 1988). If gender itself is historically and culturally constructed (Wicks and Mills, 2000), and organizations contribute to the formation and reconstitution of these gender norms, then issues of gender and organizational culture are inextricably linked. Many organizational cultures are characterized as 'masculine' in that they typically privilege heterosexual masculinity at the expense of all other positions (cf. Connell's (1987) notion of hegemonic masculinity and Hofstede's (1980) masculinity index). Our desire to move beyond describing or categorizing cultures as 'masculine' encouraged us to examine the specific aspects of organizational culture that are gendered; that is, aspects that are inequitable to women and men and contribute to the construction of our ideas of 'masculine' and 'feminine'. These gendered norms are sometimes resisted (Bradshaw and Wicks, 1997), but nonetheless create a discriminatory climate for both women and men.

Gender and organizational cultures

Relatively little mainstream research has attempted to elaborate on the connections between gender and culture or analyse their combined effects on organizational actors, despite the calls for exactly this type of research for many years (Alvesson and Due Billing, 1992; Calás and Smircich, 1991; Hearn and Parkin, 1983; Mills, 1988). Or if it has, it treats gender in a static, unproblematic way (e.g. Hofstede, 1980) that reflects stereotypical notions of women and men (for instance in the nurturing/self-interested, acquiescent/assertive distinctions). Historically, organizational research has been largely oblivious to issues of gender, assuming either that organizational arrangements impacted men and women equally, or that only the experiences of men mattered since they occupied the majority of important jobs. More recently, however, it is becoming increasingly accepted that organization theory in general is sexist, either neglecting issues of gender and sexuality completely or treating them as variables that can be manipulated and/or controlled. The contributions of a gender-based perspective of organizational analysis therefore include revealing the ways in which organizations, through cultural mechanisms, create and perpetuate discriminatory practices and behaviours. More specifically, organizational cultures typically favour maleness, organizations socialize their members to adopt particular gender identities, and organizational practices conform to sex-biased values (Mills, 1988); clearly the issues of gender and organizational culture are inseparable. A consequence is that the concept of a job itself assumes a gendered structure, one neither uniformly distributed nor easily observed (Acker, 1990). The result of such arrangements, no matter how gender-neutral they are espoused to be, is often a climate that marginalizes the abilities, perspectives and behaviours associated with femaleness (or what departs from the masculine) and institutional arrangements that perpetuate inherently discriminatory cultures.

Gendered processes, as cultures are increasingly thought to be, create systems of relative advantage/disadvantage, agency/constraint, and autonomy/dependence in terms of a distinction based on sex and gender, contributing to institutionalized systems of equality and inequality. It is precisely these processes that form the core of gendered organizational cultures, and help explain how a wide variety of social institutions have incorporated gender (by accident or design) into both their ideologies and day-to-day practices. The use of gender as a perspective from which to analyse organization is somewhat problematic because of the ambiguity surrounding the meaning of gender, and how gender relates to the sexes. We use gender in a way that suggests that information about women is at the same time about men because notions of masculine and feminine traits and behaviours tend to be relationally defined. Gender-based discrimination therefore cannot be studied without examining how organizational arrangements impact women and men as well as the relationships between them. Gender, then, designates social relations between the sexes, or a set of social constructions that create ideas about appropriate roles for women and men (Scott, 1988). Gender and sex are therefore related phenomena, but gender refers to the social origins of subjective identities rather than biological ones. We use gender in a way that utilizes a broad system of relationships that includes sex, but is not solely determined by it. If we view gender as a set of differences between men and women (however they arise), then we typically see the experiences, beliefs and values of women subjugated to those of men in a way that creates a hierarchical ordering (Acker, 1992).

The essence of cultural approaches to understanding organizational phenomena, whether they be symbols, stories, rituals, interactions or attitudes, is to understand the day-to-day work activities of organizations. Although direct observation can identify formal structures and policies that dictate behaviour, more detailed study is necessary to identify how, or to what extent, both formal structures and informal norms are constructed in terms of gender and sexuality. Because gender is viewed as the manifestation of power relations that contribute strongly to an organization's culture, formal rules (because they are easily observed) are often fallaciously presumed to be the primary determinants or constraints of organizational members' behaviours. Despite the formal or rigid appearance of these rules, they are in fact negotiated and culturally mediated (Ramsay and Parker, 1992). One of the ways in which power imbalances can persist in organizations is through the obfuscation of their sources, with attention being paid to the more formal elements of the organization instead. The metaphor of the Saturn's rings phenomenon appears to be an apt one in illustrating how gendered premises can be omnipresent, yet invisible (Delamont, 1989). The components of an organization's formal system of structures and processes provides the illusion of rationality, objectivity and equity that form the 'dust' that comprises Saturn's rings. Because these formal elements are both easily observed and those the organization would feel most pressured to display, gendered values, rules and taken-for-granted assumptions are hidden, at least in part, by a dust (i.e. an illusion) of objectivity and gender-neutrality. When the formal aspects of the organization are so highly visible and socially desirable, they are often construed to be the primary determinant of individual behaviour in organizations, while cultural influences (being largely invisible and informal) remain unacknowledged and unquestioned. This type of phenomenon is operational when, for example, justifications are made concerning the lack of women in sales positions because of the presumed emotionality that in theory would make them unsuitable for these high-pressure, competitive jobs (Knights and Morgan, 1990), or the unsuitability of women for positions as steelworkers because they lack the toughness, strength and willingness to accept risks necessary to perform certain tasks (Livingston and Luxton, 1989).

Extant theorizing suggests not only that a cultural approach is important to understanding day-to-day workplace behaviours but also that gender-based assumptions are important dimensions of an organization's culture. An objective of this study is to identify a way to document the existing values present in organizations, and use this to suggest ways in which change can be effected in order to address the systematic and systemic inequities that many cultures produce and/or reproduce. We have therefore designed this study in an attempt to identify the types of values that are present in the cultures of work organizations, the extent to which these are gendered, and the extent to which organizational members find this problematic. This study therefore addresses the following broad research questions:

1   In what ways are the cultures of work organizations inherently gendered, reflecting sex-based beliefs or assumptions?
2   Do individuals perceive that values reflected in existing organizational cultures need to be changed in order to create more equitable workplaces, and if so what types of changes would be required?
3   Do individuals perceive that men and women are rewarded for showing different values in their behaviour in the workplace, and if so how do these values correspond with existing organizational cultures and those that fully incorporate women most effectively?

In this study we use Schein's (1991) conceptualization of organizational culture consisting of various levels, each of which provides its own meaning and is studied in different ways. From this perspective, there are three fundamental levels at which culture manifests itself: observable artefacts, values and basic underlying assumptions. The value surveys we use in this study assess culture at the middle level, the culture's espoused and documented values. These values are important aspects of culture because they frequently form the bases of taken-for-granted assumptions as they stand the test of time, and become institutionalized in the practices and mindsets of organizational members (Schein, 1991). This model has been so widely supported because of its view of culture occurring simultaneously on different levels, something that is intuitively very appealing. In order to understand how organizational culture can be gendered, one needs to understand the assumptions and values that provide the grounding for the more visible and tangible cultural artefacts and symbols.

If there is a certain amount of disagreement about defining what organizational culture is, there is even greater debate about how it should best be studied. Because the notion of culture is based on concepts borrowed from theories of anthropology, sociology and social psychology, a tremendous variety of cultural concepts have been appropriated by organizational researchers (Smircich, 1983a) and used for a variety of purposes (Meyerson and Martin, 1987). We believe that values (conscious and unconscious) are the place to start inquiry because they act as 'the defining elements around which norms, symbols, rituals, and other cultural activities revolve' (O'Reilly *et al.*, 1991: 491–492). Because values represent an enduring belief of something being preferable or desirable they can sensibly be viewed as internalized, normative beliefs that influence individual behaviour. At an extreme, when these values are shared by an organization, a unified organizational culture or value system exists. Our study therefore follows others who examine culture by focusing on norms (e.g. Cooke and Rousseau, 1988; O'Reilly, 1989) with an effort to determine what organizational decisions and practices are reinforced through ongoing social interactions. This view of a homogeneous or shared organizational culture is what Meyerson and Martin (1987) refer to as an 'integrative paradigm' – one that focuses on similarity and ignores difference. Operating from within this paradigm (which we do to a certain extent) researchers seek to identify things such as shared understandings of normative rules, common language, shared values and agreement on notions of appropriate behaviour. Our particular focus is on the deeper manifestations of culture that underlie behavioural norms and observable artefacts (similar to Barley, 1983; Schein, 1985;

Smircich, 1983b) with an aim of *understanding* the extent to which agreements on values exist rather than just *assuming* that this sort of agreement is either inevitable or desirable. We also operate within what Meyerson and Martin (1987) refer to as a 'differentiation paradigm' – one that focuses on lack of consensus and diversity. So in addition to looking at similarities in perceptions of values, we also look to see differences between certain groups (women and men) to reveal the tensions that may exist within an organization's culture, especially if the culture is as inherently gendered as our literature review suggests. Despite our interest in looking at differences between women and men in terms of how they perceive current and future organizational cultures, we resist the temptation to engage in the type 'body counting' that has been aptly criticized by Alvesson and Due Billing (this volume and 1997) and Calás and Smircich (1996). There is nothing necessarily important about the biological being of a respondent that makes us venerate the results of between-group comparisons. It is not the actual comparisons (or the statistical techniques used to make them) that have been criticized, rather the belief that sex says something fundamentally important about a person. In this study we build on Scott's (1988) definition of gender that is based on social relations between the sexes. Although this directs our attention to how women and men perceive their work environments, we do so with the aim of detecting the presence of differing social norms relating to women and men and the possibility of uncovering patterns of perception within a seemingly heterogeneous sample. Our study was therefore designed to incorporate aspects of each of the 'integrative' and 'differentiation' paradigms as they relate to the pervasiveness of particular values and the ways in which they are differentially held in women and men.

The remainder of this chapter presents the findings of quantitative data analyses of the values present in the cultures of a cross-section of Canadian work organizations. By identifying the specific values that individuals are rewarded for showing in their behaviours and the extent to which these limit organizations' abilities to create more equitable and tolerant workplaces, the results of this study suggest ways in which the underlying values, norms and ideologies of many work organizations are gendered.

Methodology

Sample

Because this study is concerned primarily with how individuals perceive the culture of their organizations, a sample was chosen that represented a cross-section of organizations from a variety of industries. Sampling was conducted using a cluster sampling technique that progressed in two stages. In the first stage, each of 36 participants attending a seminar on organizational change completed a survey. The initial respondents were from 27 different Canadian organizations, representing a wide variety of publicly funded federal and provincial government departments, educational institutions and crown corporations, as well as private sector companies from industries as diverse as insurance, chemicals, retailing and consumer products, ranging in size from 600 to over 20,000 employees. In the second stage, each participant was asked to collect completed surveys from five male and five female managers in their organizations. The resultant sample consisted of 362 completed responses, with approximately equal representation of women and men.

This sample provides sufficient size for data analysis to be performed within acceptable tolerances for error, and yields theoretically useful data from which the objectives of this research can be accomplished. We suspect, however, that organizations and individuals such as these may be an unrepresentative group because of their participation in a seminar on organizational change, the way respondents in the second stage of sampling were chosen and their supportiveness as evidenced by taking the time to complete our survey. The cultures of other, non-participating organizations may even more strongly reflect both tendencies to be discriminatory and non-inclusive, and a limited desire to recognize organizational cultures as gendered in ways that are inequitable and detrimental to organizational members.

Measures

The survey instrument used is SYMLOG (Systematic Multiple Level Observation of Groups), and was developed over several decades by Robert Bales (Bales, 1970, 1988). The questionnaire is based on 26 statements that reflect a range of values, each rated for frequency. The SYMLOG instrument has high statistical reliability and validity, hence one of the reasons for its use in this application. It also has demonstrated applicability for the study of organizational culture, socialization and leadership (e.g. Polley *et al.*, 1988 is an edited collection of 164 applications of SYMLOG in different organizational contexts) and an ability to be modified easily for particular research applications without diminishing its psychometric properties. In this study data were collected from each respondent under the following customized scenarios:

1   The kinds of values currently shown in the culture of their organization (coded CUR).
2   The kinds of values that need to be shown in the culture of the organization in the future in order to create equity in the workplace (coded FUT).
3   The kinds of values women are presently rewarded for showing in their behaviour (coded RWW).
4   The kinds of values men are presently rewarded for showing in their behaviour (coded RWM).

The SYMLOG instrument was developed by a series of factor analyses that reduced the 26 survey questions into three broad categories or factors. These procedures have resulted in three dimensions that have consistently been found to be important factors in the understanding of interpersonal behaviour and group functioning. They have been labelled and defined as follows (Polley *et al.*, 1988: 5):

1   Dominance versus Submissiveness. Includes behaviours such as differences in how many people talk and share airtime, capturing such concepts as personal influence, perceived status and power.

2   Friendliness versus Unfriendliness. Associated with behaviours and values which are perceived to be bad (e.g. self-interested or self-protective) or good (e.g. equalitarian, co-operative or protective of others).
3   Acceptance versus Nonacceptance of Authority. Reflects the extent to which people are prepared to accept the restraints and constraints of what is generally perceived to be legitimate.

The purpose of reducing the 26 items into three factors is to simplify the process of interpreting similarity among and differences between respondents. This is a very popular data reduction technique used in business-related research where multidimensional phenomena exist. In studying a value structure of an organization we know that there are many instances of what outcomes or attributes an organization prefers, but oftentimes there are underlying commonalities that make it both easier and more sensible to talk about broader categories or clusters of values than a large number of small, detailed ones. For instance the three scale items 'popularity and social success, being liked and admired', 'individual financial success, personal prominence and power' and 'giving up personal needs and desires, passivity' reflect differing amounts of the broader factor dominance/submissiveness. As such, in the remainder of the chapter we will refer exclusively to the three factors that emerged as important behaviours and the values which they aim to realize.

Data analysis procedures

In order to address the three broad research questions guiding this study we developed a multi-level data analysis procedure which would detect differences in the values that organizational members perceive to exist in the cultures of their organizations. Each level of data analysis uses different statistical techniques and examines a specific set of differences in individual perceptions, resulting in an empirical depiction of the gendered nature of organizational culture. The first objective of data analysis was to explore the perceptions of respondents of the current culture of their organizations and the values currently reflected. The second objective was to assess the differences between the reports of the current culture and of the ideal future if women are to be equitably treated. The third objective was to explore the values that respondents perceive they are rewarded for showing in their organizations at the time of data collection. Finally, perceptual differences in the perceptions of male and female managers were explored to identify the extent to which individuals experience the effects of the organization's culture differently. All of these combine to demonstrate in what specific ways organizational cultures are gendered.

The ratings of all respondents ($n = 362$) were combined and plotted on a field diagram in order to assess respondents' perceptions of their organization's culture. Paired t-tests of population means were used to test differences between pairs of summary image locations (specifically CUR vs. FUT and RWW vs. RWM), with multivariate analysis of variance (MANOVA) and univariate analysis of variance (ANOVA) used to detect differences between men and women for each of the four final image locations and among the three factors of the SYMLOG scale.

Strengths and limitations of research design

Culture is a basic pattern of assumptions that helps form a set of espoused and documented values which become manifested in artefacts such as language, behaviour and feelings (Sathe, 1983). Cultural researchers are presented with one of many options with respect to how to understand the influence of culture, none of which clearly dominates; the choice should depend on the level of culture being examined, and the practical constraints faced by researchers and organizational members (Schein, 1991). Methodologically this research shares the potential problems of other quantitative studies of organizational culture, particularly as it concerns the appropriate level of analysis and definitions of culture (O'Reilly *et al.*, 1991). Debates about whether it is even possible to measure cultural values using quantitative methods have been stridently articulated (e.g. Rousseau, 1990), although there appears to be no consensus on the debate. We hope that this analysis reveals something about the systematic effects of culture, as many aspects of organizational culture are not easily accessible (O'Reilly *et al.*, 1991). Our focus on central values of the organization and its members is one particularly well suited to quantitative analysis because of the variety of instruments with which values can be reliably and validly measured. Recognizing the difficulties of using respondents' perceptions as a basis for analysis, we make the plausible assumption that these self-reported values are reflections of the deeper structures of basic assumptions underlying cultural artefacts and observable behaviours (Schein, 1991). Although much research has been criticized for examining individual perception (ostensibly because they are intangible and subjective), what is organizational culture other than what organizational members perceive it to be? In fact Ashkanasy *et al.* (2000) point to the usefulness of survey methods based on their ability to allow respondents to report on their own perceptions of reality, and not have this filtered through the lens of a researcher. Because attitudes and behaviour are influenced primarily by actors' perceptions of reality (Rentsch, 1990), the use of a reliable and valid survey instrument is extremely valuable to the cultural researcher, and should not be restricted to the shallower (ostensibly less meaningful) levels of organizational culture. Although survey research has been criticized for giving too much credence to what organizational members think and feel (versus what 'truly' exists), observational studies are themselves influenced by the values of the researcher(s) which determine, to a large extent, the way in which data are observed, described, classified and understood (Hofstede, 1980). Clearly there are strong arguments for and against the choice of any particular research method.

Additional sources of methodological debate surround the appropriate level of analysis for cultural research (Rousseau, 1990). The data used in this study is a type of 'pan cultural' data, the interpretation of which is susceptible to a 'reverse ecological fallacy' (Hofstede *et al.*, 1993: 485). By sampling individual perceptions of cultural phenomena (which by definition are holistic), we run the risk of interpreting these data as reflective of organizational cultures in general (or in Hofstede's words, treating social systems as king-size individuals). The primary problem here is how data collected at one level of analysis (the individual) are used to draw conclusions at a different level of analysis (a community of organizations) – a classic cross-level fallacy (Rousseau, 1985). Additionally we need to be cognizant of committing a reverse ecological fallacy so we can be sure in this study that we are actually finding out about organizational cultures and not just cognitive processes in the respondents themselves. Given the objectives of this research, the nature of the data collection and the survey instrument used, we are unable to analyse these individual perceptions while simultaneously controlling for differences between organizations, industries or professions. While recognizing the limitations embedded in this research design, our objective in this study is to determine the extent to which gendered elements are present in the culture of Canadian work organizations, and the potentially differing reward structures of women and men that result. Consequently we appropriately aggregate data across all individuals surveyed rather than conduct an equally interesting between-organization or between-industry comparison. Because all respondents are from Canadian firms, we have avoided the problems associated with cross-national differences, although there may be some variances attributable to provincial, industry, sector or functional differences that are not being captured in this analysis. The findings of this research must therefore be interpreted with an understanding of both the contributions and limitations of an individual level of analysis and a quantitative analysis of perceptual data.

Results

The three bipolar dimensions (dominance vs. submissiveness, friendliness vs. unfriendliness, and acceptance vs. non-acceptance of authority) are represented in three-dimensional space with directional labels. The three dimensions used in the field diagram are the factor scales that are used as co-ordinates against which the location of the images are plotted. Only two dimensions can be shown on the plane of the field diagram (friendliness and acceptance), so the location of the third (dominance) is represented metaphorically by the size of the image circle, with a large circle indicating a high average rating. Plotting the average scores of the perceptions of all respondents yields the summary field diagram presented in Figure 8.1, with average factor score ratings and standard deviations on each dimension presented in Table 8.1.

In the first stage of data analysis we examined these data for all respondents together, rather than attempting to make distinctions between any specific demographic groups. To examine the extent to which individuals perceive the cultures of their organizations to be gendered, there should be differences between the values women and men are rewarded for demonstrating in their behaviours (RWW and RWM) as well as between the perceptions of their current organizational culture and some ideal future culture that would more equally treat women and men (CUR and FUT). Ostensibly differences in either of these comparisons would give credence to the argument that the cultures of these work organizations contain gendered foundations that are perceived by a wide variety of organizational members, regardless of their sex. Each of these comparisons can be made using t-tests (matched-pair), demonstrating the confidence with which inferences to the population at large can be made about the extent to which individuals concur in their beliefs of these gendered aspects of

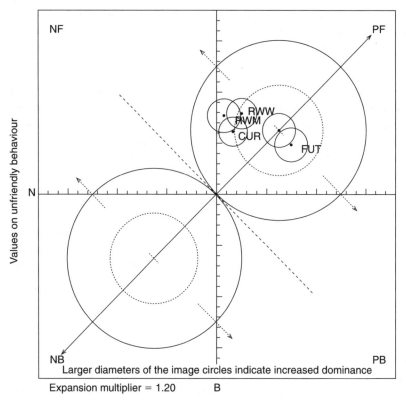

Final image locations
All respondents' perceptions

Dimension/ Scenario	UD	PN	FB
CUR	0.1	1.6	6.2
FUT	2.4	7.5	4.9
RWM	3.1	0.8	7.9
RWW	1.1	2.6	8.0

UD: dominance vs. submissiveness
PN: friendliness vs. unfriendliness
FB: acceptance vs. non-acceptance of authority

Figure 8.1 Summary field diagram of all respondents' perceptions of organizational culture survey images

Table 8.1 Cell means and standard deviations

Focus	Mean	Std. Dev.	N	95% confidence interval
CUR				
Dominance	0.155	2.851	362	(−0.140, 0.449)
Friendliness	1.448	4.556	362	(0.977, 1.918)
Acceptance	5.199	3.664	362	(4.820, 5.578)
FUT				
Dominance	2.476	2.520	361	(2.209, 2.744)
Friendliness	6.341	3.111	361	(6.019, 6.663)
Acceptance	4.147	3.391	361	(3.796, 4.498)
RWW				
Dominance	1.135	3.113	362	(0.814, 1.457)
Friendliness	2.268	3.921	362	(1.863, 2.673)
Acceptance	6.790	3.830	362	(6.394, 7.186)
RWM				
Dominance	3.188	2.840	361	(2.894, 3.482)
Friendliness	0.803	4.193	361	(0.369, 1.237)
Acceptance	6.598	3.798	361	(6.205, 6.991)

organizational culture. As the results in Table 8.1 indicate, statistically signific-ant differences ($\alpha = 0.05$) exist in both comparisons across all dimensions but one (i.e. there is no apparent difference in the extent of acceptance of authority rewarded in the behaviours of women and men). This observation provides support for the claim that organizational cultures contain embedded gender-based values that constrain the agency of women and men differently. By rewarding different behaviours in women and men, and recognizing that current cultures fail to be equitable and inclusive, the perceptions of organizational members themselves suggest a pervasive set of gendered norms that are sup-ported by the values and day-to-day workplace behaviours in the organizations sampled. In summary, organizations are not equitable places for these respon-dents. This interpretation of our results is based on two observations: (a) that women and men are expected to behave differently and display different values in their behaviours, and (b) that significant changes to current organizational cultures are necessary in order to enhance equity in the workplace.

The data presented in the summary field diagram (Figure 8.1) represent an aggregation of the entire data set, focusing on average scores rather than the variability between respondents' perceptions. The scatter plots presented in Figure 8.2, for current and future images, contain one circular image for each element of the sample. The wide range of perceptions which were averaged to produce the summary field diagram are thus graphically presented here to illus-trate the extent to which respondents consistently perceive values present in their current culture, or those needed in an ideal future organizational culture.

A second interesting observation is that although the images reported by respondents in Figure 8.2 for the current culture are widely dispersed, there seems to be much more consensus about the ideal future, reflected by a denser distribution of images. This difference is reflected in the differences in standard deviations presented in Table 8.1, suggesting that perceptions of an ideal future culture that treats women and men more equitably is much more consistently

Current
culture

Values on accepting task-orientation of established authority

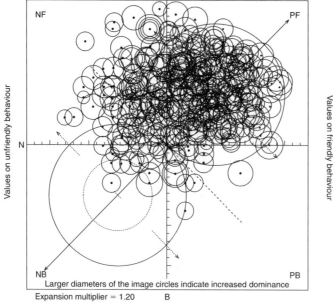

NF

PF

Values on unfriendly behaviour

N

Values on friendly behaviour

NB

PB

Larger diameters of the image circles indicate increased dominance

Expansion multiplier = 1.20   B

Values on opposing task-orientation of established authority

Ideal
culture

Values on opposing task-orientation of established authority

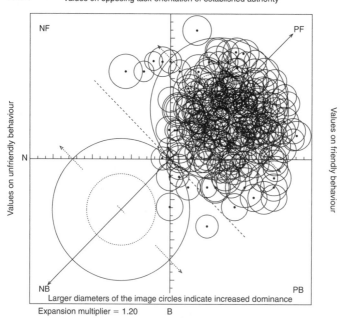

NF

PF

Values on unfriendly behaviour

N

Values on friendly behaviour

NB

PB

Larger diameters of the image circles indicate increased dominance

Expansion multiplier = 1.20   B

Values on opposing task-orientation of established authority

Figure 8.2 Scatter plot field diagram for men and women combined, current culture and ideal future

envisioned than perceptions of current organizational cultures. Although differences in the sector type and industries that comprise this sample can account for some of the variability in the current condition it is interesting to notice the convergence in the perceptions of the ideal future. The average scores reveal that the respondents felt that the kinds of values which need to be shown in the culture of organizations in the future are more friendly, more dominant, and less accepting of established authority than in the current culture. This observation suggests that most organizational members perceive a particular type of culture being one that would value women and men more equally. This finding was somewhat unexpected, given the diversity of the sample used in this study, but does reflect widespread belief that changes across all three value factors are probably necessary to create the sorts of workplaces more accepting of diversity. So, despite marked differences in existing cultures, there is considerable consistency in the belief that cultural change is required in the future if women are to be included and valued in their organizations.

Comparing women's and men's perceptions reveals other differences that relate to their workplace experiences. In order to determine whether the four images on the field diagram (Figure 8.1) are different for women and men across the three value factors simultaneously, MANOVAs were calculated, with the results presented in Table 8.2.

The results of this data analysis indicate that although there is no statistically significant difference between the ratings of the current culture as seen by women and men, there are significant differences ($\alpha = 0.05$) in all other conditions (RWM, RWW and FUT). The lack of sex-difference in the ratings of the current culture is consistent with both the variability of perceptions of current cultures, and the belief that respondents in general will perceive the values displayed in their organization's culture in similar ways. If women and men perceive their cultures in similar ways, what suggests that these cultures are based on gender-biased assumptions and values? This can be explained, in part, by the differences in how women and men rate their cultures under other scenarios.

For the conditions in which there were sex-based perceptual differences (RWM, RWW and FUT), ANOVAs were calculated to determine the statistically significant differences between the ways in which women and men rate the three dimensions (see Table 8.3).

The results of this stage of data analysis indicate numerous differences in how women and men perceive the cultures of their organizations. First, although there is no significant difference in how women and men perceive their

Table 8.2 Multivariate analysis of variance, male–female differences on ratings of image locations

Focus	F-ratio	Degrees of freedom	Significance
CUR	1.84	3,358	0.139
FUT	4.08	3,357	0.007**
RWW	4.51	3,358	0.004**
RWM	10.44	3,357	0.000**

** signifies p = 0.01

Table 8.3 Analysis of variance, male–female differences in perceptions

Focus	F-ratio	Degrees of freedom	Significance
CUR			
Dominance	0.02	1,360	0.09
Friendliness	5.18	1,360	0.02*
Acceptance	0.19	1,360	0.66
FUT			
Dominance	3.48	1,359	0.06
Friendliness	4.86	1,359	0.03*
Acceptance	5.52	1,359	0.02*
RWW			
Dominance	1.59	1,360	0.21
Friendliness	11.79	1,360	0.00**
Acceptance	0.04	1,360	0.85
RWM			
Dominance	3.03	1,359	0.08
Friendliness	14.63	1,359	0.00**
Acceptance	12.07	1,359	0.00**

* signifies p=0.10; ** that p=0.01

current cultures (CUR) across all dimensions simultaneously, there is a difference in the friendliness factor. More specifically, women perceive current cultures to be less friendly than men do. This again suggests an environment in which women feel less welcome or somewhat disadvantaged by what they perceive as self-serving, domineering cultures. Rather than simply an exercise in 'body counting', making this type of comparison gives credence to the observation that organizations, through cultural mechanisms, create and sustain environments that typically favour maleness, and result in practices that conform to sex-biased values. This is the essence of Kanter's (1977: 22–23) 'masculine ethic' that acts as an exclusionary principle for women by elevating the traits assumed to belong to men as necessary for managerial success. As such, the more 'masculine' attributes of being domineering, tough-minded and powerful are noticed more by women to the extent that they are taught or socialized to display different values in their behaviours. If cultures were more tolerant, gender-neutral or androgynous, then women would likely find them more friendly, resulting in smaller differences in this type of statistical analysis.

Second, differences in notions of an ideal future (FUT) suggest that women's perception is one that is more friendly and less accepting of established authority than is men's. More specifically, on two dimensions we see women and men differing in terms of the ways in which they believe cultures should be changed. This is particularly interesting because both groups ostensibly have the same interest in accomplishing this objective, yet arrive at different routes to change. This may be explained by the fact that gender, as a system of social relationships, typically sees the experiences, beliefs and values of women subjugated to those of men (Acker and van Houten, 1974; Kanter, 1977; Mills, 1988; Wicks and Mills, 2000). It is therefore not surprising that women perceive the ideal future to be one that is less accepting of formal authority, the foundation of the systems that have contributed to their subjugation in the past. The belief in the need for increased friendliness is mirrored in the explanation for perceptual differences in the current cultures; namely, that a movement is required towards more positive, friendly relationships in which individual expression is more freely offered and accepted.

Third, there is overwhelming empirical support for sex-based perceptual differences on the friendliness factor in terms of the values women and men are rewarded for showing in their behaviour. Once again we see differences in terms of how women and men perceive these values in their organization, with women reporting men being rewarded for relatively unfriendly behaviour and women for relatively friendly behaviour, and men reporting exactly the same patterns, but on a fundamentally different scale. That is, although there is agreement that women are rewarded for displaying more friendly values in their behaviours, the magnitude of this friendliness is perceived to differ between women and men. This finding is particularly supportive of omnipresent sex-based assumptions because our respondents perceive that women are rewarded differently from men in terms of displaying friendliness. These cultural conventions, however they may have developed, will likely continue to treat women and men differentially, with behaviours being rewarded to the extent to which they conform to stereotypical feminine and masculine traits. This type of value is especially problematic for women because significant perceptual differences permeate all four cultural scenarios measured in this study. Regardless of formal policies and practices that may be in place in organizations, there remains widespread belief in both the presence and desirability of expecting women to be friendlier (ostensibly more womanly) than men.

In summary, the results of this data analysis provide strong support for the claims that organizational cultures are strongly gendered. Based on a diverse sample of managers from a wide variety of Canadian work organizations, the findings of this study indicate that organizational cultures privilege stereotypically masculine values at the expense of feminine ones. That is, discriminatory practices are alive and well in Canadian work organizations despite anti-discrimination and employment equity public policy. Additionally there is broad support for the need to change existing cultures in order to create more equitable and tolerant workplaces. These findings illustrate the impact of gendered assumptions and beliefs that oftentimes operate so invisibly that their presence and effect are rarely questioned. Our very strong statistical results show the severity of these problems, the specific values and behaviours that unfairly discriminate, and the particular change agendas required in order to create a more equitable workplace.

Implications

Assumptions and values form the basis of an organization's culture(s), and as such are extremely important to the understanding of day-to-day workplace behaviours. An important finding of our study is that current cultures are perceived to be less than ideal in terms of the equitable treatment of women and men. The ideal future is envisioned as much friendlier, more dominant and less accepting of established authority than in current cultures. The descriptive adjectives which describe this location on a field diagram are 'well-balanced', 'many-talented', 'inspirational' and 'highly integrated', in contrast to the current cultures which are characterized as largely 'rationalistic', 'task-oriented' and 'analytic'.[1] This suggests that, on average, current cultural values in these Canadian organizations can be described as largely consistent with a 'masculine ethic', a result that is not surprising and is consistent with descriptions of our patriarchal world (Dodson Gray, 1982). As reflected in the literature review, others have described organizations as 'gendered' in that they are dominated by masculine values and perspectives. They have had, however, very little empirical data to support their contentions, nor have they shown how these are manifest in the behaviours and practices of organizations, or specified changes required to redress discriminatory practices. The findings of this study provide this empirical support, and through the identification of desired cultural changes that will promote the equitable treatment of women and men, suggest a more desirable future for these organizations and their members, both women and men alike.

The ideal future is apparently quite a different world according to the managers surveyed in this study. The adjectives which describe this future as not stereotypically feminine values, rather ones such as 'well-balanced' and 'highly-integrated'. This suggests that the ideal future seems to value a diversity of perspectives rather than reversing the privileging of masculine and feminine. This finding is in direct opposition to the exhortations of Martin (1994) and Fondas (1997) that either call for increased 'feminization' of organization and management, suggest its absence is detrimental to organizations, or assert that is has already happened. Men and women do in fact see this ideal future quite differently from one another in statistical terms, although one can see that the general direction of the future is similar for both groups. When thinking about diversity in organizations and the equitable treatment of women and men (and other underrepresented groups), the future image for all respondents appears to represent an optimum location to value diversity.

One consequence of these types of gendered cultures is the systematic privileging of typically 'masculine' values over characteristically feminine ones in ways that women and men alike seem unsatisfied with. Both in terms of how organizational members think cultures should be and what they are currently rewarded for doing, our findings suggest that formal organizations are the sites of harmful cultural practices that unfairly discriminate against men not displaying 'masculine' traits and characteristics, and women 'feminine' ones. The nature of our research design prevents us from making processual claims about the cultural practices that give rise to the reproduction of gendered practices. But because we produce culture through ongoing interaction it is important to be able to document the stereotypes and expectations that organizational members encounter, even if they are not static (Schein, 2000). Given the research design we have chosen, we cannot say how current cultures got to be the way they are. This type of finding could only be discovered through an observational and/or interview study, which we chose not to perform because our primary concern was documenting the specific ways in which cultures are experienced in gendered terms. To be able reliably to assert that organizational cultures are gendered because they (a) are widely understood to be inequitable for women and men and (b) reward women and men for showing different values in their behaviour, a quantitative research design was necessary. The trade-off we made is that the processes by which cultural conventions were formed and institutionalized remain unclear. Our findings do, however, show that organizational cultures continually reproduce notions of women and men, helping its members understand 'proper' attitudes and behaviours (Helms Mills and Mills, 2000). Change, in order to enhance equity between women and men, therefore appears to require a shift in these values towards ones which are more valuing of diversity, specifically more friendly and less accepting of formal authority. These findings are significant because of the prescriptions for change embedded in them. More specifically, all respondents agreed on the gendered nature of organizational culture and in the changes necessary to create a more balanced organizational culture. Gendered cultures have persisted despite a great deal of legislation and consciousness-raising regarding equal opportunity, suggesting the presence of deeply held assumptions and values which more tacitly guide individual behaviour in ways that inhibit change.

Several organizational implications are suggested by these data. First, existing efforts to problematize the discourse on culture, and to challenge the dominance of notions that cultures are inherently gender-neutral, are supported by our findings. The pervasiveness of a masculine ethic is illustrated, and the entrenched nature of these gendered values is reflected. In-depth research on the gendered nature of organizational cultures being carried out through observational studies is clearly required (e.g. Gherardi, 1995; Mills, 1994), and the data suggest that the dynamics go well beyond the single organization in a particular industry. We are therefore not content merely to identify the particular discriminatory practices embedded in organizational cultures, and point to change agendas that make sense in theory only. As Schein (2000) suggests, it is impossible for a single study to identify both the desired changes in organizational cultures and determine what underlying assumptions might enable or constrain organizational adoption of these norms. We therefore propose an investigation of cultural values as a complement to participative studies of cultural processes.

Second, implications of these findings for change are suggested as a result of identifying the cultural mechanisms based on gendered assumptions and values that can create and perpetuate discriminatory practices. The respondents in this study reflect the need for change in terms of the values they believe their organizations will be required to display if women and men are to be equitably treated. They also indicate that current reward structures are working to actually reinforce the status quo, which for the most part privileges masculine values over feminine ones, rather than acting as a force for change. Conceptualizations of culture based on assumptions that values are deep and resistant to change, and that culture is largely taken for granted, invisible and preconscious (Schein, 1985) are important to reflect upon when discussing cultural change. The meaning systems which are reflected in gendered cultures logically affect the issues individuals think about, how problems are framed, the specific change strategies that are developed, and how they are implemented (Marshall and McLean, 1985). Thus while change is clearly called for, whether couched in terms of individuals' view of an ideal future or that of anti-discrimination legislation, the ways in which change can be effected are extremely problematic and thus require a sensitivity to the forces sustaining stability and reinforcing the status quo (Bradshaw and Wicks, 1995). What of course cannot be captured by this type of research are the existing power relations in organizational cultures, and how patriarchal values work to the benefit of some, and concomitantly at the expense of others. A certain degree of pessimism about the possibility of change seems appropriate when the embeddedness of the status quo and the relationship between larger socio-cultural influences and organizational dynamics are considered. Because gender does not operate uniformly, and gender is itself a cultural construction, we will expect to see differences between cultures as a result of the struggles for power within the various discursive fields of organizations (Ramsay and Parker, 1992). Although organizations do reflect the historical dominance of masculine principles, they do not necessary reflect a uniformly coherent pattern in society in general. And because of this, there is always the possibility for change of a more localized nature rooted in the diversity of individuals in society.

Third, these data help us understand why women talk about the chilly climate they often experience in the workplace. Metaphors portraying women as prisoners of men's dreams (S. Gordon, 1991) or as travellers in a male world (Marshall, 1984) are easier to understand when one looks at the values perceived to exist in the cultures of these Canadian work organizations. What we also find, however, is that men are similarly rewarded, and both women and men in fact may have little choice but to conform to existing (gendered) values (Mills, 1988). Thus both men and women may be suffering from being trapped by dominant organizational cultural conventions, illustrating how gender as an analytical framework necessarily involves both women and men simultaneously. The findings of this study show both women and men calling for an ideal future that is more tolerant of diversity. To advocate the concomitant study of gender and culture we therefore reinforce the connections between the two, suggesting that both formal structures and policies and cultural norms act as constraints on agency, yet local conditions result in different manifestations of the gender-based inequalities present in most organizations.

We hope that the findings of this study, in addition to the growing body of research using a variety of observational methodologies, help support future research in gender and culture by demonstrating that conceptualizations of culture necessarily involve gender considerations. By drawing attention to the gendered nature of organizational cultures we see the need to extend the discussions of gender, sexuality and culture by examining the interactions between historical and cultural influences, and organizational structures and processes. Because cultural influences permeate the lives of individuals, it is unrealistic to expect that they will not in turn influence organizational practices. A dynamic approach to understanding organizational culture (Hatch, 1993) is likely a suitable one to use in order to see specifically how the attitudes, values, artefacts and symbols that constitute culture are created and sustained, and how gender plays a role in the processes of realization, symbolization, interpretation and manifestation. In recognition of this, the impact of such influences on organizational structures and processes becomes an important area of study, along with the effects of these on women and men alike.

Note

1 A set of descriptive adjectives characterizing final image locations has been developed in order to better interpret and describe the sets of values observed. The adjectives used in this chapter are excerpted from this set (Polley *et al.*, 1988: 81).

References

Acker, J. (1990). Hierarchies, jobs, bodies: a theory of gendered organizations. *Gender and Society*, 4(2): 139–158.

Acker, J. (1992). Gendering organizational theory. In A.J. Mills and P. Tancred (eds), *Gendering Organizational Analysis* (pp. 248–260). Newbury Park, CA: Sage.

Acker, J. and van Houten, D.R. (1974). Differential recruitment and control: the sex structuring of organizations. *Administrative Science Quarterly*, 9(2): 152–163.

Allaire, Y. and Firsirotu, M.E. (1984). Theories of organizational culture. *Organization Studies*, 5(3): 193–226.

Alvesson, M. and Due Billing, Y. (1992). Gender and organization: towards a differentiated understanding. *Organization Studies*, 13(2): 73–102.

Alvesson, M. and Due Billing, Y. (1997). *Understanding Gender and Organization*. London: Sage.

Ashkanasy, N.M., Broadfoot, L.E. and Falkus, S. (2000). Questionnaire measures of organizational culture. In N.M. Ashkanasy *et al.* (eds), *Handbook of Organizational Culture and Climate* (pp. 131–146). Thousand Oaks, CA: Sage.

Bales, R. (1970). *Personality and Interpersonal Behavior*. New York: Holt, Rinehart & Winston.

Bales, R. (1988). *Overview of the SYMLOG System: Measuring and Changing Behavior in Groups*. San Diego, CA: SYMLOG Consulting Group.

Barley, S. (1983). Semiotics and the study of occupational and organizational cultures. *Administrative Science Quarterly*, 28: 393–413.

Bradshaw, P. and Wicks, D. (1995). The oppression of women in Canada: from denial to awareness to resistance. In S.E. Nancoo and S. Ramcharan (eds), *Canadian Diversity: 2000 and Beyond*. Mississauga, Ontario: Canadian Educators' Press.

Bradshaw, P. and Wicks, D. (1997). Women in the academy: cycles of resistance and compliance. In P. Prasad, A. Mills, M. Elmes and A. Prasad (eds), *Managing the Organizational Melting Pot: Dilemmas of Workplace Diversity* (pp. 199–225). Thousand Oaks, CA: Sage.

Calás, M.B. and Smircich, L. (1991). Voicing seduction to silence leadership. *Organization Studies*, 12(4): 567–602.

Calás, M.B. and Smircich, L. (1996). From the 'women's' point of view: feminist approaches to organization studies. In S.R. Clegg, C. Hardy and W.R. Nord (eds), *Handbook of Organization Studies* (pp. 218–257). London: Sage.

Child, J. (1981). Culture, contingency and capital in the cross national study of organizations. In L.L. Cummings and B.M. Staw (eds), *Research in Organizational Behaviour* (Vol. 3, pp. 303–356). Greenwich, CT: JAI Press.

Connell, R.W. (1987). *Gender and Power: Society, the Person and Sexual Politics*. Stanford, CA: Stanford University Press.

Cooke, R. and Rousseau, D. (1988). Behavioral norms and expectations: a quantitative approach to the assessment of organizational culture. *Group and Organization Studies*, 13: 245–273.

Crozier, M. (1964). *The Bureaucratic Phenomenon*. Chicago, IL: University of Chicago Press.

Delamont, S. (1989). *Knowledgeable Women: Structuralism and the Reproduction of Elites*. London: Routledge.

Dodson Gray, E. (1982). *Patriarchy as a Conceptual Trap*. Wellesley, MA: Roundtable.

Fondas, N. (1997). Feminization unveiled: management qualities in contemporary writings. *Academy of Management Review*, 22(1): 257–282.

Gherardi, S. (1994). The gender we think, the gender we do in our everyday organizational lives. *Human Relations*, 47(6): 591–610.

Gherardi, S. (1995). *Gender, Symbolism and Organizational Cultures*. Newbury Park, CA: Sage.

Gordon, G.G. (1991). Industry determinants of organizational culture. *Academy of Management Review*, 16(2): 396–415.

Gordon, S. (1991). *Prisoners of Men's Dreams*. Boston, MA: Little, Brown & Company.

Hatch, M.J. (1993). The dynamics of organizational culture. *Academy of Management Review*, 18(4): 657–693.

Hearn, J. and Parkin, P.W. (1983). Gender and organizations: a selective review and a critique of a neglected area. *Organization Studies*, 4(3): 219–242.

Helms Mills, J.C. and Mills, A.J. (2000). Rules, sensemaking, formative contexts, and discourse in the gendering of organizational culture. In N.M. Ashkanasy *et al.* (eds), *Handbook of Organizational Culture and Climate* (pp. 55–70). Thousand Oaks, CA: Sage.

Hofstede, G. (1980). *Culture's Consequences: International Differences in Work-Related Values*. Beverly Hills, CA: Sage.

Hofstede, G., Bond, M.H. and Luk, C. (1993). Individual perceptions of organizational cultures: a methodological treatise on levels of analysis. *Organization Studies*, 14(4): 483–503.

Kanter, R.M. (1977). *Men and Women of the Corporation*. New York, NY: Basic Books.

Knights, D. and Morgan, G. (1990). Management and control in sales forces: a case study from the labour process of life insurance. *Work, Employment and Society*, 4(3): 369–389.

Livingston, D.W. and Luxton, M. (1989). Gender consciousness at work: modification of the male breadwinner norm among steelworkers and their spouses. *Canadian Review of Sociology and Anthropology*, 26(6): 240–275.

Maier, M. (1991). Evolving paradigms of management in organizations: a gendered analysis. *Journal of Management Systems*, 3(4): 147–169.

Marshall, J. (1984). *Women Managers: Travellers in a Male World*. Chichester: John Wiley & Sons.

Marshall, J. and McLean, A. (1985). Exploring organizational culture as a route to organizational change. In V. Hammond (ed.), *Current Research in Management*. London: Frances Pinter.

Martin, J. (1990). Deconstructing organizational taboos: the suppression of gender conflict in organizations. *Organization Science*, 1(4): 339–359.

Martin, P.Y. (1994). Bringing women in, keeping women down. *Journal of Contemporary Ethnography*, 23(2): 150–184.

Meyerson, D. and Martin, J. (1987). Cultural change: an integration of three different views. *Journal of Management Studies*, 24(6): 623–647.

Mills, A.J. (1988). Organization, gender, and culture. *Organization Studies*, 9: 351–369.

Mills, A.J. (1994). The gendering of organizational culture: social and organizational discourses in the making of British Airways. *Proceedings of the Annual Conference of the Administrative Sciences Association of Canada. Women in Management Division*, 15(11): 11–20.

Mumby, D. and Putnam, L. (1992). The politics of emotion: a feminist reading of bounded rationality. *Academy of Management Review*, 17(3): 465–486.

O'Reilly, C.A. (1989). Corporations, culture, and commitment: motivation and social control in organizations. *California Management Review*, 31(4): 9–25.

O'Reilly, C.A., Chatman, J. and Caldwell, D.F. (1991). People and organizational culture: a profile comparison approach to assessing person–organization fit. *Academy of Management Journal*, 34(3): 487–516.

Peters, T. and Waterman, R. (1982). *In Search of Excellence: Lessons from America's Best-run Companies*. New York, NY: Warner.

Pettigrew, A. (1979). On studying organizational cultures. *Administrative Science Quarterly*, 24: 570–581.

Polley, R., Hare, P. and Stone, P. (1988). *The SYMLOG Practitioner: Applications of Small Group Research*. New York, NY: Praeger.

Ramsay, K. and Parker, M. (1992). Gender, bureaucracy and organizational culture. In M. Savage and A. Witz (eds), *Gender and Bureaucracy* (pp. 253–276). Oxford: Blackwell.

Rentsch, J.R. (1990). Climate and culture: interaction and qualitative differences in organizational meanings. *Journal of Applied Psychology*, 75: 668–681.

Rousseau, D.M. (1985). Issues of level in organizational research: multi-level and cross-level perspectives. In L.L. Cummings and B.M. Staw (eds), *Research in Organizational Behavior* (Vol. 7, pp. 1–37). Greenwich, CT: JAI Press.

Rousseau, D.M. (1990). Quantitative assessment of organizational culture: the case for multiple measures. In B. Schneider (ed.), *Frontiers in Industrial and Organizational Psychology* (Vol. 3, pp. 153–192). San Francisco, CA: Jossey Bass.

Sathe, V. (1983). Implications of corporate culture: a manager's guide to action. *Organizational Dynamics*, 12(2): 4–23.

Schein, E. (1985). *Organizational Culture and Leadership*. San Francisco, CA: Jossey-Bass.

Schein, E. (1991). What is culture? In P.J. Frost, L.F. Moore, M.R. Louis, CC. Lundberg and J. Martin (eds), *Reframing Organization Culture* (pp. 243–253). Newbury Park, CA: Sage.

Schein, E. (2000). Sense and nonsense about culture and climate. In N.M. Ashkanasy *et al.* (eds), *Handbook of Organizational Culture and Climate* (pp. xxiii–xxx). Thousand Oaks, CA: Sage.

Scott, J.W. (1988). *Gender and the Politics of History*. New York, NY: Columbia University Press.

Smircich, L. (1983a). Concepts of culture and organizational analysis. *Administrative Science Quarterly*, 28: 339–358.

Smircich, L. (1983b). Organizations as shared meanings. In L. Pondy, P. Frost, G. Morgan and T. Dandridge (eds), *Organizational Symbolism* (pp. 55–65). Greenwich, CT: JAI Press.

Strati, A. (1992). Organizational culture. In G. Szell (ed.), *Concise Encyclopedia of Participation and Co-management*. Berlin: de Gruyter.

Trice, H.M. and Beyer, J.M. (1993). *The Cultures of Work Organizations*. Englewood Cliffs, NJ: Prentice-Hall.

Wicks, D. and Mills, A.J. (2000). Deconstructing Harry: a critical review of man, masculinity and organization. *LTA/The Finnish Journal of Business Economics*, 3: 327–349.

9 Reporting gender

Representations of gender in financial and social annual reports

Yvonne Benschop and Hanne E. Meihuizen

Introduction

The 1996 external financial report of Philips provides many representations of gender relations. Philips illustrates the slogans 'Let's be partners in success' and 'Let's be the best' (Plate 9.1) by pictures of exclusively male employees enthusiastically conversing and profoundly frowning. The slogans 'Let's put more

Plate 9.1 'Let's be the best'.

Source: Reproduced from the Philips financial report, 1996, with permission

Plate 9.2 'Let's start the day with a smile'.

Source: Reproduced from the Philips financial report, 1996, with permission

pleasure into leisure' and 'Let's relax on the move', on the other hand, are illustrated by pictures of male customers accompanied by smiling women to brighten up their leisure time. The slogan 'Let's start the day with a smile' (Plate 9.2) shows a man at home next to a toaster while a woman is lovingly feeding him breakfast, literally lifting the bread to his mouth. Women and men are portrayed here in traditional positions, with women symbolizing men's private lives as opposed to their professional lives. Opportunities to break through traditional gender images remain unutilized throughout this annual report.

This example of Philips inspired us to a cross-sectional research project on representations of gender in annual reports. Annual reports are under-researched documents (Hopwood, 1996). This holds even more when issues of gender, identity and organizational culture are concerned. Yet annual reports are interesting study objects in that respect, since they provide an entrance into the network of interrelationships between organizations and their workforces, investors, competitors, customers, suppliers, government officials, men and women (Kleinberg-Neimark, 1992). We consider annual reports cultural products of organizations (Aaltio-Marjosola, 1994). They contribute to the construction of an organization's values, norms and beliefs both at a symbolical and at a practical level. Annual reports have something to say about organizational culture, but cannot be seen as an accurate reflection of the way people engaging in everyday organizational activities experience organizational culture (Helms Mills and Mills, 2000). Annual reports are corporate publications, strategically planned self-presentations that enable organizations to create a particular corporate identity. Preston *et al.* (1996) argue that annual reports are a 'carefully manipulated sales pitch'. Mock (1992) agrees that annual reports have gradually become organizations' business cards, expressing their identity to external and internal contacts. We use the concept of corporate identity to refer to the symbolic, emotional and aesthetic meanings organizations hold for multiple constituencies (Schultz and Hatch, 1997). Our study of annual reports is directed towards this construed corporate identity; we are interested in how gender is represented in it. As various empirical studies reviewed by Lovdal (1989) suggest, exposure to gender-stereotyped media contents reinforces stereotypical perceptions, attitudes, and behaviour. Hence, inequality in the portrayal of men and women in organizations' annual reports communicates traditional gender relations and may reinforce differences in opportunities for men and women within these organizations. In this chapter we examine how these corporate publications contribute to the gendering of organizations through representations of women and men, femininity and masculinity in texts, figures, and photographs.

While the law prescribes which data should be contained in the accounts in financial reports, organizations have considerable freedom regarding the contents of the accompanying management report. Most financial reports contain information about the organization's profile, the organization's structure, and the compositions of the Board of Directors and the Board of Commissioners. Financial reports primarily aim at (potential) investors and usually underexpose the social aspects of the organization. Though not required by law, many organizations additionally publish social annual reports providing information on issues such as human resource management policies, social policies, reward systems, and the composition of the workforce. These social reports primarily aim at (potential) employees. Both types of annual reports serve as a dual communication instrument: both as provider of information and as representation of corporate identity.

In this chapter we analyse annual reports as formulations and interpretations of corporate identity, focusing on representations of gender in that corporate identity. The next section presents the theoretical frameworks used to link the central concepts of corporate identity, annual reports and gender representations.

Critical perspectives

The theoretical perspectives employed in this study are derived from three approaches to organization studies. First, we draw on the perspectives of critical organization theory to study representation and corporate identity. Critical organization theories question the neutrality of organization theory and the impartiality of management practice, critically investigating social processes of organizing, including processes of power and domination (Alvesson and Wilmott, 1992). Second, we build on notions about the nature, place, and function of the information in annual reports stemming from a critical accounting perspective. This term refers to the work of critical accounting scholars (see, for instance, Baker and Bettner, 1997), who view the public accounting profession's claims to neutrality and independence with scepticism. These scholars deal with the issue of social accountability and view annual reports in a broad historic and cultural context. And third, we use concepts and insights about manifestations and meanings of gender developed in feminist approaches to organization studies. Feminist theories recognize male dominance in social arrangements and articulate a desire to change these patterns of domination (Calás and Smircich, 1996). We are especially interested in feminist theories concerning the gendering of organizations (Acker, 1992; Mills and Tancred, 1992; Gherardi, 1995; Wilson, 1996) that study how gender is produced and reproduced in organizations. Although these theoretical perspectives differ in scope and research topics, they share a critical stance towards organizations as effective, goal-oriented, efficient sites. They all draw attention to the social, historical, and political construction of knowledge, people, and social relations and question the neutrality, rationality, and objectivity of the existing world (Alvesson and Deetz, 1996). We will build on the collective project of these theoretical perspectives that address power relations and processes of inclusion and exclusion in organizations.

Annual reports are not considered unproblematic statements about balanced accounts, but viewed as human products, social constructs, and hence as value-laden (Graves *et al.*, 1996). This emphasis on the social construction of annual reports allows us to analyse how they express and constitute organizations' corporate identities. Annual reports communicate more than bare facts, especially since visual design and imagery play an important part in shaping the form and content of contemporary annual reports (Graves *et al.*, 1996). Both in the United Kingdom and in the United States, authors have called attention to the transformations in annual reports, where accounting data are increasingly embedded in catchy texts and glossy visual design (Hopwood, 1996; McKinstry, 1996; Preston *et al.*, 1996). In The Netherlands, Hagens and Hassink (1995) observe a similar trend for social annual reports, and they point at the increasing attention paid to appearance and styling, using photographs and graphics to improve readability and aesthetic attractiveness. Hopwood (1996: 55–56) argues that annual reports have become a corporate design product used by organizations for the active management of their corporate identity.

Van Rekom (1994: 91) describes corporate identity as 'the total offer of signals an organization sends out to stress her distinctive features to her stakeholders'. He argues that such signals can be expressed consciously or unconsciously, pertaining to both strategically planned self-presentations and actual organizational behaviour. Van Rekom's conceptualization of corporate identity enables us to capture both the formulations of the organization's distinctive features and the social actions of communicating those formulations to internal and external relations, like managers, employees, stockholders, financial institutions, clients, competitors, government policy-makers, and lobby groups.

As stated before, we analyse annual reports as specific social constructions of corporate identity. Critical organization theories (Alvesson and Deetz, 1996) and postmodern theories of accounting (Nelson, 1993) call attention to the multiplicity of corporate identities. The two types of annual reports strategically project their construction of corporate identity for different audiences with different interests. Financial reports aim primarily at (potential) investors and financial analysts, who are mainly interested in the companies' future financial affairs. Corporate identities represented in these reports tend to radiate financial solidity and prosperity. Social reports, on the other hand, aim primarily at employees interested in the organization's social climate and their personal quality of labour. Corporate identities represented in social reports may stress the organization's appreciation of and care for its employees. Hence, our study focuses on representation, variation and differentiation with respect to gender both between and within the corporate identities represented in different types of annual reports.

While annual reports are a medium in which organizations publicly account for their affairs, the public accountability in these reports does not necessarily or explicitly stretch to gender relations. Since gender distinctions are deeply embedded in organizations' social relations and practices (Alvesson and Due Billing, 1997; Acker, 1992; Calás and Smircich, 1996; Wilson, 1996), however, annual reports do provide information about gender relations. Feminist studies have called attention to the significance of gender relations presented in annual reports for organizational practice. Hammond and Preston (1992) found that accounting in the US typically does not recognize the complexity and importance of power differentials and modes of exclusion according to class, ethnicity, and gender. Similarly, Van den Hoeven and Visser (1993) indicate that organizations' annual reports in The Netherlands are coloured by current (sexual) power relations and implicitly (re)produce traditional images of gender relations in texts and images. In their classic longitudinal study of General Motors, Tinker and Neimark (1987: 71) studied annual reports 'to monitor the evolution of managerial ideology regarding women over some sixty years'. Tinker and Neimark do not consider annual reports as neutral reflections of reality, nor as strictly controlled manipulations, but rather as vital parts in the social production of meaning about gender and class relations in organizations: as 'ideological instruments for promoting policies, beliefs, attitudes, and practices that perpetuate the inequality of women and other disadvantaged groups' (1987: 73). Where Tinker and Neimark emphasize the interconnection between class relations and gender relations against the background of capitalism as the 'big picture', critics of their work have questioned their emphasis on capitalist oppression, arguing that the systematic exclusion and sexual oppression of women and the organization of gender in general deserve attention in their own right (Burrell, 1987; Crompton, 1987). So, several studies show that although gender is not an explicit issue in annual reports, these reports do contain representations of gender relations that contribute to the gendering of organizations.

Analogously to the studies mentioned above, we expect no explicit referral to gender inequality in annual reports. Benschop's (1996) study in the banking sector, for instance, suggests that organizations do not acknowledge their (re)production of gender inequality. They often consider cultural norms and values about gender neutrality and equality as their organizational practice. Some annual reports may even proudly communicate an emancipatory image and present the organization as a woman-friendly employer. Benschop and Doorewaard (1998) show, however, that despite the pervaded myth of gender equality, gender inequality persists. The authors impute both the persistent practices of gender inequality and the dominant perception of gender equality to a gender subtext: the opaque, power-based processes systematically (re)producing distinct views of femininity and masculinity. We use this concept of gender subtext to analyse how representations of gender, both in employment figures and in discussions and portrayal of the workforce and clientele, contribute to the gendering of organizations.

These concepts from the critical accounting approach, critical organization theory, and feminist organization theory provide us with useful insights to conduct our empirical study of gender representations in texts, figures, and images in annual reports. Before presenting the empirical results, we describe the methodology and present some background information of the annual reports selected for our study.

Methodology

As stated above, we consider annual reports an entrance into the way organizations define and communicate gender relations. We explore how representations of gender in texts, figures and photos in corporate financial and social annual reports contribute to the gendering of organizations. Our analysis is limited to the annual reports as they are published; the actual process of producing annual reports, the decision-making process about which texts and images make it into the publication and the role of the actors involved are beyond the scope of this study.

We address the informal and often-concealed processes of gendering embedded in everyday organizational symbols, practices and routines as they are expressed in the annual reports. This focus leads us to examine representations of gender in annual reports not as reflections of gendering processes in organizations, because representations do not neutrally reflect reality, but as actively constituting that reality. We are interested in how gender is 'done' (Gherardi, 1995; Wilson, 1996) in annual reports, both in material inequalities and in discursive constructions. Our approach connects to the symbolic approach to gender (see also Chapter 2 by Bruni and Gherardi); the cultural representations of gender in annual reports produce meanings that relate to a symbolic gender order in organizations. We start with a quantitative analysis of the various modes of representations of gender in texts, figures and pictures. We discuss the implications of the quantitative findings and complement them by a more qualitatively oriented analysis that allows for more profound insights in the processes of gendering. We then interpret our findings in terms of the contribution that annual reports make to the gendering of organizations and will discuss how a symbolic order of gender is produced and maintained by particular meanings of masculinity and femininity.

Thirty organizations that have published both a financial and a social annual report over 1996 in the Dutch language are randomly selected from the firms listed on the Amsterdam Stock Exchange. The sample holds firms from a broad spectrum, representing the financial, chemical, construction, nutrition, publication, graphical, amusement, electronics, transport and retail sector. To analyse gender representations in all reports consistently we construct a score card with closed-ended questions. We use this score card on all 60 financial and social annual reports to obtain a consistent quantitative overview of the material and to compare the results between the financial and social reports. We examine texts, figures and pictures. Constructing the score card we build on studies on gender representations in television programmes, schoolbooks and learning materials, and commercial advertising. The studies by the Dutch Bureau of Representation of Men and Women (1995) in the media, Mottier's (1996) general guidelines for emancipatory aspects in language and illustrations in education material, and Zhou and Chen's (1997) categories in the portrayal of males and females in Canadian magazine advertisements, overlap considerably. From these studies we derive questions about women's and men's presence, quantitative representations, activities, occupations and dress, and about stage settings and locations. Finally, Michielsen *et al.*'s (1995) checklist for the construction of gender images in media and advertisements is also useful for our task of unravelling these images in annual reports.[1] Michielsen *et al.* make a convincing plea for playful crossing of gender boundaries and avoidance of gender stereotypes in favour of diversity. We employ their suggestions of alternative representations of gender to uncover the silences, the diverse representations that are excluded from the annual reports.

In the texts we search for direct references to gender and analyse the gender of the pronouns and nouns used to indicate people. Next, we look for discussions of issues and policies concerning the numerical presentation of men and women in the workforce, part-time work possibilities, childcare facilities, flexibility of working hours, pregnancy, maternity and parental leave of absence, career development, training and education, and inflow and outflow of personnel. We check if the texts differentiate between men's and women's access to and utilization of these issues and facilities. Our analysis of tables and graphs involves checking if data are provided on the number of employees, functions, salary levels, employment duration, weekly working hours, absenteeism, and age. If such data are provided, we examine whether they distinguish between women and men.

We study the visual imagery in annual reports, focusing on the relative frequencies with which men and women appear, on the roles, locations and clothes they are portrayed in, on their relative hierarchical positions, their relative physical positions, the relative size of the space they cover, and on who is talking. The total number of pictures in our analysis is 1,251; 518 of which are found in financial and 733 in social annual reports. The quantitative results for each type of report are obtained in four steps. First, using our score card we analyse each picture of people. Second, we group the pictures into three categories: (a) pictures with only women; (b) with only men; and (c) pictures showing men and women together. We study how men and women are portrayed individually and how they relate to others in the picture. Third, since we are interested in an overview of gender images within each report, per report within each category we compute the score percentages on each question in the score card distinguishing between male and female main characters. If the answer to a question is undetermined for a certain picture, the picture is not taken into account when determining the score percentages. Last, to shed light on gender images over all reports, in each category we drop reports without pictures in the category and average the score percentages over the remaining reports. Thus, we obtain weighted average score percentages over all pictures in a category, using the inverse of the total number of pictures within that category in each report as relative weights.

Having analysed texts, tables, and pictures of each individual report we check if gender statements in the text are consistent with the tables and picture material. Below we discuss how annual reports represent gender, comparing between financial and social reports.

The gender subtext of annual reports

Mainstream literature on annual reports deals primarily with balanced accounts and typically ignores issues of gender. The proposition is that annual reports are not about gender, and, if they are, that they are gender-innocent because they endorse gender-neutrality as the prevailing norm for addressing people. Yet gender is represented in annual reports in multiple ways, as studies from feminist and critical accounting scholars interrogating the gendered nature of accounting theory and practice show (for instance, Cooper, 1992; Hammond and Oakes, 1992; Shearer and Arrington, 1993; Oakes and Hammond, 1995; Broadbent, 1998). There are quite obvious and explicit referrals to gender and to visible differences between men and women, like the imagery in the reports that obviously features women and men. There are also implicit and more subtle gender distinctions in annual reports – for instance, pertaining to where gender is or is not mentioned in the texts of the reports. With the notion of gender subtext we are able to explore the more opaque aspects of gender relations in organizations, the symbolic representations and the various meanings of masculinity and femininity in annual reports.

Financial reports: presumed gender innocence

Texts, figures and graphs

Our analysis of the representations of gender in the texts of annual reports focuses on the referral – or lack thereof – to women and men. First, we examine the gender of nouns and pronouns used in financial reports to refer to employees, stockholders, and customers. We find that all referrals to gender in texts have been carefully avoided. Yet, the consistent use of the plural 'they' in texts remains a gendered language practice. Though it resonates the feminist critique on the repressive and exclusionary effects of using the masculine singular 'he' as a universal reference to people, it continues to silence very real gender differences between people by presenting them as generic categories of 'human resources', 'stockholders' or 'customers'. Next, we consider whether financial reports discuss the social policies of organizations. As Table 9.1 shows, hardly any financial reports mention such policies, and if they do they do not distinguish between male and female employees. As Table 9.2 illustrates, in

Table 9.1 Number of reports mentioning issues

Issue	Financial reports			Social reports		
	Not mentioned	Mentioned		Not mentioned	Mentioned	
		M/F together	M/F split		M/F together	M/F split
Part-time work	30	0	0	2	13	15
Childcare	30	0	0	22	5	3
Flexible work hours	29	1	0	18	7	5
Leave of absence	30	0	0	14	11	5
Career development	26	4	0	12	11	7
Training and education	22	8	0	6	20	4
Inflow and outflow	25	5	0	7	18	5

Table 9.2 Number of reports presenting data on issues in tables and graphs

Issue	Financial reports			Social reports		
	Not mentioned	Mentioned		Not mentioned	Mentioned	
		M/F together	M/F split		M/F together	M/F split
Number of employees	9	21	0	2	13	15
Functions	30	0	0	22	5	3
Salary levels	30	0	0	18	7	5
Employment duration	29	1	0	14	11	5
Weekly hours	28	2	0	12	11	7
Absenteeism	29	1	0	6	20	4
Age	30	0	0	7	18	5

graphs and figures more than two out of three of the financial reports show the total number of employees, but none distinguishes between the sexes. Hence, as in the texts, we find that graphs and figures in financial reports are silent about employees, let alone account for gender issues.

The workforce is clearly beyond the scope of financial reports, and firms do not recognize human resources in their balance sheets. Further, as Pfeffer (1997) argues, the benefits from social policies are often hard (or impossible) to measure or even estimate. Apparently, accountants do not give these intangible issues a place among the hard figures in financial annual reports. From a critical accounting perspective, we conclude that the present accounting conventions seriously limit the public accountability of financial reports.

Pictures

Texts and figures in financial reports, as we have seen above, provide hardly any information on the workforce. Five of the 30 reports under investigation do not represent people in pictures either, remaining silent about the human factor in their organization altogether. Our analysis focuses on the 25 financial reports that do show people in a total of 518 pictures. On average financial reports contain 21 pictures of people. Tables 9.3a–e provide a quantitative overview of the sex, role, location, dress, and setting of the main character(s) in these pictures.

Table 9.3a shows that most pictures in financial reports (71 per cent) show exclusively men, only 15 per cent show exclusively women, and 12 per cent shows people of both sexes. Further, men are more likely to be shown individually (61 per cent) then women (50 per cent) (see Tables 9.3b and 9.3c). Pictures of women accompanied by other women are rare: only seven pictures. We conclude that financial reports are reluctant to show more than one woman unaccompanied by men. We observe that 72 per cent of the pictures feature

Table 9.3a Cast composition in pictures

	Financial reports		Social reports	
	Pictures	%	Pictures	%
Pictures featuring exclusively men	366	71	397	54
Pictures featuring exclusively women	81	15	161	22
Pictures both men and women	66	12	165	23
Pictures of people with undetermined sex	5	1	10	1
Total number of pictures of people	518	100	733	100

Table 9.3b Pictures featuring men

	Financial reports		Social reports	
	Pictures	%	Pictures	%
Pictures of men individually	265	61	274	49
Pictures of men with other men	101	23	123	22
Pictures of men with women	66	15	165	29
Total	432	100	562	100

Table 9.3c Pictures featuring women

	Financial reports		Social reports	
	Pictures	%	Pictures	%
Pictures of women individually	74	50	116	36
Pictures of women with other women	7	5	45	14
Pictures of women with men	66	45	165	51
Total	147	100	326	100

Table 9.3d Pictures of employees, financial report

	Financial report					
	Pictures	% of total	% male	% female	% both	% undet.
Pictures of top or division managers	134	26	99	0	1	0
Pictures of other employees	236	46	70	17	13	1
Total pictures of employees	370	72	81	11	8	0

Table 9.3e Pictures of employees, social report

	Social report					
	Pictures	% of total	% male	% female	% both	% undet.
Pictures of top or division managers	61	8	87	10	3	0
Pictures of other employees	537	73	56	22	21	1
Total pictures of employees	598	81	59	21	19	1

employees (Table 9.3d). Men have a higher probability to be singled out for representation of the workforce in financial reports than women: the probability that a picture of an employee shows a man is 81 per cent, that it shows a woman only 11 per cent. The average relative proportions of men and women in the actual workforce, however, are 70:30.[2] When representing employees financial reports display a strong preference for male characters. This difference in numerical representation has to do with the standard inclusion of portraits of the top executives – virtually always male. Organizations apparently believe that accounting figures gain credibility when presented in combination with a portrait of a trustworthy male top manager, responsible for those figures. We observe that 26 per cent of all pictures in financial reports feature managers, who are almost always male. As Graves *et al.* (1996: 75) put it, 'the inclusion of photographs of the board members and officers in annual reports is ... ultimately a rhetorical strategy intended to persuade the reader of the credibility of the reports'. We add that this rhetorical strategy is gendered. Portraying male top managers in financial reports (re)produces a gender subtext, since it carries a symbolical message that associates masculinity both with the power at the top and with the organization's credibility. The purpose of financial reports is clearly not to provide an accurate representation of the workforce. We interpret this dominance of men in representations of the workforce as a construction of cultural meanings that include men as organizational beings and is very selective in its inclusion of women.

Having discussed the numerical representation of the sexes, we now turn to the way men and women are depicted. As Table 9.4 shows, men and women in these pictures tend to take up quite different roles. Whereas men are relatively more often depicted as employees (81 per cent of men, 57 per cent of women), women feature relatively often as clients[3] (31 per cent of the women vs. 10 per cent of the men). Men also have a higher probability to be portrayed in their job environments (89 per cent of men, 75 per cent of women), in their factories or offices, whereas women are relatively more frequently pictured on other locations: at home, outdoors, with their families (21 per cent of women, 8 per cent of men).

The biggest difference in how the sexes are portrayed is found in their clothing. Most men (83 per cent) are especially dressed for their job in industrial clothing or formal suits, and only 10 per cent wears casual clothing. Women wear industrial clothes or formal dress in 55 per cent of their pictures and are dressed informally in 37 per cent of the cases. Food company Nestlé's financial report provides a striking example of these different portrayals. All employees shown in this report are dark-suited male directors and top managers comfortably posing on the top floor of their office building (Plate 9.3). But the report also illustrates the successful launch of a new acne medication, with a voyeuristic peak in a bathroom mirror reflecting a clear-skinned, scarcely dressed woman (Plate 9.4). Though men may suffer from acne as much as women, Nestlé may not expect equally to impress financial analysts with an intimate shot of a man in this type of body stocking. The contrast between these two pictures could hardly be a more stereotypical contribution to the gendering of organizations. The male 'group of management' symbolizes the power of the

Plate 9.3 Management group, Nestlé.

Source: Reproduced from the Nestlé financial report, 1996, with permission

Plate 9.4 Différine, a new treatment for moderate acne.

Source: Reproduced from the Nestlé financial report, 1996, with permission

company, a company that reverts to the ancient marketing trick of invoking
female sexuality to seduce clients into buying products.

The analysis above shows similarities in how pictures of individuals in financial reports represent men and women. Both sexes, for instance, feature mostly
as employees. We also observe some striking differences, however. Men are
relatively more frequently presented as providers of goods and services, women
as consumers. This image seems a modern representation of the classic male
breadwinner–female caretaker pattern. Further, men tend to be portrayed as
professionals: the right(ly dressed) man in the right place. The pictures suggest
that lives of men are concentrated on, or even restricted to, their profession.
Women on the other hand hop from job, to shop, to family, to social activities,
conveniently dressed for all occasions. Women's lives seem to cover a broader
range of social circles. Though women are portrayed more realistically, leading

more varied lives than men, at the same time the differences in portrayal point precisely to what is keeping women from breaking through 'the glass ceiling'. The imagery entails a gender subtext. It reflects organizations' expectations that women get distracted from their careers by care responsibilities for family and others, whereas men can devote themselves entirely to their jobs, and hence be more reliable, dedicated, productive employees. This gender-specific role division perpetuates gender inequalities.

Next we discuss how men and women are portrayed when they feature together in one picture. When men and women are shown together, they are more often in a non-working situation than in a working one, and they are more often clients than employees. This is a strong contrast with the predominant location in the single-sex pictures. Hence, the work environment is presented as a sex-segregated one, where men and women hardly meet. The contrast in representation in pictures where only one of the sexes is represented, versus where both sexes are presented, is strongest for men. Without women, men are depicted as clients in only 10 per cent of the pictures, but with a woman in 46 per cent of the pictures. This differentiation in composition (re)produces a gender subtext in which the addition of a woman symbolizes man's private life as opposed to his professional life. Whenever a man steps out of the professional environment, a woman stands ready to provide for all his needs. So a gender subtext is underlying the pictures of men and women together, rendering the professional environment a masculine sphere and the private environment a feminine sphere. A clear example of this gender subtext is provided by the Philips' report we discussed in the introduction.

While, as Table 9.4 shows, most of the pictures of men and women together feature approximately equal numbers of men and women, men are in the majority in 26 per cent of these pictures, with women being in the majority in only 13 per cent. These pictures also allow us to compare the physical positions of men and women. It is remarkable that men take up a higher physical position than women in 47 per cent of these pictures; for instance, the man stands while the woman is sitting, or the man stands on a step while the woman stands on the floor. Women are rarely depicted higher than men (in only 7 per cent of these pictures). Further, men fill more space than women in 35 per cent of these pictures, whereas the reverse occurs only in 6 per cent. The highest hierarchical position is filled by a man in 28 per cent of the pictures, whereas this position is never allowed to a woman. And in 19 per cent of the pictures a man is talking, versus only 3 per cent in which a woman talks. These results suggest that in pictures with both men and women, men and women are depicted equally and silently most of the time. When one person is in a dominant position or talking, however, this person is most frequently male. Such cultural representations of tall, large and talking men that fill higher hierarchical positions together with smaller silent women, symbolize that men have 'more to say' in organizations. This mode of representation emphasizes the power gap and the differences in status between men and women: a higher or larger physical position symbolizes a higher social position; a lower position symbolizes submission. With the visual differences in physical positions, the financial reports reinforce classic stereotypes of masculinity and femininity.

A typical picture of a man in a dominant position and talking to a quiet,

Table 9.4 Portrayal of men and women in pictures, percentages

Pictures of main characters	Financial reports				Social reports			
	Men only	Women only	Men and women		Men only	Women only	Men and women	
	Men	Women	Men	Women	Men	Women	Men	Women
Role								
Employee	81	57	42	35	88	76	71	61
Client	10	31	46	53	4	5	12	11
Other	6	8	10	10	7	11	8	19
Undetermined	0	2	0	0	1	5	9	9
Location								
Job location	89	75	49	43	90	79	64	62
Non-job location	8	21	49	54	7	21	33	34
Undetermined	0	2	0	0	3	0	3	4
Dress								
Work clothes	40	30	13	7	26	14	9	7
Formal wear	43	25	39	34	45	30	37	32
Casual	10	37	36	44	17	36	50	57
Other	2	3	10	10	3	9	3	3
Undetermined	3	3	0	0	6	11	1	1
Talking	6	5	19	3	9	4	8	3
Majority			26	13			36	20
Higher physical position			47	7			30	7
Larger picture area			35	6			33	17
Hierarchically higher position			28	0			6	9
Number of pictures	366	81	66		397	161	165	
Number of reports	25	18	17		28	23	25	

devoted female audience is found in the brewer and leisure company Scottish & Newcastle report (Plate 9.5). The caption reveals that this man, posing outdoors dressed in a formal suit and tie, is the chair of the leisure division. The man is standing in bright sunshine, broadly gesturing while talking to a woman who is sitting near by in the shade with her back to the camera looking up at him. The text does not even hint at the woman's presence, she seems to serve merely as an anonymous decorative attribute to make him shine.

Our analysis above shows that pictures in financial reports featuring both men and women tend to represent classic gender-role patterns. A few pictures break with these classic patterns, however. Financial specialist Fortis's report, for instance, provides a picture in which a woman addresses a meeting (Plate 9.6). The full-page picture also shows three men at her side listening attentively.

Plate 9.5 John Dalgety, Chairman of the Leisure Division.

Source: Reproduced from the Scottish & Newcastle financial report, 1996, with permission

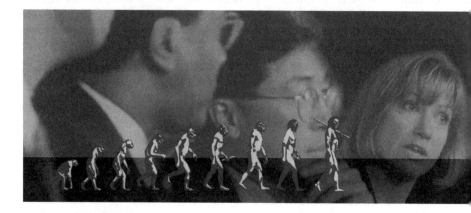

Plate 9.6 Perspectives for an interesting career.

Source: Reproduced from the Fortis financial report, 1996, with permission

Although the woman sits the furthest in the background and takes up the leas space in the picture, she is the only one brought into focus. The accompanying text discusses Fortis's management development programme and the need fo: versatile, flexible managers. The picture is cut through by a series of drawings representing the evolution from ape to *homo sapiens*. Curiously, the series are printed over the men in the picture, but stop just before the woman. This por trayal leaves the suggestion that Fortis's management development programme is responsible for the most recent breakthrough in evolution: from *homo sapien. sapiens* to the versatile, flexible, female manager.

Résumé

Gender representations in financial reports show a sharp contrast between the text and figures and the pictures. Texts and figures are silent about gender rela tions and seem to present organizations as gender-neutral sites. Financia reports carefully avoid any explicit referral to gender and, to indicate people use gender-neutral nouns and pronouns. The proposition that gender is not ai issue in financial reports is hard to maintain, however, when images and photo graphs in them are taken into account. Though these images show some simi larities in the portrayal of men and women, they (re)produce a gender subtext They represent organizations as male-dominated sites where men call the shots and women are distracted from their careers by extra-organizational tasks.

Social reports: pride and prejudice revisited

Text, figures and graphs

Like financial reports, social reports generally refer to employees and customers using gender neutral (often plural) nouns and pronouns. In the social reports o three companies in the financial sector, however, a gender subtext can be found ince employees in general are referred to in a gender-neutral plural way, but the masculine singular pronoun is used to refer to managers. The ABN-AMRO bank's social report, for instance, although proudly stating the increase of the relative number of women in management functions (p. 19), at multiple occasions refers to managers exclusively as men. Discussing the management development programme the report (p. 10) states 'Employees are responsible for their own careers, but their manager plays an important role also. The bank expects him to indicate which steps are required to develop good employees into good (top) managers ... In other words he has to look beyond job openings ...'

Obviously, social reports pay considerable attention to social issues (see Table 9.1). Like financial reports, however, most social reports are surprisingly silent about distinctions between women and men, even when such distinctions are as obvious as in part-time work, which is currently a predominantly female matter.

As Table 9.2 indicates, figures and graphs in social reports almost always show the number of employees, but only half of them provide the division between the sexes. Those that do show this division display a variety of ways to account for their workforce composition. Some reports, for instance, show colour bars in traditional blue and pink for male and female employees, while others use a rather neutral green for both sexes. Some reports put all the information in one graph, but others provide separate graphs for men and women so that the proportional representation of the sexes cannot be seen in one glance. The division of employees over age groups is provided in 18 social reports. In five reports this division is provided for women and men separately. Only three reports indicate how the sexes are distributed over different functions and function levels. Slightly more social reports provide an overview of the division over salary levels (five) and average hours worked per week for men and women (seven). Though 24 reports provide data on absenteeism, only four reports split them out between the sexes. Even when social reports do provide data on men and women separately, these data end up in a void because the texts hardly ever discuss the differences. The reports do not reveal the organizations' interpretations of those facts, whether they are content or concerned, whether the data represent intentional policies, or whether policy is considered to change them. Apparently, organizations provide data on gender differences as inconsequential trivia to readers of social reports, failing to express their responsibility for the underlying social impacts.

The lag of discussion of gender relations implies that our expectation that some organizations would use their social report to communicate an emancipatory image did not come true. Publisher Elsevier, for instance, employing as many women as men, does not mention emancipatory success in the text. Since Elsevier does not provide information on the division of functions or salary levels between the sexes, we cannot judge whether the equality between the sexes extends beyond numerical representation (i.e. whether an emancipatory image is warranted). A few organizations mention affirmative action policies aiming to enhance the proportion of women in higher functions. For instance, financial corporations such as ABN-AMRO (p. 18) and ING (p. 4) explicitly state that the composition of their workforce should reflect the diversity in the society and that they value the quality a diverse workforce will bring. Also, without referring to formal policy, some other reports proudly proclaim an increase in the number of women in formerly all-male functions or departments. The report of dredge specialist Koninklijke Boskalis Westminster (p. 4), for instance, does not mention a specific gender policy, but it does announce with some pride that 'although the ratio of men to women has hardly changed in the past years, 1996 has shown a remarkable change since two women were hired in technical functions among the weekly wage personnel: a third mate and a third mechanic. Among the monthly salaried personnel women have already been employed in technical functions for some years.' The social report of IT firm SIMAC shows an example where emancipatory progress is applauded on the shop floor. This report presents the results of an employee-satisfaction survey. 'The Maintenance & Installation Department was unanimous in their opinion that the best thing that had happened to them in 1996 was the arrival in their department of a female employee.' It is striking that these organizations, which have relatively few female employees, are paying attention to gender relations. By mentioning these events, the organizations emphasize their appreciation and pride of the small steps taken on the emancipatory road. Yet mentioning these women can also be interpreted as a message of little substance, since they are unique, visible exceptions in a male-dominated organization.

Besides the pride concerning gender relations that is sometimes found in social reports, we also found indications of prejudice lingering. Some social reports contain short interviews in which employees discuss their careers within the organization, including possibilities for future career steps. It is remarkable that women are cited commenting on the role of their partner in case a future career step would require moving residency (e.g. HBG (p. 10), ING (p.5)) whereas in interviews with male employees only challenging projects are mentioned, never partners. Apparently, whether (male) partners are willing to follow their female partner is considered doubtful, whereas (female) partners are still tacitly assumed to 'follow their man wherever he may go'. The gender subtext here entails an organizational message that families may get in the way of women's careers, but will adjust to the best interests of men's careers.

Pictures

We have discussed how gender is an issue in texts and figures of social reports. To study the pictures in social reports we use the same method as in the financial reports described above: the right half of Table 9.4 shows the results. More social reports than financial reports use pictures of people (28 vs. 25), and the average number of pictures per report is also higher (on average social reports contain 26 pictures, financial reports 21). Apparently, organizations consider pictures an adequate medium to communicate social aspects: they show their human face by showing a human face.

Compared to pictures in financial reports, pictures in social reports are more likely to feature people in the role of employee than in other roles. This result is in accordance with the social report's function to demonstrate the company's care for and appreciation of its employees. Chemical company AKZO Nobel's social report explains the purpose of the pictures, stating that its 'photographic material displays the individual employees' dedication to their jobs' (1996, p. 1)

The cover of the AKZO social report shows a female employee working in a lab-coat and concentrating on a machine to represent this dedication, while inside the report similar pictures are found of serious-looking men in combination with machines. Also, managers feature far less prominently in social than in financial reports (8 per cent vs. 26 per cent of all pictures). When managers do show up in pictures, in social reports they are even allowed to be women. The scarcity of pictures of (male) managers brings along a more accurate numerical representation of the sexes. Whereas in financial reports, female employees are strongly under-represented, the relative numbers of men and women depicted in social reports generally resemble the organization's numerical workforce composition closely. Wanting to appeal to all employees, social reports display a workforce both men and women can identify with. A clear example of the relative prominence of (accurate) representation of the labour force in social reports is provided by the financial institution ING. ING's financial report does not use any pictures of actual people, yet shows drawings of stylized human-shaped puppets that are usually sexless, yet sometimes equipped with male genitals, as insignificant links in a complex financial world evolving around technology. The only mammal in the report is ING's corporate logo: the clearly male lion. Texts and figures should suffice to convince investors of ING's financial well-being. The pictures in ING's social report, on the other hand, neglect technology and suggest that ING evolves entirely around its employees. In accordance with ING's workforce composition and its explicit policy for equal opportunities for all, the social report depicts 40 per cent women and 60 per cent men in a very similar fashion. Some reports, however, fail to acknowledge women's contributions to the companies. Tyre producer Vredestein, for instance, where 5 per cent of the employees are women, depicts 18 male employees in their job environment, but not a single woman. Like a few other organizations, brewer Heineken overrepresents women in its pictures, suggesting more balance in the workforce than there actually is.

As in financial reports, pictures featuring only one of the sexes depict men as employees and in job environments relatively more often than women, who are depicted relatively more often as clients and in non-job environments. Men tend to wear industrial clothes and formal dress more frequently, women informal dress, and again men do most of the talking. So here again we find a gender subtext in the picture material, where men tend to be portrayed more career-oriented than women, yet not as strongly as in financial reports.

When men and women are portrayed together in a picture in social reports (as in financial reports), their roles, environment, and dress style match rather closely. Whereas women in financial reports seemed to accompany men predominantly in the private sphere, in social reports men and women are predominantly portrayed as colleagues working together in professional environments. Although here too men dominate more often than women, this does not happen as frequently as in financial reports, and domination alternates more between the sexes. Women more frequently fill the largest area in the picture, yet still not as often as men do. A clear example of the relative equality and diversity in portrayal appears in Fortis's social report. The report witnesses much interaction between men and women on the shop floor, where men and women sit and stand, talk and listen, and give and take instructions interchangeably (see Plate 9.7).

Plate 9.7 Growth opportunity and real estate development.
Source: Reproduced from the Fortis social report, 1996, with permission

Surprisingly, Table 9.4 indicates that women fill higher hierarchical positions than accompanying men in 9 per cent of the pictures featuring both sexes, whereas men appear higher in rank in only 6 per cent. This result does not mean that women frequently rank higher than men do. Rather, male managers are portrayed individually, whereas female managers are portrayed amidst members of their departments. So, even though female managers may be rare expressed as an average percentage of pictures showing men and women, they appear relatively common.

Résumé

Our analysis of social reports shows that the gender subtext of these reports is ambiguous and complex. Various, sometimes inconsistent representations of gender are found in the different parts of the reports we examined. Gender relations may be proudly discussed in the texts, yet subtle expressions of prejudice and references to traditional gender roles occur simultaneously. Graphs sometimes account for the proportional representation of women and men, yet the social implications or relevant policies are rarely discussed. The picture material suggests that social reports represent a diverse workforce both men and women can identify with. The proportions of male and female employees shown in the pictures closely resemble the actual workforce. Further, though male employees still dominate more often in pictures showing both sexes, reports also show pictures where the reverse holds. Hence, although male employees still dominate the pictures in social reports, the reports regularly cross gender boundaries and favour differentiated representations of gender in their visual imagery.

Representations of gender and corporate identities

We now interpret our findings in terms of the implications for corporate identities. Corporate identity refers to the verbal, written and symbolic representations used by a company in its communication with various constituents (Gioia *et al.*, 2000). The corporate identity is not only expressed through carefully designed and actively managed corporate symbols but also encompasses self-presentations and actual organizational behaviour that are not so strategically planned. In that respect we argue that gender is done as a routine and ongoing accomplishment in the corporate identities of the organizations studied. Texts and figures in financial reports hardly ever mention people, let alone the issue of gender. When people do feature, they feature in a seemingly gender-neutral way. When it comes to pictures, however, financial reports lose their presumed innocence of gender. These pictures portray grey-suited men as organizational beings, while the occasional woman often serves as an organizational outsider, as an ornament or as a customer. Interpreting these results in the light of corporate identity, the symbolic meanings of masculinity and femininity entail multiple, even contradictory, corporate identities within financial reports. The reports send stakeholders textual messages about gender neutrality that are inconsistent with visual messages proclaiming traditional gender relations. The corporate identity captured in visual signals generally reflects male grey-suited, businesslike, reliable managers, who devote their lives to their careers. When women are represented in the corporate identity, the diversity of their lives is generally recognized. Yet they pay a price, either by featuring at the lower organizational levels or by being excluded from the organization altogether. The representations of gender in corporate identities are limited. Crossing of gender boundaries rarely occurs. For instance, representations of female managers and male customers are often excluded from financial reports.

In contrast to financial reports, social reports explicitly provide information on gender, discussing equal opportunity programmes or differentiating numerical data between the sexes. However, the texts of social reports usually do not clarify the numerical data presented in figures and graphs, so they end up in a void.

We argue that the corporate identities regarding gender relations in social reports are also multiple and contradictory: the proud comments on the increasing number of women occur simultaneously with the prejudices questioning women's devotion to their careers and the organization. And the pictures tell yet another tale about gender relations in the corporate identities, bringing a symbolic message of gender equality in which representations of men and women resemble each other quite closely: both are generally portrayed as employees, in job locations, and in alternating dominant positions.

So, organizations communicate multiple corporate identities regarding gender representations within financial and social annual reports. Yet not surprisingly, the most substantial differences in the gender subtexts of the corporate identities are found when comparing the two types of corporate publications. While organizations in their financial reports differentiate between men and women and the place they are allowed in the organization, in the social reports they open all positions for both sexes. Financial reports, directed towards (potential) investors and financial analysts, have a masculine connotation, reinforcing the masculine logic of accounting (Broadbent, 1998). A clear manifestation of this is the gendered rhetorical strategy of portraying male top executives, which associates masculinity with the power of the top, with sound financial policy and with the credibility of the reports. Social reports, addressing (potential) employees, have a much more feminine connotation, communicating values like the appreciation of and care for the workforce. The rhetorical strategy of portraying women and men in similar ways is gendered as well for it calls upon the feminine logic of care (cf. Tronto, 1993), to signal to the employees that equality matters and that the organization cares.

With the linking of masculinity to accounting and of femininity to care in their annual reports, organizations (re)produce traditional meanings of masculinity and femininity that serve to maintain or even reinforce the traditional gender order. These social meanings of gender contribute to the perpetuation of gender inequalities and hinder alternative meanings come to the fore. They build on fossilized norms that lag behind the current developments in gender relations in organizations.

Potentially, annual reports are a powerful medium to break through traditional representations of gender and to start accounting for the diversity in gender relations in organizations. It is a shame that this potential is not yet met, though the differentiated representations of gender in the social reports leave some room for future optimism. If organizations would actively search for alternative modes of representation they could break with traditional gender roles and stereotypes and even engage in playful crossing of gender boundaries. Yet this should be done with great care and acuity to avoid women being depicted as trophies of non-existing equality. It is important that there is room for diversity, variation and pluriformity in the annual reports' representations of gender, so that the multiplicity of the experiences and concerns of organizational women and men can be acknowledged. From our study, the lesson can be drawn that organizations need to be aware that annual reports contain inadvertent signals, messages and meanings concerning gender relations. The careful consideration that obviously goes into the design of the imagery and texts of annual reports should be stretched to gender relations, so that gender can be done differently and traditional meanings of masculinity and femininity no longer dominate these corporate publications.

Notes

1 The main categories in our analysis are 'women' and 'men'. We realize that with our choice of aspects we do not do full justice to the differentiation and variation within these categories. Other aspects, like class, race and age are also represented in annual reports. We have left these issues out of our analysis, because identifying them objectively solely based on visual information without textual elaboration appeared to be problematic.

2 Since we want to compare the percentages of women and men depicted in reports to the percentages of women and men working in the organizations, we have calculated the later. As far as provided we have used the data from the reports and obtained the missing data upon request from the organizations. We found that these forty organizations on average employ 30 per cent women and 70 per cent men.

3 Our data do not distinguish between different types of customers that belong to the different product groups represented in our sample. Therefore, in our analysis we concentrate on the role of customers as organizational outsiders as opposed to members of the organization.

References

Aaltio-Marjosola, I. (1994). Gender stereotypes as cultural products of the organization. *Scandinavian Journal of Management*, 10(2): 147–162.

Acker, J. (1992). Gendering organizational theory. In A.J. Mills and P. Tancred (eds), *Gendering Organizational Analysis* (pp. 248–260). London: Sage.

Alvesson, M. and Due Billing, Y. (1997). *Understanding Gender and Organizations*. London: Sage.

Alvesson, M. and Deetz, S. (1996). Critical theory and postmodernism approaches to organizational studies. In S. Clegg, C. Hardy and W.R. Nord (eds), *Handbook of Organization Studies* (pp. 191–217). London: Sage.

Alvesson, M. and Wilmott, H. (1992). *Critical Management Studies*. London: Sage.

Baker, C.R. and Bettner, M.S. (1997). Interpretive and critical research in accounting: a commentary on its absence from mainstream accounting research. *Critical Perspectives on Accounting*, 8(4): 293–310.

Benschop, Y. (1996). *De mantel der gelijkheid. Gender in organisaties*. Assen: Van Gorcum.

Benschop, Y. and Doorewaard, H. (1998). Covered by equality. The gender subtext of organizations. *Organization Studies*, 19(5): 787–805.

Broadbent, J. (1998). The gendered nature of 'accounting logic': pointers to an accounting that encompasses multiple values. *Critical Perspectives on Accounting*, 9(3): 267–297.

Bureau Beeldvorming m/v (1995). *Informatieve programma's: beeldvorming van vrouwen en mannen*. Hilversum: NOS.

Burrell, G. (1987). No accounting for sexuality. *Accounting, Organizations and Society*, 12(1): 89–101.

Calás, M.B. and Smircich, L. (1996). From 'the woman's' point of view: feminist approaches to organization studies. In S. Clegg, C. Hardy and W.R. Nord (eds), *Handbook of Organization Studies* (pp. 218–257). London: Sage.

Cooper, C. (1992). The non and nom of accounting for (M)other Nature. *Accounting, Auditing, Accountability Journal*, 5: 16–39.

Crompton, R. (1987). Gender and accountancy: a response to Tinker and Neimark. *Accounting, Organizations and Society*, 12(1): 103–110.

Gherardi, S. (1995). *Gender, Symbolism and Organizational Cultures*. London: Sage.

Gioia, D.A., Schultz, M. and Corley, K.G. (2000). Organizational identity, image and adaptive instability. *Academy of Management Review*, 25(1): 63–81.

Graves, O.F., Flesher, D.L. and Jordan, R.E. (1996). Pictures and the bottom line: the television epistemology of U.S. annual reports. *Accounting, Organizations and Society*, 21(1): 57–88.

Hagens, M.J. and Hassink, H.F.D. (1995). Trends in de sociale jaarverslaggeving. *Tijdschrift voor Bedrijfsadministratie*, 99(1179): 214–222.

Hammond, T. and Oakes, L. (1992). Some feminisms and their implications for accounting practice. *Accounting, Auditing, Accountability Journal*, 5: 52–70.

Hammond, T. and Preston, A. (1992). Culture, gender and corporate control: Japan as 'other'. *Accounting, Organizations and Society*, 17(8): 795–808.

Hatch, M.J. (1997). *Organization Theory*. Oxford: Oxford University Press.

Helms Mills, J.C. and Mills, A.J. (2000). Rules, sensemaking, formative contexts and discourse in the gendering of organizational culture. In N. Ashkanasy, C. Wilderom and M. Peterson (eds), *International Handbook of Organizational Climate and Culture*. Thousand Oaks, CA: Sage.

Hoeven, J. van den and Visser, P. (1993). De vrouw in het jaarrapport. In M.N. Hoogendoorn and R. van der Wal (eds), *Jaar in – jaar uit* (pp. 179–189). Groningen: Wolters-Noordhoff.

Hopwood, A. (1996). Introduction to making visible and the construction of visibilities: shifting agendas in the design of the corporate report. *Accounting, Organizations and Society*, 21(1): 55–56.

Kleinberg-Neimark, M. (1992). *The Hidden Dimensions of Annual Reports. Sixty Years of Social Conflict at General Motors*. Princeton: Markus Wiener.

Lovdal, L. (1989). Gender roles messages in television commercials: an update. *Sex Roles*, 24: 715–724.

McKinstry, S. (1996). Designing the annual reports of Burton Plc from 1930 to 1994. *Accounting, Organizations and Society*, 21(1): 89–111.

Michielsen, M., Celis, K. and Delhaye, C. (1995). *Beeld voor beeld: vrouwen in media en reclame*. Brussel: Ministerie van tewerkstelling en Arbeid en Gelijke Kansenbeleid.

Mills, A.J. and Tancred, P. (eds) (1992). *Gendering Organizational Analysis*. London: Sage.

Mock, H. (1992). *Financiële public relations/investor relations: naar betere betrekkingen tussen bedrijf, beurs en belegger*. Deventer: Kluwer Bedrijfswetenschappen.

Mottier, I. (1996). Taal en beeldvorming in leermiddelen. In Ministerie van Onderwijs, Cultuur en Wetenschappen. *Taal en beeldvorming over vrouwen en mannen* (pp. 63–73). Den Haag.

Nelson, J.S. (1993). Account and acknowledge, or represent and control? On postmodern politics and economics of collective responsibility. *Accounting, Organizations and Society*, 18(2–3): 207–229.

Oakes, L. and Hammond, T. (1995). Biting the epistemological hand: feminist perspectives on science and their implications for accounting research. *Critical Perspectives on Accounting*, 6: 49–75.

Pfeffer, J. (1997). Pitfalls on the road to measurement: the dangerous liaison of human resources with the ideas of accounting and finance. *Human Resource Management*, 36(3): 357–365.

Preston, A.M., Wright, C. and Young, J.J. (1996). Imag[in]ing annual reports. *Accounting, Organizations and Society*, 21(1): 113–137.

Rekom, J. van (1994). Corporate identity. Ontwikkeling van concept en meetinstrument en de betekenis ervan voor concernpositionering. In C.B.M. van Riel (ed.), *Handboek corporate communicatie* (pp. 85–121). Houten/Zaventem: Bohn Stafleu van Loghum.

Schultz, M. and Hatch, M.J. (1997). A European view on corporate identity. An interview with Wally Olins. *Journal of Management Inquiry*, 6(4): 330–339.

Shearer, T.L. and Arrington, C.E. (1993). Accounting in other wor(l)ds: a feminism without reserve. *Accounting, Organizations and Society*, 18(2–3): 253–272.

Tinker, T. and Neimark, M. (1987). The role of annual reports in gender and class contradictions at General Motors 1917–1976. *Accounting, Organizations and Society*, 12(1): 71–88.

Tronto, J. (1993). *Moral Boundaries. A Political Argument for an Ethic of Care*. New York, NY: Routledge.

Wilson, F. (1996). Research note: organizational theory: blind and deaf to gender? *Organization Studies*, 17(5): 825–842.

Zhou, N. and Chen, M.Y.T. (1997). A content analysis of men and women in Canadian consumer magazine advertising: today's portrayal, yesterday's image? *Journal of Business Ethics*, 16(5): 485–495.

10 Self in research

Hopelessly entangled in the gendered organizational culture

Saija Katila and Susan Meriläinen[1]

Introduction

There is no escape – the term 'feminist' is written across our foreheads – probably for the rest of our academic careers. We must admit, though, that we did something to deserve it. We are members of a rather easy-going academic organization. We have been doing research in the department for nine and eleven years respectively. During that time, we have felt that we were treated differently from our male counterparts. Our occasional claims of discrimination produced mainly angry and frustrated reactions and demands to prove our claims. The attempts to bypass our complaints made us angry and frustrated. All this operated as a catalyst for us to reflect on our own experiences and write a paper about the gendered discursive practices taking place in our own work organization (Katila and Meriläinen, 1999).

In this chapter, we will discuss how placing self in the centre of research – that is, seeing self both as the subject and the object of research – can be a meaningful and fruitful research strategy when dealing with the gendered practices of academic work (see also Bruni and Gherardi, Chapter 2 this volume). Even though we perceive that this methodological choice is useful in general, we maintain that it is even more useful when we are dealing with discriminative organizational cultures. There is ample evidence that different forms of negative discrimination exist, be they based on sex, ethnicity, religion, sexual orientation or any other axis of identity. There are, however, very few studies that show how people discriminate and are discriminated against in our everyday organizational life, and how this happens even in organizations that try to avoid it. One reason for the lack of studies reporting on discriminatory *processes* in organizations is that the easily accessible methods and techniques of research, like questionnaires and interviews, are seldom suitable for this purpose.

We will begin this chapter by briefly discussing some features of academic culture in general and its gendered nature in particular. We will also discuss in the first section how the gendered nature of academic work influences the professional identity construction processes of female academics and their self-concept and consciousness of their own abilities. This discussion is based on an action-oriented research project that we have carried out in our own work community (see Katila and Meriläinen, 1999). To give you an idea of the kind of data we have used in our study, we will present one of the stories described in our previous paper in the 'Storytelling' section of this chapter. With this particular extract, we want to show how we have contextualized the stories and analysed them. From the very beginning of our research process, we have perceived writing about the gendered discursive practices taking place in our own work organization as part of our own identity work, something which is both personal and emotional. This does not, however, mean that we are only dealing with our individual experiences. By embedding the discourses in the social situation and the cultural fabric of the organization, we are able to tell a story that is as much collective as it is personal.

In the latter part of this chapter, we will discuss our methodological choice of placing ourselves in the centre of research in more detail by analysing one critical review that we have received for such writing. We will show how the review comment vaguely touches on the classical scientific virtues of objectivity, neutrality and separation. And finally, we will problematize such criticism by highlighting its ambivalent nature. We will show how the perceived weaknesses of this type of research, such as a researcher's emotional involvement in the research process and with the members of the work community under study, may turn out to be its strengths.

Academic culture, gender and identity

When we became researchers some ten years ago, we had both just acquired a master's degree. We did not know much about research or science, although we had internalized its core values. We believed that a good piece of research is one that is neutral, objective and value free. In a similar vein, we believed that a good researcher is one who is rational and independent, one who can distance herself/himself from the research object; in other words, (s)he is a disembodied knower. It is not so that we had been intensively socialized to believe in these values during our university studies but rather that these values are inscribed on Western civilization. You breathe these values from the moment you are born. You are brought up to believe in the superiority of scientific knowledge over other kinds of knowledge throughout the educational system. The belief in scientific knowledge and its purity is something that distinguishes the Western world from other 'less advanced' civilizations. As Loomba (1998: 104) has pointed out, we need images of the outsider to construct the insider, the 'self'.

Being born in the Western world means that you are an insider of the 'civilized world' *ipso facto*. Yet it does not mean that you are self-evidently accepted into its core, as part of the scientific community. As a novice, you have to strive towards full membership in the world of science (Ylijoki, 1998). Like any other culture, academic cultures can be seen as moral orders where rituals, confirmations of respect and contempt and displays of proper character and moral commentary are permitted only to those who are members of these communities (see Harré, 1983: 245). After a successful presentation of proper personhood in an academic context, one can acceptably feel pride tempered with a public display of humility. In case of failure, one is expected to feel ashamed (Harré, 1983: 236–237; see also Mäntylä, 2000).

Different academic communities do, however, adhere to the core values of academic moral order in various degrees, depending on the field of study and even depending on the departmental culture. Academic fields also differ in their perception of what kind of academic practices would produce an end product that would conform to these values. For example, in economics it is believed that the goal of objectivity is accomplished by abstract and highly formalized analysis. These practices are believed to set economics apart from the 'softer' fields (Nelson, 1995) like organization studies. Thus, your first task in academia is to figure out the values and norms of your own scientific field and of your own departmental culture, and then act accordingly.

We sought full membership in academia mostly by imitating and repeating practices that we believed would take us there. Often we failed, but did not understand why. As novices in the scientific community, it took us years to realize that the core values of scientific knowledge production – that is, the values of objectivity, separation and neutrality – are powerful myths which have for the most part been used to produce, control and normalize reality rather than explain it (Foucault, 1980). It took us even longer to realize that the norms and values of scientific thought, as well as our everyday academic practices, are gendered and as such limit women's opportunities for full membership in academic organizations.

We did not clearly comprehend at the time we started our postgraduate studies that values such as subjectivity, connection and emotion lie outside the realm of formal knowledge because they conflict with the image of pure science as emotionally and sexually neutral (Keller, 1983). We were also unaware of how the cultural values associated with masculinity, such as competitiveness, aggressiveness and visibility, are favoured in most academic organizations (see Morgan, 1986; Katila and Meriläinen, 1999). Neither did we realize how gender bias in the evaluating of scientific competence was, and still is, common practice (Wennerås and Wold, 1997). We were also completely unaware of the various ways in which organization analysis has neglected gender (Hearn and Parkin, 1983) and how policy, curricula, career paths and even management are gendered in higher education (see Acker, 1994; Evans, 1995; Fogelberg *et al.*, 1999; Husu, 2001; Martin, 1994; Stolte-Heiskanen, 1991).

In the beginning of our university studies, we did not even have the capacity to start thinking about how science could also be gendered on the level of language. Even today, the belief in the intrinsic masculinity of science finds daily expressions in the language and metaphors we use to describe science. Let us think, for example, about the distinction between 'hard' and 'soft' sciences. By defining the objective sciences such as economics as 'hard', as opposed to the 'softer' branches of knowledge like organization studies, we implicitly invoke a sexual metaphor where 'hard' is associated with masculinity and 'soft' with femininity. Another illustrative example is the distinction between facts and feelings. While facts are associated with the 'hard' sciences and, hence, with masculinity, feelings are associated with 'soft' sciences and, hence, with femininity. The innocence and neutrality of such distinctions are, however, questionable. The categories selected are socially constituted; they are also constitutive in the sense that they reproduce relations of power that create, sustain or transform particular identities and interests. The use of such discursive constructions is selected for purposes of elevating the 'hard' sciences carried out predominantly by men over the 'soft' sciences, where the majority of the researchers are female (see Keller, 1983; Knights and Richards, 2000).

Regardless of the lack of knowledge of the issues described above, we felt that male and female academics were treated differently in our department and that this had an impact on the identity construction processes of female academics in general, and on our identity construction processes in particular. Thus, we raised the question of gender equity in our department, which did not, however, get us anywhere. This is when we decided to write a paper about the gendering processes taking place there. We believed that gendering was done especially through discursive practices. Thus, we took as our starting point the idea that gender is culturally enacted and 'positioned', especially through the discursive practices. Gender is something we, both females and males, do and think (Gherardi, 1994). The advantage of such an approach is that it renders possible the exploration of gender at the micro-level of interaction; that is, the examination of how gender is performed as a routine accomplishment in our daily organizational practices.

Storytelling

The empirical data of our study is based on naturally occurring conversations, some of which we have written down on site, and some of which we have recorded from memory afterwards. Our strategy has been to utilize any and all situationally available techniques to gather data (Lundman and McFarlane, 1976). In our earlier study (Katila and Meriläinen, 1999), we described how women in our department and in academia in general are presented as lacking the qualities needed in academic work. The characteristics required for professional identity seemed to be tied to a system of values in which identities defined as masculine were prioritized. The study further indicated that after years of hearing how women are lacking in one respect or another, many women start to believe in it as an objective fact, while men get support for their often unconscious assumptions of women as the other sex, the inferior one. The study also showed how women's gender positions are often made explicit through categorizing them as girl, seducer, or just plain beautiful in an academic context. The image of incompetent women is further strengthened by the behaviour of all organizational members. Men display masculinity by being public, visible, and aggressive whereas women tend to adopt a feminine position by being more private, invisible and submissive. According to the academic standards of professionality, women's behaviour is regarded as unprofessional (ibid.).

The following extract is a direct quotation from our article (Katila and Meriläinen, 1999). The purpose of presenting it in this connection is to illustrate what kind of contextualized stories we have written, and how we have analysed them:

> *Silence of the lambs*
> The weekly doctoral seminar starts in a usual, rather constrained atmosphere. A doctoral student gives his presentation, and then there is silence ... To break the silence one of our full professors takes the floor, thanking the presenter, after which he starts commenting on the male student's work. Later on the other male members of our community join the discussion.

One of the more active male participants takes the floor – whether he has anything relevant to say or not. He starts: 'When I was the executive of the company ...' Soon after his comment another eager male steps up to speak: 'In the book I published last month I said ...' The women are still quiet. Finally, one of them opens her mouth: 'This is probably not relevant to the issue but I was thinking ...', and she continues: 'I am not really sure but I personally think that ...'

The story describes how women and men are actively collaborating in the reproduction of the gendered organizational culture in our department, if not consciously. Men as well as women are behaving in accordance with the expectations embedded in the dominant discourse. To take the public space by referring to one's credentials in the field of management and academia reflects that men are expressing values contiguous to their relationship with masculinity – visible, aggressive, successful. Women, on the other hand, tend to adopt the role of an outsider. They keep silent as if they had nothing to contribute to the discussions, even if the topic concerns their own field of expertise. The silence of women reflects ambivalent behaviour, however. On the one hand, women are adopting a subordinate feminine role which is in accordance with the expectations embedded in the dominant discourse but, on the other hand, some women use the silence as a sign of solidarity and power. As pointed out by Tannen (1996), silence alone is not a self-evident sign of powerlessness, nor volubility a self-evident sign of domination.

But what is disturbing in these seminar situations is the imbalance of male and female voices heard which works against women in the long run. Additional problems arise when women take part into the discussions. Taking over the public space and adopting the position of a competent professional in the field is hard after years of silence. Women most often start by asking for a permission to intrude. In other words, women indirectly request authorization, protection and benevolence. Consequently, they give up their autonomy to define the discussion. Apologizing also reflects the fact that women undervalue their competence to speak about any subject matter but the personal. Men, on the other hand, retain their authority, assuming that women had an equal chance to define the matter but were not able to, or chose not to (see also Gherardi, 1994). It seems that women are more inclined to take the role of a listener and men that of a lecturer (see also Tannen, 1996). These roles are not, however, pre-given but created over and over again in the seminar context in our interaction. The problem of the asymmetrical nature of the seminar conversations has been discussed openly several times, but as a collective we have been unable to break it.

(Katila and Meriläinen, 1999: 168–169).

Taking into account the fact that the discussion we opened up was not a pleasant one, the reception of our paper was surprisingly positive. We were encouraged, and there were no further demands to prove whether discrimination existed. We had made our case. We felt self-satisfied and happy, but also relieved. We were not crushed like some people had anticipated. Our colleagues seemed to understand how in our everyday discourses we position women as lacking the qualities needed in academic work. Neither did they find our method of inquiry problematic. Our departmental culture could be characterized as one that is open both to new areas of research and to new methods of conducting them. Our paper passed the first level in the institutional hierarchy of cognitive authority, but there were others ahead.

Gatekeeping

Academic disciplines and organizations could be characterized as reputational systems that collectively co-ordinate what tasks are carried out, how they are carried out and how performance is evaluated (Collins, 1975: 496). Organization studies, like management studies, could be characterized as a fragmented adhocracy where there is a wide variety of work techniques, approaches and audiences. Even though the field has a variety of publication outlets, getting your paper published in an academic journal demands that you are able to convince your fellow specialists of the importance and correctness of the result (Whitley, 1984). Our strategy of using self both as an object and subject of research was bound to create tension between innovation and tradition.

We submitted our paper to an international journal and received a letter containing the following message. '*The associate editor felt this should be published in the journal under the heading Research Notes as it is clearly a piece written from the practical experience of the authors, rather than a conventionally researched study. We have no objection to such writing but feel it fits better under the Research Notes nomenclature.*' Another time we received a commentary that was pretty much in line with what Richardson (1997: 300) received for her work. Her article was described as self-indulgent informal biography that was not much more than 'table talk'. What does this kind of criticism actually tell us?

First of all, in the text a distinction between unconventional and conventional research is made. Our work is characterized as unconventional, but the criteria for a conventional study are left unsaid. The only thing that is explicitly stated in the text is that our practical experience does not form sufficient bases for a conventionally researched study. After discussing the commentary, we came to the conclusion that the academic values of detachment, objectivity and neutrality underlie this message. In the next paragraph, we will use our imagination and freely interpret in more detail what kind of implicit meanings this message might convey.

The text could be seen to imply that we have been unable to separate ourselves from the field. This lack of detachment has resulted in a confusion of the subjects and objects of the study that has kept us from making neutral observations and reliable interpretations of the researched reality. Furthermore, the text could be seen to imply that our obviously emotional involvement in the process and with the members of our work community has prevented us from doing 'objective' analysis of the research material. Research is not supposed to be personal and emotional, nor should it be perceived as identity work (see Coffey, 1999; Bruni and Gherardi, Chapter 2 this volume). The text further constructs our experience as an individual body of knowledge rather than as a collective accomplishment. It could also be interpreted that the data collection method was not rigorous enough. It has been produced as a by-product of our everyday organizational life rather than as an end product of a systematic data ollection process. The text further questions whether practical experience ould be considered knowledge with any relevance to academic audiences. hus, the question is do the findings of our study have any relevance beyond the rganization in question? All of the above-mentioned arguments could be seen s rather standard criticism raised against studies where self is both the subject nd the object of research. They might be seen to weaken the overall validity of he study and, thus, it might be deprived of the status of a full article. In the next ection we will problematize the bases of such criticism and point out how these weaknesses' can turn out to be the strengths of a study.

Turning weaknesses into strengths

We have emphasized in all our writings that the meanings of organizational dis-ourses arise from the social situations and the cultural settings that frame them. Such a view is in accordance with a Foucauldian understanding of discourse as a et of related statements that produce and structure a particular order of reality, nd which within that reality makes available specific subject positions. In this ense, discursive practices could be seen as a frame within which identities are onstructed, as it is difficult for individuals to think outside them. Discourses are exercises in power and control regardless of the intentions of their producers see Loomba, 1998: 39).

It could be argued that to be able to place discourses in their social setting vould demand an ethnographic approach. There are interesting ethnographies hat have been done 'at home' (see Kunda, 1993; Van Maanen, 1991; Frost *et al.*, 991). The problem of the time-consuming nature of ethnography has, however, been acknowledged. There also seem to be difficulties in arranging financing for studies that require lengthy periods in the field. When the obstacle of financing s resolved, the questions of entry and gaining the confidence of the informants till remain. Given all these difficulties, we wonder why taking one step further by using yourself as a research instrument to gain access to and understanding of the organizational culture to which you belong raises such objections.

As a member of the community you have researched for years, you become an important carrier of cultural knowledge. The question is how to access this knowledge so that it can serve as the basis for relevant research. To gain the evel of cultural knowledge we carry within ourselves, an outsider would often pend years in fieldwork and hundreds of hours in interviewing, transcribing and analysing the transcriptions. Why would interviewing others on their subjective experience be more valid than our own experience on the same issue? We will start the following section by highlighting the practical benefits of placing self in the centre of research and continue with more profound epistemological issues. We will end this section by raising some political and ethical considerations con-cerning the chosen research strategy.

Easy entry and access to 'table talk'

Doing ethnographic research in your own organization and using yourself as he research instrument has several advantages. One of them, of course, is ease of entry. Another advantage is that you are not a social stranger to the organizational setting. You speak the language and know the general culture in there (see Coffey, 1999: 33–34). When we, for example, have carefully conducted research in our own occupational setting, we have had the opportunity to address issues of gendered occupational and organizational culture while making sense of our own occupational identity. Furthermore, researching yourself and the work community you are a member of gives you access to discussions that you might have great difficulty in gaining access to as an outsider. You have access to discussions just by being there. As an 'insider', you understand what people are talking about and who they are talking about, which gives you the ability to place the stories in a larger cultural and social setting.

We argue that using yourself as a research instrument is especially fruitful in organizations like academia, where formal designators of organizational identity are few. The nature of academic work in our field tends to be highly individual. People work alone in individual projects in the solitude of their offices. People working in the same department even compete with each other, and there are few, if any, goals that organizational members strive to achieve collectively. Furthermore, all organizational members rarely meet, except at departmental meetings, seminars and parties. Thus, the sense of community in academic organizations is often rather weak. In our department, researchers escape the solitude of their rooms by going out for lunch in pairs or in larger groups. We argue that in settings like this, the more informal and even private organizational gatherings are important sites where organizational reality is constructed. Thus gaining access to such situations is of great importance. As Hearn and Parkin (1987: 7) note, regardless of being public, work organizations offer opportunities for private discussions behind closed doors – enclaves for intimacy. Thus, the undervalued 'table talk' becomes more than relevant information, perhaps even the major forum where organizational reality is constructed.

In all our writings, we have emphasized that the meanings of organizational discourses arise from the social situations and the cultural settings that frame them. We use the stories, like the one described earlier, to depict the gendered social and discursive practices in terms of the social and cultural settings in which they belong. To write such highly contextualized stories and analyse them in detail, you must constantly be there in the field yourself. It demands knowledge of the persons in question as well as the history of the organization and its members; in other words, something that goes beyond the piece of text at hand. Swepson (1999) notes that when you are doing research in your own work organization you are a participant first, prior to, during and after the research process. As such, you share a history with the people you study, you know the key stakeholders and you are familiar with the language they use. All this enables you to place the discourses in a larger cultural and socio-historical context, which guides the meanings we attach to them.

The collective nature of experience

Another possible reading we gave to the criticism we received was that we were seen to be too intimately involved with the organization under study and its members to be able to distance ourselves from the field. Our inability to separate the object and subject of research produces an unreliable and biased account

of the reality under study. Thus, the objectivity of our observations and interpretations of what is going on could be questioned. In addition, it could be
argued that what we claim to be a collective and cultural phenomenon merely
represents our individual experiences that have no generalizability beyond the
organization in question.

We could start refuting these arguments by quoting Helen Longino (1999),
who argues that there is no essential difference between the subjects and objects
of knowledge. Knowers do not stand outside the world we seek to know. We
can continue arguing that our analysis is objective because we have made our
standpoint clear in all our papers; we have clarified where we are coming from
and what are the assumptions and values of our study, and how they affect our
beliefs and theorizing (see Harding, 1993). This does not, however, mean the
acceptance of an individualized, apolitical notion of experience. While using
ourselves as research instruments, we have realized that the experiences formerly perceived as merely individual are in fact social and, in a larger perspective, historical. Therefore, we nowadays understand that experience is more than
something belonging to one and exclusively her/his own. Rather, we would use
the term 'experience' in the general sense of a process through which one places
oneself, and is placed, in social reality – as a set of social relations which
produce both the possibilities and limitations of that experience (Acker *et al.*,
1983; de Lauretis, 1984).

While writing about our personal experiences, we have organized our autobi-
ographical memory through socially shared resources. We have drawn on cultural meanings and language to shape our memories (see Coffey, 1999: 127). As
Atkinson (1996) has noted, the memory that is brought to bear is both uniquely
biographical and collective. By writing about the gendered discursive practices
of our own work community, we have positioned ourselves within a set of discursive possibilities, which we have criticized and challenged. We have positioned ourselves in relation to our colleagues, their responses, criticisms,
agreements, and contributions, which also makes our knowledge production a
communal activity (see Code, 1991).

Furthermore, our everyday actions, experiences and emotions are framed by
different sets of cultural norms and expectations prevalent in our organizational
setting. For example, people's interactions at work are more or less influenced
by pre-existing experiences of gender roles (e.g. as husband/father,
mother/daughter, etc.) (Collinson, 1988; Pollert, 1981 in Helms Mills and Mills,
2000: 64). Different values and norms that govern our behaviour in organizations are developed through formal and informal group processes. Although
we seldom have unity of values, norms or beliefs in organizations, we might
nonetheless experience a communality of action. Our behaviour can be seen as
rule-governed. Organizational rules are influenced by extra-organizational rules
that become embedded in organizational rules; the rules that reflect dominant
social beliefs about the relative nature of women and men in our society (Helms
Mills and Mills, 2000) are a good example. These rules are manifested for
example in organizational discourses.

Through a cyclic process of immersion in the field and separation from it, we
have been able to access some of the rules that manifest gendered cultural
norms and expectations in our organization and in academic settings in general.

We have been able to detect some of the rules that contribute to the development, establishment and forms of gender relations in our everyday organizational lives. Some rules have become visible by the exercise of self-reflexivity, such as the rules of friendship, whereas some have become visible by accident when we have broken the rules (see Katila and Meriläinen, 2002). Making tacit rules visible and changing them demands active participation in the field. Mere observation is not a sufficient means to meet this goal. Our emphasis on keeping up the issue of the gendered practices in academia can be seen as an attempt to establish a rule that would value self-reflexivity and make it possible to change the undesirable organizational practices. The process of exploring and understanding the rules constraining and controlling our organizational behaviour has been epistemologically meaningful to us, yet at times personally burdensome.

A lot of the discourses that we produce in our everyday interaction are unconscious. They just happen. During this process of making gendered discursive practices visible, we have noticed that gendering of academic work is not so much a result of conscious and deliberate discrimination but rather a result of a strong belief in the neutrality and objectivity of academic practices in general and in the gender equality and even neutrality of one's own thinking and actions in particular (Katila and Meriläinen, 2002). There seem to be few rules or values in academic organizations that regulate the production of gendered discourses, because androcentric assumptions are invisible in our everyday organizational lives. The patriarchal structures that affect the way in which women and men feel about themselves and each other are deeply internalized (see Flax, 1987). Organizational rules are not stable, however. They can be changed and developed through the actions of organizational members. Rules can be established, enacted, enforced, misunderstood, resisted or broken (Helms Mills and Mills, 2000). Seldom can they be legitimately changed and established by outsiders, however (see Meyerson and Kolb, 2000; Coleman and Rippin, 2000; Ely and Meyerson, 2000). They have to be changed from within by the insiders.

Emotions as knowledge

The letter of the editor implies that we are too emotionally involved in the field and that this prevents us from reasoning clearly/purely. As newcomers to the field of academic work some ten years ago, we both started doing research believing that our own orderly, coherent and logically organized descriptions of organizational life and those of others were reasonable representations of that reality. But when we started doing research on our own work organization, we came to realize that people (including researchers) are emotionally vested in their work organizations and that disregarding this gives an anorectic picture of our organizational lives (Katila and Meriläinen, 2002; see also Fineman, 1993, 2000; Mäntylä, 2000). Furthermore, we realized that emotions play a key role in sustaining and reproducing academic moral orders (see Harré, 1983; Ylijoki, 1998).

Even though the language of social science makes little room for emotions in organizations in general, we are more concerned here that there is almost no place for the emotions of social scientists (Coffey, 1999; Meyerson, 2000; Mäntylä, 2000). There is an unwritten rule in the social sciences according to which researchers are supposed to suppress their own feelings. They are considered disturbances that prevent objective analysis of the subject matter. Talking about one's feelings towards participants and the research process in more general terms might be interpreted in a scientific context as a sign of subjectivity and, thus, of untrustworthiness (Kleinman, 1991).

We contend, however, that researchers' feelings are essential resources in understanding the phenomenon under study. Our research project on the gendered organizational practices started precisely because of our emotional involvement. As Jaggar (1989) has argued, our emotions are sources of knowledge about their objects. Our anger and frustration operated as a catalyst for us to write a paper about the ways in which gendered discourses and social practices influence women's professional identity in academia. We did not, however, understand in the early phases of our research project that the emotions we experienced reflected not only our individual emotions but also the emotions of academic women more generally. Our emotions were understandable to other women through a cultural communality of reaction. Ruth and Vilkko (1996) have noted that in addition to conveying the collective subjectivity of specific groups, emotional expressions in autobiographies tell us about issues that are shared by humans in general.

We have learned that 'touching' gender calls forth loads of emotions that have to be dealt with within your own organizational setting. Even though our gendered social and discursive practices are cultural in nature, making them visible on an organizational level always involves individuals, which makes the job difficult – not to mention how difficult it is to change one's own social and discursive practices. Changing is uncomfortable and threatening, in different ways, for all concerned. Thus, importing change to the gendered practices of organizations seldom produces any significant results, as Coleman and Rippin (2000: 586) unhappily learned during their action research project. According to them, people prefer not to talk about the gender issue, or they keep the discussion at the policy level with gender equality as a distanced concept. We have, however, learned that as long as gender discrimination remains an issue that happens somewhere else or by somebody else, it does not call forth emotions, which are important sources of change.

Political and ethical considerations

In addition to conveying relevant information about the norms, values and emotions of academic organizations, our personal and emotional texts have carried political potential as well. Our texts, for example, resonate with the experiences and emotions of other academic women, thus, also serving the political aim of consciousness-raising. The academic women who have read our paper have felt relieved and empowered after realizing that their position in the academic scene is not so much a question of their individual incapabilities and weaknesses but rather something more structural. Our writings have also helped women in similar situations to gain access to their own feelings. The stories that reflect our feelings of anger and frustration serve as a legitimization for expressing such feelings – feelings that are very often experienced as a threat to organizational stability.

Developing feminist consciousness has not, though, been the primary aim of our research project but rather a by-product of our intervention politics. This does not, however, mean that our research project was not political right from the beginning. On the contrary, in our first paper (Katila and Meriläinen, 1999) we listed two political aims that we wanted to accomplish. First, by opening up the discussion about gender discrimination taking place in our department, we wanted to help the members of our work community, whether male or female, to make better sense of our daily organizational lives. Second, we wanted to place the organization in a state of flux and to tweak the power relationships. Such a political orientation is a characteristic of participatory action research, which is closest to the method we are using. In the case of feminist participatory action research this has often meant a commitment to a transformational project that makes visible, and challenges, the web of forces that (re)produce and sustain any forms of gender oppression (see Gatenby and Humphries, 2000; Lather, 1991; Maguire, 1987, 2001).

Not to give too rosy a picture of the research strategy we have chosen, we will discuss some of the problems we have confronted. The first concerns the reactions that our research project has brought about in our work community; the second, the nature of the community we are building through our action-oriented project. First, using our seminars, meetings and table talk as examples in our academic papers (Katila and Meriläinen, 1999, 2002) has brought about feelings of uneasiness among some of our colleagues. They feel that they are under constant surveillance. When we went public with our first paper, we could not enter the room unnoticed for a while. Our colleagues called attention to our arrival for coffee breaks and other informal discussions, remarking that we were making notes of what they were saying. It often happened that the conversation changed and became more cautious. This cannot be considered a positive reaction because nothing fundamental had changed. Rather there was a tendency to divert the conversation along more politically correct lines if we were present. In some cases, though, our intervention seemed to heighten the sensitiveness to the gendered nature of our daily organizational practices. Our presence served as a reminder to focus on the discourses utilized. Also some members of our work community gradually became aware of how unconscious most of the way we talk is, and how we unintentionally produce meanings that we do not mean to produce. During the course of our research project we have noted that though we have attempted to contribute to the practical concerns of all members of our work community, it has been women who have found our writings most empowering. For some men this exercise has been a more disturbing and ambivalent experience.

Our second concern is related to the question of the kind of community we are actually building through our interventions if the reactions of the members of our work community are split according to traditional gender lines. Are we building a community that is exclusive rather than inclusive (see Grimes, 2000)? By reflecting specifically on our own experience, as long-standing female members of our work community, we run the risk of overriding experiences of the Other that might be of relevance in challenging the forces that (re)produce any forms of gender oppression. At this point of the process we see that in order to be able to understand and appreciate others' dilemmas on the subject matter t is crucial for us to understand our own ambivalence in relation to it. However, his does not mean an acceptance of an individualized, apolitical notion of experience as discussed earlier in this chapter (p. 193).

Conclusion

n this chapter we have discussed the benefits of a research strategy that places elf in the centre of research. By reporting on our identity work as female academics in a male-dominated academic community, we have been able to highlight he gendered nature of academic work in general, and the difficulties women ace in constructing their professional identity in particular (Katila and Meriläinen, 1999, 2002). By doing research on our own work community and using ourelves as research instruments we have highlighted the fluid boundaries between he subject and object of research, personal and collective experience, as well as political and apolitical streams of research. We have shown how individual experiences and emotions are always partly collective and how individual actions are constrained and controlled by organizational rules. We have argued hat through our personal experience we can gain access to collective organizational reality.

By writing about our own personal experiences we have advocated a political strategy based on the exploration of micropolitics and contests over meaning. We have found that the challenges and changes placed by the academic culture of our own work community on our professional identity construction process and the sense of self have been both methodologically and personally significant. We must remember, though, that even though we are striving for change, he direction of change cannot be known (see Mulinari and Sandell, 1999: 292). Resisting by writing about our personal experiences, we are entering into the struggle over meanings – using our power to signify (see Haraway, 1991). Entering the struggle does, however, mean that we might contribute to dominance in spite of our liberatory intentions (see Lather, 1991: 150). To be able to develop a work community that is more open to difference would demand that we, as well as other members of our work community, are aware that we have 'multiple and contradictory selves, selves that contain the oppressor as well as the oppressed' (Harris, 1991: 252).

Our identities as researchers are co-constructed within the communities we practice research in (see Katila and Meriläinen, 1999; Räsänen and Mäntylä, 2001), and what kind of identities we are constructing is not an irrelevant issue. Gendered practices have costs both to individuals and scientific communities, but also to science in general as Rolin (1999) has pointed out. According to her, he archaic cultural and social practices which function as obstacles to inclusive and responsive practices constitute a serious threat to the epistemic integrity of science. It is not sufficient that the individual members of a scientific community are honest, competent, conscientious, and capable of epistemic self-assessment. A trustworthy community practice involves social norms, which are designed to promote inclusive and responsive dialogue in science.

Note

1 The authorship is alphabetical; this chapter was produced in full collaboration.

References

Acker, S. (1994). *Gendered Education. Sociological Reflections on Women, Teaching and Feminism.* Philadelphia, PA: Open University Press.
Acker, J., Barry, K. and Esseveld, J. (1983). Objectivity and truth: problems of doing feminist research. *Women's Studies International Forum*, 6: 423–435.
Atkinson, P. (1996). *Sociological Readings and Re-readings.* Aldershot: Avebury.
Code, L. (1991). *What Can She Know?: Feminist Theory and the Construction of Knowledge.* Ithaca, NY: Cornell University Press.
Coffey, A. (1999). *The Ethnographic Self.* London: Sage.
Coleman, G. and Rippin, A. (2000). Putting feminist theory to work: collaboration as a means towards organizational change. *Organization*, 7(4): 573–587.
Collins, H.M. (1975). *Conflict Sociology.* New York, NY: Academic Press.
Collinson, D.L. (1988). Engineering humour: masculinity, joking and conflict in shop floor relations. *Organization Studies*, 9(2): 181–199.
De Lauretis, T. (1984). *Alice Doesn't: Feminism, Semiotics, Cinema.* Bloomington, IN: Indiana University Press.
Ely, R.J. and Meyerson, D. (2000). Advancing gender equity in organizations: the challenge and importance of maintaining a gender narrative. *Organization*, 7(4): 589–608.
Evans, M. (1995). Ivory towers: life in the mind. In L. Morley and V. Walsh (eds), *Feminist Academics – Creative Agents for Change.* London: Taylor & Francis.
Fineman, S. (ed.) (1993). *Emotion in Organizations.* London: Sage.
Fineman, S. (ed.) (2000). *Emotion in Organizations* (2nd edn). London: Sage.
Flax, J. (1987). Postmodern and gender relations in feminist theory. *Signs*, 16(2): 621–643.
Fogelberg, P., Hearn, J., Husu, L. and Mankkinen, T. (eds), (1999). *Hard Work in the Academy.* Helsinki: Helsinki University Press.
Foucault, M. (1980). *Power/Knowledge.* New York, NY: Pantheon Books.
Frost, P., Moore, L., Reis Louis, M., Lundberg C. and Martin, J. (eds) (1991). *Reframing Organizational Culture.* London: Sage.
Gatenby, B. and Humphries, M. (2000). Feminist participatory action research: methodological and ethical issues. *Women's Studies International Forum*, 23(1): 89–105.
Gherardi, S. (1994). The gender we think, the gender we do in our everyday organizational lives. *Human Relations*, 47(6): 591–610.
Grimes, D.S. (2000). Essentialism and Difference in Community Building. http://www.mngt.waikato.ac.nz/RES. . ./Vol6_2/Vol6_2articles/grimes.asp
Haraway, D. (1991). *Simians, Cyborgs, and Women: The Reinvention of Nature.* New York, NY: Routledge.
Harding, S. (1993). What is strong objectivity? In L. Alcoff and E. Potter (eds), *Feminist Epistemologies.* New York, NY: Routledge.
Harré, R. (1983). *Personal Being.* Oxford: Basil Blackwell.
Harris, A.P. (1991). Race and essentialism in feminist legal theory. In K. Bartlett and R. Kennedy (eds), *Feminist Legal Theory: Readings in Law and Gender* (pp. 235–262). Boulder, CO: Westview Press.
Hearn, J. and Parkin, P.W. (1983). Gender in organizations: a selective review and critique of a neglected area. *Organization Studies*, 4(3): 219–242.
Hearn, J. and Parkin, P.W. (1987). *'Sex' at 'Work' – The Power and Paradox of Organizational Sexuality.* Brighton: Wheatsheaf.

Helms Mills, J.C. and Mills, A.J. (2000). Rules, sensemaking, formative contexts, and discourse in the gendering of organizational culture. In N. Ashkanasy, C. Wilderom and M. Peterson (eds), *Handbook of Organizational Culture and Climate* (pp. 55–70). Thousand Oaks, CA: Sage.

Husu, L. (2001). *Sexism, Support and Survival. Academic Women and Hidden Discrimination in Finland.* Social Psychological Studies 6. Helsinki: University of Helsinki, Department of Social Psychology.

Jaggar, A. (1989). Love and knowledge: emotion in feminist epistemology. In A. Jaggar and S. Bordo (eds), *Gender/Body/Knowledge.* New Brunswick, NJ: Rutgers University Press.

Katila, S. and Meriläinen, S. (1999). A Serious researcher or just another nice girl?: Doing gender in a male-dominated scientific community. *Gender, Work and Organization*, 6(3): 163–173.

Katila, S. and Meriläinen, S. (2002). Metamorphosis: from 'nice girls' to 'nice bitches'. Resisting patriarchal articulations of professional identity. *Gender, Work and Organization*, 9(3): 336–354.

Keller, E.F. (1983). Gender and science. In S. Harding and M.B. Hintikka (eds), *Discovering Reality: Feminist Perspectives on Epistemology, Metaphysics, Methodology, and Philosophy of Science* (pp. 187–205). London: D. Reidel Publishing Company.

Kleinman, S. (1991). Field-workers' feelings: what we feel, who we are, how we analyze. In W.B. Shaffir and R.A. Stebbins (eds), *Experiencing Fieldwork – An Inside View of Qualitative Research* (pp. 184–195). Newbury Park, CA: Sage.

Knights, D. and Richards, W. (2000). Sex Discrimination in UK Academia. Paper presented at the American Academy of Management Meeting, 4–9 August, Toronto, Canada.

Kunda, G. (1993). *Engineering Culture. Control and Commitment in a High-Tech Corporation.* Philadelphia, PA: Temple University Press.

Lather, P. (1991). *Getting Smart: Feminist Research and Pedagogy with/in the Postmodern.* New York, NY: Routledge.

Longino, H. (1999). Feminist epistemology. In J. Greco and E. Sosa (eds), *The Blackwell Guide to Epistemology* (pp. 327–353). Oxford: Blackwell Publishers.

Loomba, A. (1998). *Colonialism/Post-colonialism.* London: Routledge.

Lundman, R.J. and McFarlane, P.T. (1976). Conflict methodology: an inquiry and preliminary assessment. *The Sociological Quarterly*, 17: 503–512.

Maguire, P. (1987). *Doing Participatory Research: A Feminist Approach.* Boston, MA: University of Massachusetts.

Maguire, P. (2001). Uneven ground: feminisms and action research. In P. Reason and H. Bradbury (eds), *Handbook of Action Research: Participative Inquiry and Practice* (pp. 59–69). London: Sage.

Mäntylä, H. (2000). Dealing with shame at academic work – a literary introspection. *Psychiatria Fennica*, 31: 148–169.

Martin, J. (1994). The organization of exclusion: institutionalization of sex inequality, gendered faculty jobs and gendered knowledge in organizational theory and research. *Organization*, 1(2): 401–431.

Meyerson, D.E. (2000). If emotions were honoured: a cultural analysis. In S. Fineman (ed.), *Emotion in Organizations* (pp. 167–183). London: Sage.

Meyerson, D. and Kolb, D. (2000). Moving out of the 'armchair': developing a framework to bridge the gap between feminist theory and practice. *Organization*, 7(4): 553–571.

Morgan, G. (1986). *Images of Organization.* London: Sage.

Mulinari, D. and Sandell, K. (1999). Exploring the notion of experience in feminist thought. *Journal of the Scandinavian Sociological Association*, 42(4): 287–297.

Nelson, J. (1995). Feminism and economics. *Journal of Economic Perspectives*, 9(2): 131–148.

Pollert, A. (1981). *Girls, Wives, Factory Lives*. London: Macmillan.

Räsänen, K. and Mäntylä, H. (2001). Preserving academic diversity: promises and uncertainties of PAR as a survival strategy. *Organization*, 8(2): 301–320.

Richardson, L. (1997). Skirting a pleated text: de-disciplining an academic life. *Qualitative Inquiry*, 3(3): 295–303.

Rolin, K. (1999). Gender and Epistemic Trust. Paper presented in the American Philosopical Association Eastern Division Meeting.

Ruth, J.-E. and Vilkko, A. (1996). Emotion in the construction of autobiography. In C. Magat and S. McFadden (eds), *Handbook of Emotion, Adult Development and Aging* (pp. 167–181). San Diego, CA: Academic Press.

Stolte-Heiskanen, V. (1991). Handmaidens of the 'knowledge class', women in science in Finland. In V. Stolte-Heiskanen and R. Fürst-Dilic (eds), *Women in Science – Token Women or Gender Equality* (pp. 35–62). Oxford: Berg.

Swepson, P. (1999). Doing Action Research in My Own Organization: Ethical Dilemmas, Hopes and Triumphs, *Action Research international* (http//:www.scu.edu.au/shools/sawd/ari/ari-holian.html)

Tannen, D. (1996). *Gender and Discourse*. New York, NY: Oxford University Press.

Van Maanen, J. (1991). The smile factory: work at Disneyland. In P. Frost, L. Moore, M. Reis Louis, C. Lundberg and J. Martin (eds), *Reframing Organizational Culture* (pp. 58–76). London: Sage.

Wennerås, C. and Wold, A. (1997). Nepotism and sexism in peer-review. *Nature*, 387(22): 341–343.

Whitley, R. (1984). The development of management studies as a fragmented adhocracy. *Social Science Information*, 23(4/5): 775–818.

Ylijoki. O. (1998). *Akateemiset heimokulttuurit ja noviisien sosialisaatio*. Tampere, Finland: Vastapaino.

11 Interviewing female managers

Presentations of the gendered selves in contexts

Iiris Aaltio

Introduction

Interviews – using questions to create talk, discussion and text – are commonly used methods in social sciences, especially in qualitative research and in studying the inequality between men and women in organizations. Surprisingly, gender issues sometimes disappear when a researcher tries to capture them by means of interviews (Calás and Czarniawska, 1998). This is sometimes the case even in the interviews of female respondents, whose life-context, if assessed in advance, would imply that the topic of inequality should play a major role in their positioning in the organization and in their career histories (Czarniawska-Joerges, 1994a: 95–98). In addition, in interviews with male managers, a question regarding gender inequity at the workplace is likely to be followed by a polite, defensive or, occasionally, an embarrassed silence (Aaltio-Marjosola, 1994: 147–162). Sometimes it feels as if the topic is of more interest to the researcher than to the interviewees themselves: gender disappears during the study. This is the tendency towards 'hidden' gender, found also in a study based on interviews among office personnel, and leading to questions of whether the ways of solving problems related to gender discrimination are more real than the problems themselves (Kinnunen and Korvajärvi, 1995: 89). Is this a part of the ceremony of 'doing gender': of pronouncing the non-existence of gender inequality in society (Korvajärvi, 1998: 145), enforced by talk in informal as well as in formal organizational contexts? Or how should we interpret these findings of hidden gender?

From a naive empiricist point of view (Sayer, 1984: 51–52), we may ask whether the interviewed people are telling the truth or lying? Are they sincere or are they trying to hide something? Is there some inner truth, reality, out of which they speak, or which they try to hide? This chapter explores the paradox of hidden gender in interviews and offers some interpretations for the findings. We aim to understand how the organizational culture as a context is reflected in the findings, and argue that, rather than being paradoxical, our findings in fact make it possible to describe and interpret sensitively the gendered cultural contexts of the interviewed. To put it simply: the interviewed people tell us about issues as they see them, and we interpret their stories in various ways. This is often done by using a shadowing technique (Czarniawska-Joerges, 1992: 197; Korvajärvi, 1998: 51) – that is, we read gendering processes from material in which gender (notions of women and men) is not explicitly mentioned. As Erving Goffman states:

the performer can be fully taken in by his own act; he can be sincerely convinced that the impression of reality which he stages is the real reality. When his audience is also convinced in this way about the show he puts on ... then for the moment at least, only the sociologist or the socially disgruntled will have any doubts about the 'realness' of what is presented.

(Goffman, 1959: 17)

The performers' talk and stories are not merely unique and individual, but they take place within gendered cultural contexts and are impacted by them as well. Men and women have multiple identities within an organization, and they reach out to occupy different identities depending on their place in the organization. These identities are not described by their 'natural' selves, but by the selves that derive from the global and local organizational contexts in which they live.

From an individual's point of view to contextual identities: how to reach the gendered self

Growing critique in the 1990s has led to a discussion about the assumptions regarding individuality and personality in different organizational settings, accompanied by feminist research which has solidly criticized socio-biological theories (Aaltio-Marjosola and Kovalainen, 2001: 34). Theoretical discourse stems mainly from one crucial idea, and that has been the move away from the notion of the 'essential' individual as normatively male. This means to challenge the conventional school of thought, where identity is to be found in the individuals themselves, whether in their genotype or in their 'soul', and, according to which, to acquire one's identity therefore means to find one's true 'I' and express it. On the other hand, instead of essentializing the individual one can claim, as the social environmental school does, that it is the society which creates the individual, and, at the same time, reproduces and changes society as well. Society, its rules, its language, values and institutions build one's individual identity. The organization is a kind of 'superperson' in this transforming of identity, while the individual is 'an institutional myth developed within rational theories or choice' (Czarniawska-Joerges, 1994b: 195).

This line of thought complies at a deeper level with historical developments in the twentieth century (Ashmore, 1990; Trew, 1998: 4): first, from 1894–1936 there was a phase of sex differences in intelligence, based on seeing gender as a subject variable that can be measured in the same way as any other individual difference; second, from 1936–1974, masculinity and femininity were treated as global personality traits and as single psychological dimensions, created through family practices leading men to task-orientation and bread-winning, and making women socio-emotional, nurturant and caring; third, from 1974–1982, androgyny was a sex-role ideal, signifying both the masculine and the feminine traits of individuals; and finally, from the 1980s onwards, sex came to be seen as a social category, and the idea of masculinity and femininity as dimensions of personality, and as traits, came to be challenged. As Trew notes:

Following the paradigm shift in the 1980s ... most theoretical accounts of gender now concentrate almost exclusively on gender as a social category, thus implicating differences between men and women in terms of their relative power and prestige in society. Such societal-based realities are assumed to have an impact on how an individual thinks, acts and feels.

(Trew, 1998: 6)

However, individual subjectivity is still a key concept in the story. Elliott (1999: 2) points out that the problematization of human subjectivity is one crucial issue which has emerged in social theory at the turn of the twenty-first century, not as some pre-given substance but rather as a reflexively constituted project. The 'death of the subject' as an early postmodern idea attracts criticism, and concern is now given to the complex and contradictory ways in which men and women seek to appropriate and exert control over their lives (Elliott, 1999: 1–11). This will presumably lead to a theoretical discourse on identity and self in the creation of subjectivity, both in local and global contexts.

One of the doubts has been whether the discourse concerning organizational identities indicates a loss of individual identities, 'loss of the referent, and anchor, a sense of self with respect to participation in and interaction between organizations' (Christensen and Cheney, 1994: 233). According to Kavolis (cited by Czarniawska-Joerges, 1994b: 197), modern identity encompasses the following elements: (1) an overall coherence between an individual's experience and the way it is expressed, (2) a memory – on the part of the individual and others – of a continuity in the course of the individual's life, and (3) a conscious but not excessive commitment to the manner in which the individual understands and deals with his or her 'self'. This explanation expands beyond the 'essential self' to the idea of self-narrative as a way of achieving one's identity. Modern identity emerges from the individual's life history, presents it and separates it from the collective identity. Individual identities are shaped in the process of telling one's own story, in social conditions where discourses are no longer so grand and stable as they used to be.

In any description of the relationship between gender and social behaviour, gender identity and the gendered self are looked upon as integral components within social and personality psychology (Trew, 1998: 3–10). Gender is assumed to have an impact on how one thinks and understands the nature of one's self, whereas gender identity is a complex, dynamic and multifaceted social phenomenon. Due acknowledgement of this complexity aims at a genuine understanding of this issue. Overall, men and women tend to identify themselves differently, with men presenting themselves as separate and independent of others, while women define themselves in terms of closeness with others. Construing the self is a process, and it has been suggested (Cross and Madson, 1997) that most women develop an independent self-construct in which the self is flexible, encompassing various roles and relationships. The gender is 'done' in the process of communication, given the emphasis of language and meaning rather than the structural elements of it, seeing communication more as water than as glue (Newell, 2001: 81). Gendered discourses in organizations can, accordingly, be regarded as their essential integral dynamics.

Work, as the opposite of non-work, is a public domain. However, the boundaries between work and non-work do not divide life at the individual experimental level as sharply as they seemingly do in everyday language. In organizations, work is based on shared meanings (Smircich and Morgan, 1982: 257–273) created by individual selves that constitute the identities of the organizations and also of the individuals. The whole issue of public vs. private is crucial in the discourse concerning women's and men's places in society, in families and in work-organizations, since men 'his'storically relate to the public and women to the private spheres of life (Grosholz, 1987: 218–226). By extending their roles and breaking into public institutions women challenge the prevalent male 'grand story' and bring private issues into public and institutional spheres.

The segregation of work is based on the classical stereotypes of men's and women's behaviour and orientations (Gerzon, 1982): men are oriented towards technical and industrial work, whereas women are engaged in occupations where one needs caring ability and social integration, such as teaching and nursing. Culturally, men and women are creating, structuring and reforming our publicly as well as privately shared ideals. Statistics show clear evidence that women are still in the minority as decision-makers in working life: for example, as top managers who have broken the invisible glass-ceilings in the organization, as board members of big enterprises, as CEOs and even as top-level politicians, both world-wide and locally. Overall, there is a high degree of vertical segregation in work within organizations: that means there are few women in managerial positions compared to men (Czarniawska and Calás, 1997: 326; Acker, 1990, 1994). In addition to the figures that show the inequality between men and women as decision-makers, their work in organizations also differs from each other qualitatively; men and women end up doing different kinds of work: in terms of organizational structure, their jobs differ horizontally. Even in Nordic economies like in Finland, where 70 per cent of adult women participate in working life and thus combine their private and working-life issues, there still remains a strict segregation of work, both horizontally and vertically, in the work organizations (Veikkola, 1999).

There is also segregation of work in managerial positions: a closer look at the statistics based on body-counts within industries shows an equal number of women and men working in positions of personnel management in Finland, whereas men are predominant as managers in all other areas, such as managers in industrial enterprises and in strategic decision-making (Tienari, 1999, 2000; Kauppinen and Otala, 1999). The female ideals of relationship orientation, caring and focusing on 'personal growth' are apparent in these figures, whereas male managers find their place in strategic management where they can spread their ideas in marketing and in expanding the company. Statistics further show that women form the majority of the workforce in public administration in the Nordic countries (see Chapter 5 by Alvesson and Due Billing in this volume). The same tendency, even stronger, can be seen in Finnish data on female entrepreneurs (Kovalainen, 1995), who occupy entrepreneurial roles in line with the traditional ideals of female behaviour: women are encountered as entrepreneurs in restaurants and hotels, in nursing firms and in handicrafts, often working in small or even micro-sized enterprises, while men are in the majority in industrial enterprises and in venture-capital, growth-seeking business enterprises. Surprisingly, studies of leadership rarely analyse the sex or sex roles of the leaders. 'We read as if leaders have no sex' (Metcalfe and Altman, 2001: 104), even if a closer reading reveals realizations of masculine ideals, and an implicit male emphasis is shown as well (Calás and Smircich, 1991: 567–602; Oseen, 1997: 170; Collinson and Hearn, 1996).

A naive objectivistic approach (Sayer, 1984) tends to see organizations as 'natural', as pure empirical facts. An attempt to investigate their gendered nature means reaching over to a culturally bound understanding of them. Behind the selected research method there is the epistemology of the gendered organization, a profound idea of organizations as gendered liaisons that are qualified with cultural traits based on the masculine and the feminine, the man and the woman. While gender is a constitutive element of any social structure, and of any organizational structure, these structures become moulded by the relationships that stem from the division of work and the hierarchical nature of the organization. As Britton (2000: 422) notes, 'it becomes impossible to see one organization as somehow less gendered than another'. Organizations can be seen as inherently gendered; that is, gender has an ontological status.

When the researcher enters to study the empirical realities of a gendered organization, however, there is the dilemma and problem of experience in the study of organizations: we can study individuals and small groups directly, but we cannot experience large organizations that way. This fact has many implications for scientific theories of organizations (Sandelands and Srivatsan, 1993: 1–22); it makes them especially theory-based. Nevertheless, it should be self-evident that people working in organizations have rich experience that is gendered, and they should be able to describe this when asked.

When organizational researchers use conversation as a basic method of gaining data, this very often means that they first ask and then listen to the talk given by the interviewees. The creation and analysis of this talk depends on the methodological orientation of the study; for instance, we may study the language itself as a way of 'doing gender' (West and Zimmerman, 1987: 125–151), or focus on the studied individual cases in order to find some more general, behavioural and gendered patterns in the organization. This talk does not just take place spontaneously, irrationally and randomly, but is created and structured by the interaction processes that take place between the interviewer and the interviewees. It is contextualized, both locally in the circumstances where it is created, and more broadly within the individual life-spans of the interviewees. During the discourse that takes place in the interview, by means of talking, the respondents conceptualize, reshape and share their gendered experiences with the interviewer, usually with certain encouragement on the interviewer's part, by using either structured or non-structured interviewing technique; as a result the talk is created and texted.

Contextual mutuality between the interviewer and the interviewee

Besides being a research method, the interview is a socially constructed, localized interaction process, usually between two people, one being the interviewer and the other the interviewee. Interviewing is certainly the most widely used qualitative method in organizational research, often not merely a method in itself but also a way of gaining data to be analysed by other means. The aim of a qualitative research interview is to gather descriptions of the interviewee's sphere of life with respect to an interpretation of the meaning of the described phenomena (Kvale, 1983: 174; King, 1994: 14). A key feature of this method is the special nature of the relationship between the interviewer and the interviewee. The emphasis in earlier knowledge on research methods was on the objective nature of the situation and researchers sought ways to minimize the impact of subjective, interpersonal processes on the course of the interview. Contemporary knowledge in the field, however, presents a qualitative researcher who no longer believes in such a thing as a 'relationship-free' interview but, on the contrary, sees a mutual relationship and its sensitive and reflective study as a part of the research process, not as a distraction from it. The researcher's concern is to obtain accurate information by listening and recording the interviewee's talk, but not so that it should be free from all subjectivity (see also Chapter 10 by Katila and Meriläinen in this volume). The interviewee is a participant in the research, actively shaping the course of the interview rather than passively responding to the interviewer's pre-set questions (King, 1994: 14–15).

In the classical work on sociological paradigms, the various fields of study differed by the ontological status given to the studied phenomenon and to the researcher (Burrell and Morgan, 1979). In the paradigms the subject and object of study are either separated strictly, as in an objectivistic orientation to research, or they emphasize the dependence of the two. Interviews, which are often semi-structured, are determined by the subjectivity of the researcher in a number of ways. This is, indeed, a challenge for the researcher – not to do away with subjectivity totally, which would, of course, be impossible in social terms as well, but to reflect that subjectivity throughout the research process using the interview.

Predominant feminist methodology has challenged the masculine nature of knowledge by similar kinds of arguments, both in the United States and Europe, calling the existing institutions and social practices into question as emerging from a patriarchal value system. This critique has been extended beyond societal concerns to include the production of knowledge – specifically, science itself – both as a product and a legitimator of patriarchy (Harding, 1986, 1987; Haraway, 1988; Millman and Kanter, 1987; Keller, 1984). Science has often been characterized as being reflective of values traditionally associated with masculinity and males in Western society. Since the values of science seem to correspond so closely to just one subset of human experience – that is, the historical value system of stereotypic masculinity – then the supposedly 'real' criteria of objectivity, reliability and validity championed in the scientific enterprise can be seen as value-based in and of the one subset of human experience (Jacobson and Aaltio-Marjosola, 2001).

Taking the argument of 'strong objectivity' by Sandra Harding, scientific objectivism turns out to be weak because knowledge-makers deliberately 'turn away from the task of critically identifying all those broad, historical social desires, interests and values that have shaped the agendas, contents and results of the sciences much as they shape the rest of human affairs' (Harding, 1991: 141). Strong objectivity is gained by creating scientific knowledge about women's lives through research carried out in real, historical contexts. This means localization instead of globalization of experiences, a holistic approach to the understanding of experience, and complexity rather than simplicity. This also means telling local, contextually situated narratives instead of grand stories (Calás and Smircich, 1999).

Concepts sometimes float out of meanings, some in order to come alive later. One generation may forget their meanings while another may find them meaningful again later, as Elias has pointed out (1978). Concepts also tend to transform themselves from time to time. The concepts of subjectivity and objectivity, subject and object, are applied in research contexts but, in fact, are only seemingly separate from each other. Julia Kristeva has made an important contribution in breaking the barrier of language by promoting the concept 'abject' instead of 'object' to refer to the 'not-yet-subject'. She further uses the term to describe the way in which 'abjection' functions to avoid both separation from and identification with the maternal body, as happens in early childhood development, in the process of subjectification and objectification (Elliott, 1999; Höpfl, 1998). Object, subject and 'abject' become, in Kristeva's language, something that breaks the barriers of time, growing beyond the limits of time to become a process. When concepts fail to show the virtuality of their true nature and serve stableness instead, they may, in fact, become void of meaning. Behind language and vocabulary there is a floating from strict use to an understanding that is more insightful, that reveals the roughness of the concepts used and serves the underlying complex and vivid reality that they try to capture. Thus, as concepts, the object of study and the subject of study are interrelated concepts, not totally separate.

As argued earlier, individual stories of people frequently do not offer very rich data for analysing inequality issues within organizations. We suggest that in interviews with women, especially with female managers, the talk that is produced and recorded contains definite aspects of 'doing gender' at that given moment. The cultural aspects of the given context are evoked by the way the interviewees talk, and this process of interaction between the researcher and the interviewed people gives a special, mutually shared context to the talking. When we see that the situation between the interviewer and the interviewed, in fact, is socially constructed, we come to promote an understanding that is reflective of this mutuality and takes it as a way of reaching the gendered selves, as well as the cultural local surroundings, of the respondents.

The expressiveness of an individual appears to involve two radically different kinds of sign activity: the expression that the individual gives and the expression that he or she gives off:

> The first involves verbal symbols or their substitutes which he uses admittedly and solely to convey the information that he and the others are known to attach to these symbols. This is communication in the traditional and narrow sense. The second involves a wide range of action that others can treat as symptomatic of the actor, the expectation being that the action was performed for reasons other than the information conveyed in this way.
>
> (Goffman, 1959: 3)

Front, dramatic realization, idealization, maintenance of expressive control, misrepresentation and mystification are, thus, performances given by individuals (ibid.: 17–77). The presentation of gendered selves in a research situation is carried by multiple techniques used by those interviewed, all bound to local and institutional culturally bound contexts of that specific situation.

Female managers' presentations of their gendered selves

Female managers and organizational cultures

Organizations are culturally held liaisons, constructed through social as well as political processes. As such they are created and changed by the management of meanings, partly by organizational leaders who are given that role by the subordinates (Smircich and Morgan, 1982; Berger and Luckmann, 1966). While the gender aspects of organizations have been studied widely in recent years, many of these studies are based on a critical understanding of individual life patterns and their organizationally bound behaviour, biased because the differences between men and women are not taken into account in studies classically conducted by male researchers (Mills, 1988: 351–369). Since organizations are products of culture and they produce culture (Czarniawska-Joerges, 1992), the managers – male and female – have a significant role in this process as well as in its single gender-biased incidents. Feminist approaches have drawn attention to the inequity aspects in these cultural productions in a practical sense by asking, for instance, why there are so few female managers, and whose economic life is it – including the cultural orientations – that we are working within (Acker, 1990). Other similar questions refer to the gendered limits of scientific approaches, inquiring whose sciences, whose knowledges do we base our understandings on (Harding, 1991: 296–312), pointing out the small minority of female researchers in early classical knowledge among the various disciplines (as Hearn and Parkin, 1983; Mills, 1988 have done).

Organizational cultures are generally written as if they were gender-neutral, even if their gendered nature is demonstrated daily by a multitude of differences predicated on gender – for instance, pay, promotion, status and job segregation. Gender and organizational culture are closely knit together, and the gendered nature of the cultural values and basic assumptions has, accordingly, been recognized in a number of studies (Wilson, 1997: 289–303 and 2001: 168–188; Wicks and Bradshaw, Chapter 8 in this volume). The fact that sociological and psychological knowledge underline some basic differences between men and women (Paludi, 1992; Kanter, 1977; Gilligan, 1982; Miller, 1987; Trew and Kremer, 1998) makes it natural to ask related questions concerning business life. For instance: do men and women as managers lead to qualitatively different organizational cultures? If not, why not? Are there reasons that are due to organizational cultures for why there are fewer women than men in managerial positions?

Nevertheless, the fact that females comprise a minority as business managers, both globally and locally, is an issue of inequality, which leads to women's lower salary level and minor role as political decision-makers compared to men. It has been argued that one more reason why women should hold more managerial positions is that no class in society should end up in a decisive role over the others – for example, men should not occupy managerial positions over women. Moreover, it has been suggested that women in managerial positions could bring along alternative values and, in so doing, give a special contribution that men cannot. Women could bring 'new' cultural insights into management situations, perhaps even giving birth to 'alternative' cultures in those organizations (Alvesson and Due Billing, 1997: 153–176). The discourse in the media often emphasizes that women as leaders would show the way to 'softer', more 'humanistic', 'people-oriented' organizational cultures, and, overall, that their management style would differ from that of their male counterparts. What if women managers, who are often seen as mere tokens (Kanter, 1977), formed the majority on committees, for instance? If there were more female managers, would that mean different, maybe 'better' – according to some measure – organizational cultures?

In studies about female managers both similarities and differences are found compared to male managers. As shown by a number of studies, however, female managers do not differ so much with regard to their management styles as compared to male managers (Donnell and Hall, 1980; Marshall, 1984; Kovalainen, 1990: 143–159; Rosener, 1990: 119–125; Alvesson and Due Billing, 1997: 163; Grant, 1988: 56–63). While indicating the imbalance between men's and women's positioning at management levels in organizational hierarchies, some feministically oriented studies also argue for various differences between men and women as organizational leaders with respect to their values (Rosener, 1990: 119–125; Marshall, 1984; Bayes, 1987), their differing ethical standards (Kanter, 1977; Mumby and Putnam, 1992: 465–486; Gilligan, 1982) and, in general, their different roles in reshaping organizational realities into a more feminine-oriented direction (Zimmer, 1987; Grant, 1988).

Some of the approaches even challenge the hierarchical organizational structure itself, pointing out its masculine features (Iannello, 1992; Garsombke, 1988: 46–57) and argue for organizational practices that are less hierarchically-oriented and less embodied by masculine tones. The language that we use in research as well as in everyday organizational discourses should be dismantled from its masculine features to allow more space for female presentation; this is the statement. Methodological and method-like arguments have also been put forward in an attempt to understand why there has been so much gender-blindness in organizational studies in the past, arguing for a better understanding of private-life issues and pointing out the invisibility of women in the essence of organizational behaviour and management (Sherif, 1987: 37–56; Millman and Kanter, 1987: 29–36; Calás and Smircich, 1991: 567–602).

Interviewing as a method to study identity and self

We now proceed to issues concerning the interview as a method of studying gendered identity and self, using pieces of material gained from interviews with women working as senior managers at the top level in big Finnish organizations. The main aim of the interviews was to collect stories about how these women perceived their careers, their work, their organization and the wider business life they were involved in at the time, in terms of their female gender. What is the special context within which they talk? Why are they giving interviews? 'When an individual appears in the presence of others, there will usually be some reason for him to mobilize his activity so that it will convey an impression to others which it is in his interests to convey' (Goffman, 1959: 4).

Gender identity shapes and is shaped by country-specific struggles, and is central in the construction of the nation as an entity with a distinctive identity (Krause, 1996: 99). The talk of the interviewed senior managers can be seen in multiple contexts: in the context of Finnish business life, in the context of their own organizational culture and its ideals, and in the context of their individual life-spans. These female managers appear in the flux of privacy and working life, presenting themselves as women with private-life issues and as public persons, and portraying themselves as professional managers at the same time. As King (1994) argues, it requires a special attitude to ask for an interview from high-status interviewees such as the interviewed managers, both from an institutional and a political point of view:

> When interviewing people of high status (such as senior managers and professionals), who are used to being treated with a degree of deference in most of their daily interactions, it is important to set your relationship with them at an appropriate level. If you are over-familiar, or appear to show off your knowledge in their domain, you may cause offence. Conversely, if you are overly nervous or submissive you are likely to be patronized. Either way, it might be difficult for you to obtain anything other that the most shallow, surface level of answers to your questions. You need to be respectful – especially in regard to the areas of professional or expert knowledge – but at the same time confident of the worth of what you are doing and of your own expertise.
>
> (King, 1994: 23)

Though we should not overemphasize the demand for respect from the managers' point of view, there certainly is a lesson to be learned when we approach female managers for an interview: unavoidably, when interviewed, these women carry the identity of manager, even if from a gendered point of view. If we approach these women to give interviews as representatives of the category of 'natural women', they presumably speak themselves 'out' from that category, and essentialize their professional identity.

Even if the whole idea of a hierarchical organization and its argued patriarchy can be challenged, the context within which the interviewees speak is determined by those structures. To be able to manage the given meanings of the local organizational environment, the interviewees identify with its requirements. At the same time they shape their gendered selves and seek identification with the rest of their life-span. They socially construct the situation in which they talk, and the mutuality between the interviewer and the interviewed plays an important part in this social construction. 'Thus, when the individual presents himself before others, his performance will tend to incorporate and exemplify the officially accredited values of the society, more so, in fact, than does his behaviour as a whole' (Goffman, 1959: 35). 'I have said that when an individual appears before others his actions will influence the definition of the situation which they come to have' (ibid.: 6). The interviewed women, female managers, identify themselves in multiple ways: with the class of top managerial professionals, with female managerial professionals, and with women in global terms.

The prominent context of the talk in interviews can be understood by using the standpoint of their 'front', meaning the setting, the physical layout, the scenic parts of expressive equipment, clothing, sex, age, race – parts of the social front also in abstract terms (Goffman, 1959: 23–27). This social front tends to be institutionalized. 'The front becomes a "collective representation" and a fact of its own right' (ibid.: 27). 'It will be convenient to label as "front" that part of the individual's performance which regularly functions in a general and fixed fashion to define the situation for those who observe the performance. Front, then, is the expressive equipment of a standard kind intentionally or unwittingly employed by the individual during his performance' (ibid.: 22). Besides one's front, expressed in the interview situation, the self is presented with fluid inter-related meanings, where one's individuality, local circumstances and broader institutional context all hold a place.

Presenting the front – speaking 'away' the 'natural woman'

Surprisingly, as noted earlier, when questions of inequality are focused on, females do not present very rich data for the analysis. Even if we essentialize organizational as well as institutional dimensions of gender inequity, gender issues should become visible also at the individual level and in the making of gendered selves. In interviews the issue of gender often seemingly disappears, like in interviews with female top managers, as seen in the pieces of interview material cited below.

Again, how to understand these findings? As females are often determined as being part of the category of 'women' instead of individuals, the interview situation, and the request to talk as a female manager, challenges the professional identity of the interviewees. Their managerial professional identity competes with the identity of the 'natural' or 'essential' woman. During the interview the women perform a speech act that will be referred to here as 'speaking themselves "away" from the assumed female self ideal construct'. The use of this terminology tries to show a dynamic, active separation from the essential, 'natural' woman; that is, the women speak themselves 'away' from any that kind of assumption on the interviewer's part. The terminology emphasizes the inner dynamics of the interviewing situation that creates talking and texted talk. The talk of the interviewees can be understood by simultaneously taking their front into account.

By giving interviews these women present the idealized female manager, being females and top-level managers at the same time. For instance, as one of the female managers pointed out: 'Female managers easily become separated from the other managers and other female employees in the organization, and there are certain merits that come from my being unexceptional in the position I hold. In this respect my company differs from others.' As another of the interviewed top managers remarked: 'Sometimes you sense that you are invited to some committee mainly because you are a woman, and you get labelled from the very beginning.' Female managers search for professional identity, albeit a somewhat different one compared to that of male colleagues; they feel empowered if they are treated as 'natural women' without the professional label being added. One of the interviewees made that separation in a very solid way: 'You should not throw yourself into a woman's role. Helplessness makes knights of men, and the bipolarity of men vs. women strengthens.' Woman's role, in this citation, looks to carry the assumptions of passivity and weakness, both typical for the classic female ideal.

Also Erving Goffman describes the presenting of the female self in traditional girl behaviour in the 1950s American context:

> college girls did ... play down their intelligence, skills, and determinativeness when in the presence of datable boys ... These performers are reported to allow their boy friends to explain things to them tediously that they already know; they conceal proficiency in mathematics from their less able consorts; they lose ping-pong games just before the ending. Through all of this the natural superiority of the male is demonstrated, and the weaker role of the female affirmed.
>
> (Goffman, 1959: 39)

We can find that Goffman's description is near to the idea of 'the natural woman': the assumptions of women being nice, helpless, and empowered.

The women also talk themselves into an equal position with their male colleagues. In the words of a female university dean: 'I am firstly the dean, and I am the one who feels my femaleness. I have been voted to the position of dean of this university three times now. The first period as a dean was a difficult one, I really had to work my way in because of a difficult year economically. I had to convince the others, really get into the details of the economic situation of the university, and there were many doubts of how a woman with a humanistic background could succeed in the position. I did, and I later got my second tenure as well.' Being managers, these women differ in their lifestyles from many other women and, in some cases, they point out this distance in the interview: 'When I talk with the mothers of my daughter's friends, I sometimes feel apart and distant, as if we live in two separate worlds. I have no time, for instance, for baking as they seem to do, I usually buy my things from the store.'

The interviewed top managers emphasize their professional roles first and 'speak' themselves 'away' from any idea that their femaleness would partly contribute to their career advancement. A top manager working in a wholesale business, and leading one of its branches, says: 'I have accepted the male way to behave, it is the business culture that determines the operating model. I have made my career on my own – they did not give it to me because I am a female.' This is partly due to the front: these women feel responsible as representatives of female management and speak themselves 'away' from the requirement to be 'natural women'. 'I keep a low profile, I don't emphasize my position, I manage my life and get along, and my male colleagues appreciate this. I feel accepted here, but it is because my work is evaluated the same way as anyone else's', describes one of the interviewed female top managers.

The identity of female managers is built locally in the various contexts within which they talk in the interview situation. These contexts are built around subordinateship, around publicly held conceptions of what it means to be a female manager in regard to their subordinates, often with the requirement of presenting oneself soft, nice and empowered. The individual female managers may struggle with the global and local images by presenting themselves as gender-neutral professionals and, in that way, 'speak' themselves out of reach of the global and local requirements to lead and manage according to the stereotypes of the universal female character. The idea that the relationship between the female manager and her subordinates differs from that of the male managers is strengthened by the 'alternative values' ideology, as well as by the specific contribution ideology according to which female managers bring different values and contributions to leadership situations compared to their male colleagues (Alvesson and Due Billing, 1997: 153–176).

There are more female managers in personnel departments, which proves that professional work segregation (Acker, 1990) exists also at the management level. Looking behind the statistics shows multiple kinds of empowerment tendencies, one of them being 'glass ceilings', the difficulty of female managers to rise to board level and reach the top of the organizational hierarchy (Tienari, 1999). The stereotypes do not hinder women's career advancement to the middle management level, and also the personnel managerial positions fit well with the image of relationship-orientation of female character, but to break through the glass ceilings means to challenge the stereotypes that emphasize female passivity and being nice, over the labels that empower as well as flatter in some cases.

During the interviews there is a struggle, which encompasses all the various identities, in which the researcher tries to capture a sense of the gendered, individual self of the person presenting herself in the interview situation. What is found as a result of the talk is a self that is in process, not a stagnated self. Moreover, a 'manager' is an indefinite concept in organizational hierarchy. There are many types of managers. Also, their leadership capacity differs, from top-level managers with hundreds of subordinates to managers with none. The management contexts differ from each other, and the female managers' identity building and presentation of the self are dependent on those frontal contexts. There are multiple identities present in an interview situation; the gendered self is processed in the interaction between the researcher and the interviewed.

Discussion

Beside being a method, an interview is a socially constructed, localized interactional process. When we study inequality issues within organizations by interviewing female managers, we gain presentations and representations of their gendered selves in the local context. It is obvious that 'female management' as a universal category certainly fails to give an answer to each and every management issue. Empirical research should enable us to grasp the impact of gender in the many different situations faced by people in organizations. In the interview situations that focus on issues of gender inequity, the interviewed women speak themselves 'away' from the idea of the essential woman by making their female gender invisible, while at the same time asserting their identity as professionals.

In order to understand how organizations are gendered, it is necessary to look at the various other categories as well – for example, cross-cultural categories, class, race, age and educational background and experiences. Although the women in the interviews emphasized that their femaleness was not supportive of their managerial position nor a reason for their advancement, and gender issues did not come up in the interview situation directly, a 'front' could be discerned as the women identified themselves as representatives of female management professionals as a social and organizational category. This front is evident even at the level of local organizational identity: the wholesale enterprise where one of the interviewees had earlier encountered some difficulties with the media when the company had been labelled 'chauvinistic'. The female manager working in that enterprise talked a lot about the subject and thereby exhibited loyalty towards her colleagues, be they male or female. Thus the interviewed managers speak both within a local, organizational identity context, which has its historical background (see Chapter 7 by Mills in this volume; Mills, 1997) and in a more general, public context when asserting their careers in the interview situation.

Local organizational contexts also support the tendency of female managers to present female management in a way that is neither ideological nor manipulative. They do not see themselves as advocating any feminine ideology, but they may portray themselves as working somewhat differently to men. They exhibit and share a sense of responsibility by presenting and representing the front of idealized female management in their texted talk. Stereotypes of femaleness, describing women as nurturing, caring, soft and relationship-oriented, generally appear to lead females to managerial positions where such features are particularly emphasized in the public image – to personnel management, for instance, but not easily to top-level strategic management positions with stereotyped masculine values. Female managers are thrust to the front line of cultural change in organizations: female management gives voice to expectations towards 'better' and human ways to manage organizations. At the same time, the argued feminization of organizational cultures is a challenge from the standpoint of women managers, which may burden them as well: they may feel pressured to present a universalized feminine ideal of 'girls being nice' (see Chapter 10 by Katila and Merilainen, this volume). Women easily get the label of being ruthless when they deviate from this ideal. Accordingly, in the interview situation female managers attempt to distance themselves, to speak themselves away from those universal ideals by essentializing gender neutrality concerning any issue of their position in the organization.

Gender inequality in organizations is evidenced by body-count figures, which show that men and women are unequal as biological categories in a multiplicity of ways (see Chapter 5 by Alvesson and Due Billing, this volume). Since gender is socially constructed, the ideas about gender tend to be pervasive and are easily presented as 'natural'. Gender identity gains political significance, particularly in the presence of orthodox ideas about gender, challenged by those who have an interest in breaking down the existing gender order (Krause, 1996: 107). There are no 'natural selves', but instead our individual selves derive from various political discourses within which they are created and changed. Indeed, we learn from a gender perspective, 'genderedly', about power structures from those discourses, be they institutional or organization-specific.

In studying gender and inequality aspects, what can we gain by interviews: truths, emotional reactions, lies, hidden talk that is never spoken out loud – what is this text we obtain from the discourse? There is, in fact, a great deal to be gained. By presenting their 'selves' in the interviews, the interviewees reach far beyond the question of whether they are telling the truth or hiding something, and, in fact, speak out their cultural frames from within the organizational, interorganizational and even institutional realities they inhabit. Their speech broadens from their individual life stories, their unique realities, to outer contextual realities at the same time. To the cultural researcher these stories are contextualized data, rooted in a cultural frame with ideals, values and prejudices, which in themselves tell about the sources of inequity within those cultural contexts. The interplay between the interviewer and the interviewed creates local, contextually situated stories, the interviewee being the actor and giving the performance, and the interviewer being the invisible director of the action – metaphorically – which takes place in the study laboratory or, using Erving Goffman's words (1959: 17–76), at the theatre.

Femaleness is an institutional category, both in a local and a global context, which reaches beyond body-count issues and beyond the idea of the 'natural' woman, and turns to prevailing cultural realities as the context of any talk. Such issues gain more importance in an interview concerning gender inequality than in the case of other topics of study, and, moreover, the question relates to the gender of the interviewee and the interviewer. In order to obtain knowledge from the women's point of view, the interviewer must be reflective to the shared context of the interview participants in the research situation, to the context within which the talk is created and texted. This is not to make the data more objective in universal terms, but to make the data meaningful for the specific topic of study and truly sensitive to the cultural, local and broad contexts of the talk. In fact, this is one way of reaching beyond the individual and unique, as well as beyond the presumption of the existence of a 'natural, essential woman', to study the multiple, gendered identities and selves that are presented within the given context.

Acknowledgement

I am grateful to Marja Oravainen and Barbara Miraftabi for suggestions concerning language on an earlier draft of this chapter.

References

Aaltio-Marjosola, I. (1994). Gender stereotypes as cultural products of the organization. *Scandinavian Journal of Management Studies*, 10(2): 147–162.

Aaltio-Marjosola, I. and Kovalainen, A. (2001). Personality. In E. Wilson (ed), *Organizational Behaviour Reassessed. The Impact of Gender* (pp. 17–37). London: Sage.

Aaltio-Marjosola, I. and Sevón, G. (1997). Gendering organizational topic. In *Administrative Studies*, 16(4): 289–304.

Acker, J. (1990). Hierarchies, jobs and bodies: a theory of gendered organizations. *Gender & Society*, 5: 390–407.

Acker, J. (1994). The gender regime of Swedish banks. *Scandinavian Journal of Management*, 10(2): 117–130.

Alvesson, M. and Due Billing, Y. (1997). *Understanding Gender in Organizations.* London: Sage.

Ashmore, R.D. (1990). Sex, gender and the individual. In L.A. Pervin (ed.), *The Handbook of Personality: Theory and Research* (pp. 486–526). New York, NY: Guilford Press.

Bayes, J. (1987). Do female managers in public bureaucracies manage with a different voice? Paper presented at the Third International Interdisciplinary Congress on Women, Dublin, 6–10 July.

Berger, P. and Luckmann, T. (1966). *The Social Construction of Reality. A Treatise on the Sociology of Knowledge.* Garden City, NY: Doubleday & Co. Inc.

Britton, D. (2000). The epistemology of gendered organization. *Gender & Society,* 14(3): 418–434.

Burrell, G. and Morgan, G. (1979). *Sociological Paradigms and Organizational Analysis. Elements of the Sociology of Corporate Life.* London: Heinemann.

Calás, M. and Smircich, L. (1991). Voicing seduction to silence leadership. *Organization Studies,* 12(4): 567–602.

Calás, M. and Smircich, L. (1996). From the 'woman's' point of view: feminist approaches to organization studies. In S. Clegg, C. Hardy and W. Nord (eds), *Handbook of Organization Studies* (pp. 218–257). London: Sage.

Calás, M. and Smircich, L. (1999). Past postmodernism? Reflections and tentative directions. *The Academy of Management Review,* 24(4): 649–671.

Christensen, L.T. and Cheney, G. (1994). Articulating identity in an organizational age. Commentary on Czarniawska-Joerges. In S.A. Deetz (ed.), *Communication Yearbook/17* (pp. 222–235). Thousand Oaks, CA: Sage.

Collinson, D.L. and Hearn, J. (1996). Men managing leadership! men and women of the corporation revisited. *International Review of Women and Leadership,* 1(1): 1–24.

Cross, S.E. and Madson, L. (1997). Models of the self: self-construals and gender. *Psychological Bulletin,* 122(1): 5–37.

Czarniawska, B. and Calás, M. (1997). Another country: explaining gender discrimination with 'culture'. *Finnish Administrative Studies,* 4: 326–342.

Czarniawska-Joerges, B. (1992). *Exploring Complex Organizations.* Newbury Park, CA: Sage.

Czarniawska-Joerges, B. (1994a). Editorial: modern organizations and Pandora's box. *Scandinavian Journal of Management,* 10(2): 95–98.

Czarniawska-Joerges, B. (1994b). Narratives of individual and organizational identities. In S.A. Deetz (ed.), *Communication Yearbook No. 17* (pp. 193–222). Newbury Park, CA: Sage.

Donnell, S. and Hall, J. (1980). Men and women as managers: a significant case of no significant difference. *Organization Dynamics,* Spring: 60–77.

Elias, N. (1978). *The History of Manners.* New York, NY: Pantheon Books.

Elliott, A. (1999). *Social Theory & Psychoanalysis in Transition. Self and Society from Freud to Kristeva.* London: Free Association Books Ltd.

Garsombke, D. (1988). Organizational culture dons the mantle of militarism. *Organizational Dynamics,* Summer: 46–57.

Gerzon, M. (1982). *A Choice of Heroes: The Changing Faces of American Manhood.* Boston, MA: Houghton Mifflin.

Gilligan, C. (1982). *In a Different Voice: Psychological Theory and Women's Development.* Cambridge, MA: Harvard University Press.

Goffman, E. (1959). *The Presentation of Self in Everyday Life.* New York, NY: Doubleday Anchor Books.

Grant, J. (1988). Women as managers: what can they offer to organizations. *Organizational Dynamics,* 16(1): 56–63.

Grosholz, E. (1987). Women, history and practical deliberation. *The Journal of Speculative Philosophy*, 1(3): 218–226.

Haraway, D. (1988). Situated knowledges: the science question in feminism and the privilege of partial perspective. *Feminist Studies*, 14(3): 575–599.

Harding, S. (1986). *The Science Question in Feminism*. Ithaca, NY: Cornell University Press.

Harding, S. (1987). Is there a feminist method? In S. Harding (ed.), *Feminism and Methodology* (pp. 1–15). Bloomington, IN: University of Indiana Press.

Harding, S. (ed.) (1991). *Whose Science? Whose Knowledge?: Thinking from Women's Lives*. Ithaca, N.Y.: Cornell University Press.

Hearn, J. and Parkin, W. (1983). Gender and organizations: a selected review and critique of a neglected area. *Organization Studies*, 4(3): 219–242.

Höpfl, H. (1998). The Maternal Body and the Organization: the Influence of Julia Kristeva. Unpublished paper.

Iannello, K. (1992). *Decisions Without Hierarchy. Feminist Interventions in Organization Theory and Practice*. London: Routledge.

Jacobson, S.W. and Aaltio-Marjosola, I. (2001). 'Strong' objectivity and the use of Q-methodology in cross-cultural research: contextualizing the experience of women managers and their scripts of career. *Journal of Management Inquiry*, 10(3): 228–249.

Kanter, R.M. (1977). *Men and Women of the Corporation*. New York, NY: Anchor Press.

Kauppinen, K. and Otala, L. (1999). Tasa-arvoinen ja hyvä työpaikka. Tutkimus työpaikan tasa-arvosta ja työpaikan hengestä. Julkaisematon keskustelupaperi. Unpublished discussion paper on equality in the workplace and work atmosphere in Finland.

Keller, E.F. (1984). *Reflections on Gender and Science*. New Haven, CT: Yale University Press.

King, N. (1997). The qualitative research interview. In C. Cassell and G. Symon (eds), *Qualitative Methods in Organizational Research* (pp. 14–37). London: Sage.

Kinnunen, P. and Korvajärvi, P. (1995). Sukupuoli työpaikalla. In M. Kinnunen and P. Korvajärvi (eds), *Työelämän sukupuolistavat käytännöt*. Jyväskylä: Vastapaino, Gummerus.

Korvajärvi, P. (1998). *Gendering Dynamics in White-Collar Work Organizations*. Acta Universitatis Tamperensis 600. Vammalan kirjapaino Oy, Finland.

Kovalainen, A. (1990). How do female and male managers in banking view their roles and subordinates? *Scandinavian Journal of Management*, 6: 143–159.

Kovalainen, A. (1995). *At the Margins of the Economy: Women's Self-Employment in Finland, 1960–1990*. Aldershot: Avebury.

Krause, J. (1996). Gendered identities in international relations. In J. Krause and N. Renwick (eds), *Identities in International Relations* (pp. 99–117). New York, NY: St Martin's Press.

Kvale, S. (1983). The qualitative research interview: a phenomenological and a hermeneutical mode of understanding. *Journal of Phenomenological Psychology*, 14: 171–196.

Marshall, J. (1984). *Women Managers: Travellers in a Male World*. Chichester: Wiley & Sons.

Metcalfe, B. and Altman, Y. (2001). Leadership. In E. Wilson (ed.), *Organizational Behaviour Reassessed. The Impact of Gender* (pp. 104–129). London: Sage.

Miller, J.B. (1987). *Toward a New Psychology of Women*. Boston, MA: Beacon Press.

Millman, M. and Kanter, R.M. (1987). Introduction to another voice: feminist perspectives on social life and social science. In S. Harding (ed.), *Feminism and Methodology* (pp. 29–36). Bloomington: University of Indiana Press.

Mills, A.J. (1988). Organization, gender and culture. *Organization Studies*, 9(3): 351–369.

Mills, A.J. (1997). Practice makes perfect: corporate masculinities, bureaucratization and the idealized gendered self. *Finnish Journal of Administrative Studies*, 4: 272–288.

Mumby, D. and Putnam, L. (1992). The politics of emotion: a feminist reading of bounded rationality. *Academy of Management Review*, 17(3): 465–486.

Newell, S. (2001). Communication. In E. Wilson (ed), *Organizational Behaviour Reassessed. The Impact of Gender* (pp. 60–86). London: Sage.

Oseen, C. (1997). Luce Irigaray, sexual difference and theorizing leaders and leadership. *Gender, Work and Organization*, 4(3): 170–184.

Paludi, M.A. (1992). *The Psychology of Women*. Dubuque, IA.: Brown & Benchmark.

Rosener, J. (1990). Ways women lead. *Harvard Business Review*, November–December: 119–125.

Sandelands, L. and Srivatsan, V. (1993). The problem of experience in the study of organizations. *Organization Studies*, 14(1): 1–22.

Sayer, A. (1984). *Method in Social Science. A Realistic Approach*. London: Routledge.

Sherif, C.W. (1987). Bias in psychology. In S. Harding (ed.), *Feminism and Methodology* (pp. 37–56). Bloomington, IN: University of Indiana Press.

Smircich, L. and Morgan, G. (1982). Leadership: the management of meaning. *The Journal of Applied Behavioral Science*, 18(3): 257–273.

Tienari. J. (1999). The first wave washed up on a shore: reform, feminization and gender resegregation. *Gender, Work and Organization*, 6: 1–19.

Tienari, J. (2000). Gender segregation in the making of a merger. *Scandinavian Journal of Management*, 16: 111–144.

Trew, K. (1998). Identity and the self. In K. Trew and J. Kremer (eds), *Gender and Psychology* (pp. 3–15). London: Arnold.

Trew, K. and Kremer, J. (eds) (1998). *Gender and Psychology*. London: Arnold.

Veikkola, E.-S. (1999). *Changes at the Top. Labour Market, 12/1999, Statistics of Finland*. Helsinki: Yliopistopaino.

West, C. and Zimmerman, D. (1987). Doing gender. *Gender and Society*, 1(2): 125–151.

Wilson, E. (1997). Exploring gendered cultures. *Administrative Studies*, 16(4): 289–303.

Wilson, E. (2001). Organizational culture. In E. Wilson (ed.), *Organizational Behaviour Reassessed. The Impact of Gender* (pp. 168–188) London: Sage.

Zimmer, L. (1987). How women reshape the prison guard role. *Gender & Society*, 1(4): 415–431.

Index

Note: page numbers in *italics* refer to illustrations